flavors of puglia

flavors of puglia

TRADITIONAL RECIPES FROM THE HEEL OF ITALY'S BOOT

NANCY HARMON JENKINS

BROADWAY BOOKS
New York

"... e vanne in Puglia piana,

la magna Capitana,

la dove lo mio core nott'e dia."

Broadway Books titles may be purchased for business or promotional use or for special sales. For information, please write to: Special Markets Department, Bantam Doubleday Dell Publishing Group, Inc., 1540 Broadway, New York, NY 10036.

BROADWAY BOOKS and its logo, a letter B bisected on the diagonal, are trademarks of Broadway Books, a division of Bantam Doubleday Dell Publishing Group, Inc.

Library of Congress Cataloging-in-Publication Data
Jenkins, Nancy Harmon.
  Flavors of Puglia : traditional recipes from the heel of Italy's boot / Nancy Harmon Jenkins. — 1st ed.
      p. cm.
   Includes bibliographical references and index.
   ISBN 0-553-06675-7 (hc)
      1. Cookery, Italian—Southern style.   2. Cookery—Italy—Puglia.
I. Title.
TX723.2.S65J46   1997
641.5945′75—dc21   96-48470   CIP

FIRST EDITION

Designed by Vertigo Design
Map by Martie Holmer

Photographs © 1997 by Ellen Silverman: pages 5, 8, 20, 48, 74, 108, 138, 164, 184, 212, 228
Photographs © 1997 by Naomi Duguid/ASIA ACCESS: pages x, 29, 33, 36, 42, 53, 103, 121, 123, 151, 153, 161, 183, 222, 227, 239, 240

97 98 99 00 01 10 9 8 7 6 5 4 3 2 1

IN MEMORY OF ARLENE WANDERMAN:
GENEROUS FRIEND AND FELLOW TRAVELER,
WHO SHARED MY ENTHUSIASM FOR PUGLIA —
AND FOR EVERY OTHER PART OF THE WORLD
WHERE THE OLIVE TREES GROW

contents

introduction

i went down into Puglia in the late autumn of 1995,
and stayed through the winter and into the following
spring in a farmhouse set amid the low limestone hills
that rise west of the city of Monópoli on the Adriatic.
The house, secluded in olive groves, had an upper terrace that faced south, its back to the north wind, and
collected so much warmth on sunny winter afternoons
that I was able to take my lunch outside, basking in the
sunshine, when the weather permitted.

There was not a lot of sunshine that winter, one of
the stormiest and wettest on record, not just in Puglia
but throughout Italy. But by late January the season had
already begun to turn toward spring. The mimosas

flowered earliest, fuzzy yellow pellets cascading in great clusters from high, supple branches, quickly followed by the almond trees, their ghostly pale drifts of blossom delicately scented and brushed with pink. In the muddy, rain-soaked fields sturdy stalks of fava beans and graceful pea vines appeared even while the harvest of winter crops, broccoli and cabbage, fennel, artichokes, celery, was still under way. It was a true Mediterranean spring, each day the sun growing visibly stronger. And though there were plenty of chilly nights and blustery days and even frost and snow ahead, you could still feel, as vital and compelling as the myth of Demeter and Persephone, the return of life to the earth.

From my terrace I looked out on stony fields and walled orchards of olives, trees with trunks so thick three men with arms outstretched could not contain them, darkly gnarled and twisted into anthropomorphic sculptures. The landscape, into which other similar farmsteads were folded, fell away from the house and then rose again across the ravine of the Lama Macina, *lama* being a local word for an ancient river bed in which occasionally are found the stone implements of those who were here long before us. I was, I felt, surrounded, wrapped deep inside a Van Gogh landscape of pure, intense color, iron red and chocolate brown of freshly turned earth, bleached white of dry-stone terraces and plastered house walls, and the deeply comforting blue green and silver of cypresses, olives, carob, and eucalyptus. In the distance were the white blocks of modern Monópoli, a town whose past, though respectably long, is not readily apparent to the eye, and, stretching away to Albania, the dazzling Adriatic, ranging in color from indigo to aquamarine to stormy gray, dotted with fishing boats and the ferries that carry cars and people from Bari and Brindisi to the nearest islands of Greece. Sometimes a military jet screamed overhead, on the way to or back from what used to be Yugoslavia. The only other sounds were of dogs barking on a neighboring farm, cocks crowing in the early morning, the occasional rumble of a tractor, and the church bells at Cozzana, which rang at noon and again at six in the evening.

Puglia, or Apulia as it is often called in English, is "the heel" of the Italian boot, including the steep and rocky spur of the Gargano peninsula projecting into the sea. It is the easternmost region of Italy, eight hundred kilometers of coastline stretching down the Adriatic and around the heel into the high arch of the Ionian Sea and the Gulf of Taranto. This heel reaches out toward the Eastern Mediterranean, and at times the landscape looks and feels more like Greece than the softer, gentler Italy of Rome and the North. Especially under the harsh brilliance of the summer sun—*il solleone,* the lion sun of August—you sense the connection with the Balkans and the East. Greeks were among the earliest settlers in this region, dominating the indigenous Messapicans, the Daunians, the Peucetians, as far back as Mycenaean times, perhaps even earlier. Taranto on the Ionian was a Greek colony from the eighth century B.C., a flourishing capital of Magna Graecia, the great cosmopolitan Greek world beyond Greece itself; in Taranto's Museo Nazionale, you catch glimpses of the splendors of that lost world in the dazzling collection of antique vases illustrating in exquisitely painted detail the old stories of gods, heroes, and mortals, their lives so intimately entwined.

Puglia has known many conquerors since—the Romans, of course, and then the Byzantine Greeks, Lombards, Arabs, Normans, Angevins, Aragonese, and Spanish, the armies of the popes and of the German emperors, Bourbons who ruled from Naples, Turkish corsairs who harried the coasts, on and on, in a rich and mercilessly cruel history of conquest, betrayal, loss, and gain. Each incursion, each struggle, left its mark on this land, from the ancient dolmens scattered across the landscape to the baroque fantasies of cities like Lecce and Martina Franca. There are magnificent castles and citadels, like Castel del Monte, grand and enigmatic, an octagonal monument in alabaster-colored stone to what some say was the cabalistic vision of Frederick II, Puglia's greatest ruler. There are spectacular eleventh- and twelfth-century romanesque churches like the soaring seaside cathedrals of Trani and San Nicola at Bari, and rock-carved chapels and hidden grottoes, the walls of which were plastered by monks, saints, and hermits with feverish and apocalyptic visions. There are clusters of white-walled villages and fortified farms called *masserie,* set well back from a dangerous coast once beset by pirates and marauders. And of course there are the trulli, the characteristic vernacular architecture of the Murge, the high grassy plateau of central Puglia. Stone dwellings capped by corbel-vaulted roofs built of overlapping circles of flat stones called *chiancarelle,* the trulli are both disturbing and anachronistic, like the dwellings of a race of aliens set down in our midst. Traditionally, it is said, they were built of unmortared stone so they could be quickly torn down when the Bourbon tax-collector came around, then rebuilt just as quickly when he was gone from sight. Their roofs are often decorated with painted symbols whose meanings have long since been lost.

For all the richness of its history, however, Puglia is, has always been, a land of poverty, a land of emigration. Thousands of Pugliese left their villages for America in the early years of this century, many of them never to return. Almost everyone you meet in Puglia has cousins in America, and if you say you're from there, most people have a tale to tell.

"The California of Italy" is the phrase that chambers of commerce and tourist development agencies use to lure tourists to Puglia, but Puglia has something California lacks—a depth of history, a sense of the chiaroscuro of tragedy and loss, of the harsh side of life that counterpoints moments of joy and sweetness. There's a special poignancy to celebration when the ache of misfortune and sorrow underlies it: It seems significant that the *pizzica,* a woman's triumphal dance of seduction and conquest, is almost indistinguishable from the ritualistic rapture of the tarantella, the hypnotic trance-dance induced by the remorseless sting of a spider that lurks, one writer says, "in the labyrinths of a guilty conscience" and almost always attacks women, almost always those who have been unlucky in love or marriage.

"La cucina pugliese nasce come cucina povera," says Paola Pettini who for twenty-five years has directed a cooking school in her native Bari: The cuisine of

Puglia was born as the cuisine of poverty. What this means, she explains, is pasta made without eggs, bread made from the hard-grain durum wheat flour that flourishes locally, and a diet based on vegetables, including many wild vegetables like *cicorielle,* wild chicory, and *lampascione,* the bulb of a wild tassel hyacinth, foods that are foraged from stony fields and abandoned terraces. Meat is not much eaten and beef, until a few years ago, was almost unknown on Pugliese tables, with horsemeat being preferred. For Christmas and Easter feasting, weddings and baptisms, Pugliese cooks look to what are called *animale da cortile,* farmyard animals, especially chickens and rabbits, although this rocky landscape being sheep country, lamb is the very symbol of feasting, as it is in most of the Mediterranean.

The food of Puglia is in essence a home-based cuisine, not marked by the influence of great chefs or restaurants. Pasta manufacturer Benedetto Cavalieri says that even twenty years ago, in his home town of Lecce, there were only a handful of restaurants, mostly patronized by commercial travelers and others who had no home to go to—or, Benedetto adds with a discreet smile, were dining with ladies they could not bring home. Restaurants like Concetta Cantoro's home-style Cucina Casareccia are newcomers to Lecce, even more so because of the chef-owner's rigorous insistence on serving that very home-based cuisine that is the glory of Pugliese kitchens.

Because it is based on home cooking, this is a *cucina delle donne,* created by women cooking at home rather than male chefs in professional kitchens. It is a cuisine without rules and regulations, based solely on what's in the family larder, which is then stretched and expanded to feed those who may show up *al improviso,* at the unplanned last minute. Thus, a recipe becomes a manner of speaking rather than a rule. "How much flour do I need for orecchiette for six people?" asks Adriana Bozzi-Colonna in a kitchen in Lecce. And her assistant Silvana Camisa replies with a gesture: Using her hands as a cup she scoops up a double handful of semola. "That's for one," she says, and proceeds to add five more scoops to the pile.

It also means that a recipe changes from one village to another, even from one household to another, without the cooks themselves always being aware of it. It's almost impossible to speak of authenticity when a word like *ciambotta* describes two entirely different dishes—a mixture of vegetables in Monópoli, a mixture of fish in Bari, just thirty kilometers to the north. And while some cooks insist that the only way to make a purée of dried fava beans is with a cooked potato mixed in to give it smoothness, others raise their eyebrows in shocked consternation at the very thought.

Such individualism means there are no culinary canons, yet there are certain givens: You know what something *isn't,* if not precisely what it *is.* You know it when you see it, or more exactly, when you put it in your mouth. "Did she use onions in the stuffing?" asks Nonna Rosa when I tell her about a *scalcione,* a double-crusted savory pie, made for me in a town outside Bari. "Ah, then she did it the right way. She knew what she was doing."

Pugliese cuisine is based on olive oil, one of the great products of the region. In any given year, Puglia produces as much as two-thirds of all the olive oil in Italy, and while much of it is shipped north, more of it stays right here to be used in Pugliese kitchens. Cooks in Puglia even deep-fry with extra virgin oil, something that comes as a surprise to Americans but is routine in many parts of the Mediterranean (Sicily, Andalucia in southern Spain).

Butter is rarely used in the traditional cuisine, and even some sweets are made with olive oil and often fried. And sweets, moreover, are not an everyday occurrence but associated only with holidays, whether major ones like Christmas and Easter, or minor ones like the Feast of the Dead (All Saints) or Shrove Tuesday, or locally celebrated ones like the feasts of St. Anthony Abbot and St. Joseph.

In this culture of sparsity, nothing is wasted. Stale bread is cut into cubes or crumbled and toasted in oil to make a garnish for pasta and vegetable dishes. Vegetables themselves, at the height of their season, are dried, pickled, or preserved in oil to eke out the larder in the lean months of the year. Figs are dried or boiled down to make a syrup, and grape juice, after the first pressing, is boiled to make a thick molasses called *mosto cotto,* to be served at Christmas poured over the fried sweets called *cartellate*.

Wild greens in great variety are still harvested, especially during the brief Pugliese winter when gardens are less productive and the wildings are at their best, tender and sweet. On misty days, when the damp soil yields wild roots more easily, you'll see elderly foragers, men and women alike, stoop-shouldered as they course intently over abandoned fields, often accompanied by grandchildren who are learning to tell good from bad. Lampascioni are so precious that in recent years, it's rumored, they've been brought in from North Africa to fill Pugliese market demand. Even the green shoots of the vine, pruned in the springtime in order to concentrate the plant's energy on the developing fruit, are soaked for a few days in vinegar and water, then heated with oil and garlic, mixed with the ever-present purée of fava beans, and served with crusts of fried bread.

Three dishes come to mind when I think of this cuisine, three dishes that Pugliese cooks have prepared for me over and over again, dishes that they themselves select as exemplary, and dishes, moreover, that are linked in their ingredients as much as in their deep roots in the culinary culture of Puglia. They are:

1. **'Ncapriata** or **fave e cicoria:** A purée made from dried peeled fava beans (with or without a potato added), dressed with a thread of olive oil and eaten with steamed bitter greens, preferably wild chicory. The presentation becomes more elaborate with the addition of chopped red onions marinated in vinegar, fried or pickled green peppers, steamed lampascioni, fried black or green olives, and other condiments (page 114).

2. **Ciceri e tria:** Homemade durum wheat pasta (no eggs) in the form of flat tagliatelle or noodles (tria), cooked with chick-peas (ciceri) and mixed

with about a third of the pasta that has been kept apart and fried in olive oil until it is crisp and brown, with a surprisingly meatlike flavor (page 100).

3. **Orecchiette con cime di rape:** Again, homemade durum wheat pasta, shaped in the form of "little ears," cooked with the bittersweet vegetable we know as broccoli rabe or rapini, and dressed with oil, garlic, anchovies, and perhaps a little hot peperoncino (page 102).

Grains and greens or grains and beans, what these dishes seem to me to have in common, apart from their antiquity, is their strict reliance on familiar, everyday, domestic products of the Pugliese countryside. Pure and authentic, they are what poor home cooks have relied on to sustain their families through the centuries. Neither are they disdained by the rich, for Puglia remains one of those rare places in the world where rich and poor eat pretty much alike, except that the rich eat more of it. Fave (or broad beans) are throughout the Mediterranean *la carne dei poveri,* the meat of the poor. Along with chick-peas, they are among the oldest legumes known in Mediterranean cooking. Wild chicories and similar greens have sprung up in this dry, bleached landscape presumably since the beginning of time. Olives have been cultivated at least since the earliest Greeks brought trees to southern Italy. And hard durum wheat, while its origins are more speculative, has been one of the great products of Puglia's upland plains for centuries.

It's altogether likely that even five hundred years ago, the dishes on Pugliese tables were not all that different from what they are today, with one great exception—the tomato. There are no early cookbooks to tell us when tomatoes were first introduced to Puglia, but whenever it was, probably sometime during the long Spanish hegemony, they took to the country's arid climate and bony geography as if God had always intended them to be there. Puglia's tomatoes are sweet and acid, dense with flesh and bursting with juice. They are available year-round, fresh from the garden, sun-dried and packed in oil, put up simply in jars, whether whole or in a sauce, or strung in brilliant red clusters that, astonishingly, if hung in a cool, dry place, will keep from harvest until well into the following spring.

I could add a fourth dish to the list above, although it doesn't fit quite so neatly into this tidy scheme. It is called *tiella* or *taieddha* or *teglia,* depending on where you are in Puglia and what dialect is being spoken. Into the tiella goes a mixture, a carefully structured layering of several ingredients that may or may not contain rice (this is the problematic part, as we shall see) but will almost always contain potatoes. Another element will be a vegetable, such as artichokes, zucchini, or mushrooms, depending on the season, and the final ingredient is sometimes bits of salt cod or more usually mussels, the Mediterranean black mussels that have been cultured for centuries in the Mar Piccolo, Taranto's inner sea. Food historians and writers, in Puglia and elsewhere, often suggest that this is a Pugliese version of Spanish paella, derived from the Spanish in the centuries when they occupied

Puglia along with much of the Italian south. But tiella is really very different from paella—paella is quickly cooked on top of the fire, while tiella is baked in the oven for quite a long time. Moreover, paella is a dish that was associated, until quite recently, only with the rice-growing area around Valencia and not with other parts of Spain at all. Rice is not grown in Puglia, and is not essential to the Pugliese dish. Still, spell and call it what you will, teglia, tiella, taieddha, tiedde, or something else, and put in it what you will (as long as you include potatoes), it's a dish that is confidently and unembarrassedly Pugliese, and I've included several recipes for different versions. For more detail, see page 158.

Late one night toward the end of my stay in Puglia, I was sitting at the supper table with my landlord Pino Marchese while his wife Anna put little Totó to bed. We were finishing up a platter of fave e cicoria, rubbing crusts of bread in what remained of the fava bean purée, and musing, as we often did, about Puglia and America and the differences, and the whys of those differences. Pino is a deeply philosophical man, though his life right now leaves him little time for contemplation. Still, when he speaks he's worth paying attention to. Moreover, he's traveled widely in Europe and the Mideast. "I think," he said, with neither pride nor exaggeration, but exactly like a philosopher ruminating on the business at hand, "I think this is without question the best food in the world." He meant not just what we were eating but the whole range of Pugliese cuisine, and he meant what he said.

ingredients and basic recipes

Anchovies

*t*he best ones are salt-packed whole anchovies, available by the ounce or in large cans from Italian groceries; they keep forever, though once opened, the can should be refrigerated. To use them, rinse the whole anchovy under running water to get rid of the salt; then split down the middle into two fillets and discard the bony tail and backbone.

Bread

*a*lthough there are recipes for Pugliese-style bread in this book, even the most assiduous bakers have to buy bread from time to time. When that happens, seek out a bakery that makes what I call a good country-style loaf, not a pan bread but a bread cast right onto the floor of the oven, whether it's fired with wood or gas. Look for a loaf with a crisp crust and a firm texture to the crumb inside. Ask what ingredients were used. Barley flour might be part of the composition of the dough, but otherwise it will be made of wheat flour, whether semolina from durum wheat, unbleached white flour from regular bread wheat, or whole-wheat flour.

Avoid breads that are made with milk, eggs, or any enhancers. The best country-style bread is made with flour, yeast, salt, water, and nothing more. A sourdough bread, if it's used, should be properly made, without the intense, vinegary tang that too many sourdough bakers seem to feel is needed.

BREAD CRUMBS. Bread crumbs are made from stale bread, preferably from a loaf like the one described above that is a few days old. When a recipe calls for "freshly grated" bread crumbs, it doesn't mean grated from a fresh loaf, but rather freshly grated from a stale loaf. Stale ends of bread can be cut into smaller pieces and quickly grated in a food processor—easiest and most efficiently done in small batches—then frozen in zip-lock bags so a supply of "freshly grated" bread crumbs is always on hand. Many Italian bakeries sell bread crumbs, but the commercially available bread crumbs in a can should only be used in recipes where toasted or dried bread crumbs are called for. Don't use seasoned bread crumbs as the flavor will interfere with the dish. Toast your own bread crumbs by spreading them on a cookie sheet and baking them in a preheated 350°F. oven for 15 minutes or so. Keep an eye on them as they can go from golden brown to charcoal black very quickly.

Some recipes call for sautéed bread crumbs, a fine southern Italian technique. For a cup of bread crumbs, heat a teaspoon of olive oil in a skillet over a medium to medium-high burner, add the crumbs, and toast, stirring, until the crumbs are all golden brown and crisp. The crisp crumbs can substitute for grated cheese on pasta or to top steamed or braised vegetables. This is an especially good trick for vegans, or anyone who doesn't eat dairy products.

Capers

MOST PUGLIESE recipes call for capers packed in brine, but we don't seem to get the best quality of these in this country. I use salt-cured capers, purchased in Italian-American groceries, and rinse them in a sieve under running water before using.

Cheeses

SHEEP'S milk is the basis for the most characteristic Pugliese cheeses, whether freshly made ricotta or pecorino that's been aged several months. It's not easy to find similar cheeses outside Puglia, but diligence and determination will pay off.

RICOTTA.   Paula Lambert's Mozzarella Company (page 256) in Dallas makes excellent goat's milk ricotta, the soft, curdy cheese that is produced by cooking the whey, the liquid by-product of cheese-making. Hollow Road Farms (page 256) in the Hudson Valley is a sheep's-milk dairy producing good ricotta. Other possible sources are from local goat's milk and sheep's milk cheese producers; often all it takes to get ricotta is to let the farmer or dairy person know the market is available.

If your only choice is a commercially available ricotta, drain it overnight in the refrigerator in a sieve lined with a double layer of cheesecloth before using it in any recipes. Made from cow's milk, it has nowhere near the flavor of sheep or goat ricotta, but at least the texture will be right after you drain it.

PECORINO.   Pecorino simply means sheep's milk cheese, aged anywhere from a couple of weeks to as much as a year and a half. Most of what we see in this country is aged three to six months and much of it is not 100 percent sheep's milk, but a mixture of sheep's and cow's. Most Pugliese pecorino these days is also made from a mixture of cow's and sheep's milk.

I've never located a Pugliese pecorino in America, but if you can get pecorino sardo (from Sardegna) or pecorino toscano (from Tuscany) from your cheese shop, it's a fine substitute. I've also used manchego, a sheep's milk cheese from Spain, to good effect. Beware, however, of pecorino romano, a peculiar, sour, unpleasant cheese often sold generically as "pecorino" in this country. I don't know where it comes from (certainly not Rome) but it's pretty awful.

MOZZARELLA.   In Puglia mozzarella is usually made from cow's milk rather than the buffalo milk mozzarella of the region around Naples. It's now possible to get good imported Italian mozzarella on a regular basis in U.S. markets. In some Italian-American neighborhoods, there are cheese vendors who still make their own, kneading the curd in hot water while they stretch it—a fascinating sight, if you ever have the opportunity to watch. Fresh mozzarella is almost a porcelain white, quite soft, and chewy rather than rubbery. It usually comes in a brine that helps maintain the texture, and it should not be more than a day or two old, since the cheese deteriorates rapidly after that. Beware of the lumpy, sour, yellowish thing made from skim milk and packaged in plastic shrink wrap; it bears no resemblance to the real thing.

Olio santo

A CONDIMENT that appears on every table throughout the Terra di Bari, this is fiercely hot olive oil in which hot dried peppers (peperoncini rossi) have steeped for several weeks. To make it, simply pack a sterile jar full of small hot dried red chile peppers (first rinsing and thoroughly drying them) and fill it with extra virgin olive oil. Let sit on a cool, dark pantry shelf for a couple of weeks. Use with caution.

Olive oil

SEE pages 248 to 251 for a discussion of Pugliese olive oil. Use only extra virgin olive oil. Masseria di Sant'Eramo is the most widely distributed Pugliese brand but there are others, such as the oil that Carlo Middione puts up under his own Vivande label, or the Dentamaro available at Balducci's. When I can't find Pugliese oil, I use Colavita, which is widely available in this country and usually includes some Pugliese oil in its blend, or a flavorful Greek oil like Athena or Greek Gourmet instead.

Pancetta

A SALT-CURED, unsmoked bacon increasingly available in this country. If only smoked bacon is available, blanch it in boiling water for a couple of minutes in order to rid it of most of its smoky flavor.

Pasta

BENEDETTO Cavalieri's pasta (page 75), made in the town of Maglie south of Lecce, is one of the high-quality artisanal pastas available in this country, and the only one that's actually made in Puglia. Other brands I like are Latini, from the Marche, and Rustichella d'Abruzzo, from the Abruzzi; though not Pugliese, they are both fine pastas, made, like Cavalieri's, of nothing but first-rate *semola di grano duro* and water, with no eggs added. All three brands are produced by the *metodo delicato,* which involves long, slow drying at low temperatures to retain the nutty flavor of hard durum wheat. Further, the pasta forms are shaped with bronze dies, which give a rougher surface to the finished pasta than conventional modern Teflon dies, and allow for a more intimate marriage of pasta to sauce. All these pastas are available by mail order through a number of shops (page 255). If you can't get these artisanal pastas, a good commercial pasta, widely available, is De Cecco.

Peperoncini rossi

VERY HOT, dried, red chile peppers (sometimes called *diavolicchi,* little devils), these are used more liberally in the South than in other parts of Italy, but with far greater restraint than Americans, used to Thai and Mexican foods, are accustomed to tasting. Pleasantly warm and spicy, with a suffusion of heat but no rushing for the water pitcher—that's the balance aimed for in "hot" Pugliese food. Crushed red pepper flakes can be substituted for whole peppers.

On the other hand, sweet peppers in Puglia have a good deal more character than what we're used to here, and I find that most Pugliese recipes, like the one on page 131, are improved by the addition of a few jalapeño chiles.

Tomatoes

THE FINEST tomatoes, of course, are home-grown, harvested at their peak of ripeness, and eaten while still warm from the summer sun. Unfortunately we're not all that lucky. A local farmers' market may provide an equivalent bounty, just so long as fresh, ripe, and regional are the words on your lips.

Once the tomato season has passed, what's a cook to do? The same things cooks do in Puglia. Tomatoes are among the few fruits that take very well to canning, and canned tomatoes, whether store-bought or put up from your own garden bounty, are a perfectly acceptable substitute for fresh ones. (For a recipe for home-canned tomatoes, see page 215.) There are some recipes, mostly involving raw tomatoes, where nothing but fresh ones will do, but for the most part, high-quality canned tomatoes are fine. My favorite brand is Muir Glen, organically raised tomatoes from California that are available as whole tomatoes, chopped tomatoes, and tomato purée. Hunt's whole canned tomatoes are also very good and perhaps more widely available than Muir Glen.

TOMATO SAUCE AND TOMATO CONCENTRATE. A recipe for tomato sauce can be found on page 14. Concentrate is more problematic; I have yet to find a commercially available concentrate that tastes of anything but metal. Making your own is the best solution (see pages 218 to 219) but if that's not possible, simply leave it out.

tomato sauce
SALSA DI POMODORO

about 2 cups

A basic all-purpose tomato sauce, this may be put up in canning jars for long storage. Simply adjust the other ingredients for the quantity of tomatoes you have available and cook the sauce. Then fill clean pint or half-pint (depending on the size of your household) canning jars to within a half-inch of the top, screw down the lids, immerse them in water to a depth of one inch in a stockpot or canning pot (put a layer of newspaper on the bottom to keep the jars from banging around), bring to a boil, and process for 30 minutes. Using tongs, remove the jars from the water and set them aside on a cloth towel until the lids ping, indicating that they are fully sealed. Tighten the lids once more and secure.

2 or 3 garlic cloves, sliced

2 tablespoons extra virgin olive oil

3¹/₂ pounds fresh ripe tomatoes, cut in chunks, or one 28-ounce can whole tomatoes, with juice, chopped

1 teaspoon salt (omit if using canned tomatoes)

¹/₂ teaspoon sugar

IN a heavy nonreactive saucepan over medium-low heat, sweat the garlic in the oil until it begins to soften, about 5 to 7 minutes. Add the tomatoes, salt if you wish, and sugar, raise the heat slightly, and cook rapidly, stirring frequently, while the tomatoes give off their juice and cook down to a thick mass—15 to 20 minutes. Watch the mixture carefully toward the end to make sure it doesn't scorch.

PUT the sauce through the fine disk of a food mill, discarding the seeds, bits of skin, and other residue. If the sauce seems thin, return it to medium-low heat and continue cooking, stirring constantly and watching very carefully, until it reaches the desired consistency.

fish broth

BRODO DI PESCE

6 to 7 cups

The carcasses (head and bones) of any white-fleshed fish may be used to make a flavorful fish stock—monkfish, snapper, cod, haddock, weakfish, whatever is available at your fishmonger's. Do not use oily fish such as bluefish, mackerel, or salmon, however, because the flavor is too strong.

Head and bones of one 4- to 6-pound fish, preferably haddock, cod, or snapper

2 or 3 bay leaves

1 medium onion, halved

1 teaspoon whole black peppercorns

About 15 sprigs flat-leaf parsley

1 cup dry white wine

6 cups water

Salt and freshly ground white pepper to taste

COMBINE the ingredients in a heavy soup kettle or stockpot and bring slowly to a boil over medium-low heat. Cover, turn the heat down to a bare simmer, and continue cooking for 45 minutes. Strain the broth through a double layer of cheesecloth in a colander and discard the solids. Taste and adjust the seasoning, keeping in mind that the salt will be concentrated if the stock must later be reduced.

meat broth

BRODO DI CARNE

10 cups

About 6 pounds meaty beef bones—
ribs and shanks are good; a
knuckle bone will add richness
and body

2 yellow onions, unpeeled and
halved

2 garlic cloves, if desired, crushed

2 medium to large carrots, halved

¼ cup flat-leaf parsley leaves

3 bay leaves

1 small dried hot red chile pepper,
if desired

Salt and freshly ground black
pepper to taste

1 cup dry red wine

10 cups water

COMBINE the ingredients in a heavy soup kettle or stockpot and set over
medium heat. Bring slowly to a boil, then cover the pan, turn the heat
down to a gentle simmer, and cook very slowly, patiently skimming off the
scum that rises to the top, for at least 2½ hours.

STRAIN the stock through a double layer of cheesecloth, discarding the
solids. Taste the stock and adjust the seasoning, keeping in mind that the
salt will be concentrated if the stock must be later reduced. Place the stock
in the refrigerator to let the fat rise to the top and solidify, after which it
can be easily removed with a slotted spoon.

chicken broth
BRODO DI POLLO

about 10 cups

Using a so-called free-range or naturally raised bird is the only way to produce a good flavorful chicken broth. These are available in farmers' markets and natural-foods stores, and increasingly in supermarkets, and they make all the difference in the world. Commercial birds are often bland and don't produce a rich and aromatic stock.

One 4- to 5-pound chicken, or 4 to 5 pounds chicken parts, including wings and backs

2 unpeeled onions, quartered

1 medium carrot, quartered

$^1/_2$ cup flat-leaf parsley leaves

About 10 cups water

Salt and freshly ground black pepper to taste

PUT all the ingredients in a heavy stockpot or soup kettle, adding more water if necessary to cover the bird to a depth of one inch. Place the pot over medium heat and slowly bring to a simmer, skimming off any froth that rises to the top. Cover the kettle, lower the heat, and simmer very gently for 1$^1/_2$ to 2$^1/_2$ hours, or until the bird is falling apart.

STRAIN the broth in a colander through a double layer of cheesecloth, discarding the solids. Taste the broth and adjust the seasoning, keeping in mind that if the broth is to be reduced later it will concentrate the salt. Put the strained stock in the refrigerator to let the fat rise and solidify, after which it may be removed easily with a slotted spoon.

vegetable broth

BRODO DI VERDURA PER VEGETARIANI

About 2 quarts

You will never get the same flavor impact with vegetable broth as you do with broth made from meat, chicken, or fish, so using olive oil to unite and boost the flavors is important. Vegetable broths as such are rarely used in Pugliese kitchens—this one is for the benefit of strict vegetarians.

---

2 medium yellow onions, quartered

3 carrots, peeled and cut in chunks

3 dark green outer celery ribs, cut in chunks

3 garlic cloves, lightly crushed with the flat blade of a knife

2 tablespoons extra virgin olive oil

6 plump brown mushrooms, cleaned and quartered (cremini or shiitake are more flavorful than ordinary supermarket mushrooms; wild mushrooms, if you can find them, are best of all)

1 cup dry white wine

9 cups hot water

1 fat leek, rinsed carefully

1 fennel bulb, including the leafy green tops, chopped

1 tablespoon chopped fresh thyme, or 1 teaspoon dried, crumbled

One 3-inch cinnamon stick, optional

6 whole cloves, optional

6 slices of dried porcini mushrooms

Salt and freshly ground black pepper to taste

PREHEAT the oven to 425°F. In a flameproof glass or metal baking dish, turn the onions, carrots, celery, and garlic in the olive oil to coat them well. Roast for 15 minutes; then add the mushrooms and stir to mix well. Return to the oven for another 15 minutes, after which the vegetables should be brown and crispy on the edges and should give off a delicious aroma. Remove the dish from the oven and scrape the vegetables into a heavy stockpot or soup kettle. Add the wine to the oven dish and set over medium heat. Cook the wine, scraping up the brown bits in the pan, until it is slightly reduced, about 10 minutes, then add to the stockpot with 9 cups hot water. Add the leek, fennel, thyme, cinnamon, and cloves. Bring the stock to a simmer over medium-low heat, cover, and cook for at least 1 hour.

MEANWHILE, put the dried mushrooms in a 1-cup measure and fill with boiling water. Let soak for 15 minutes. Remove the mushrooms (do not discard the soaking liquid) and rinse under running water to get rid of grit. Chop them coarsely and add to the stockpot along with the soaking liquid, strained through a fine-mesh sieve.

WHEN the stock has finished cooking, strain it through a double layer of cheesecloth or a fine-mesh sieve. Discard the vegetables and aromatics. Taste the broth for seasoning, adding salt and pepper if necessary—be mindful of the salt, however, because reducing the broth later may concentrate the salt too much.

Roasted Peppers

CHARCOAL OR WOOD EMBERS are best for roasting peppers because they add a smoky flavor. If you have a charcoal grill, set the peppers on a grid about 4 inches above the coals, turning them frequently so the skins become thoroughly blackened and blistered. If you don't have live coals, the peppers can be roasted over a gas flame, using a long-handled fork, or under an electric broiler, always turning frequently to blacken and loosen the skins and make them easy to peel.

When the peppers are done, remove them from heat and set them aside under a dish towel until they are cool enough to handle. Slit them and drain the juices into a bowl. (Add the flavorful juices to the preparation, or save for another recipe.) Peel the peppers by pulling and rubbing away the blackened skin with your fingers. Use a sharp knife if necessary to remove remaining bits of skin. Peeling the skins under running water washes away too much of the flavor, but a bowl of water is handy for rinsing off difficult bits.

With a knife, scrape away the seeds and interior white membrane of the peppers. The peppers can be prepared in advance and refrigerated, if necessary, until you're ready to cook.

the small dishes
of Puglia

ANTIPASTI, SNACKS, AND LITTLE MEALS

*L*ittle china bowls of home-cured black, mottled green, and mauve-colored olives; platters of sliced underripe tomatoes dressed with oil, salt, and a sprinkle of dried oregano; strips of roasted eggplant and zucchini fragrant with a minted vinegar marinade; salted anchovies and brine-cured tuna; thick coins of rosy salami studded with nuggets of pork fat; wedges of mint-scented frittata; perhaps, if the season is right, a terra-cotta bowl filled with fresh pale fava beans, steamed and dressed simply with oil and lemon juice; a little pile of sweet, briny shrimp still encased in their papery husks; or an oven dish of hot and fragrant mussels plump in their shells and strewn with a crisp crust of bread

21

crumbs and oil—all the fantasy, all the considerable ingenuity of Pugliese cooks comes into play in the antipasto course.

Antipasto means literally "before the meal," though it's also called, a bit more crudely, the *apristomaco,* the stomach-opener, the aim being to prepare the stomach, and the palate, for what will come after. You are not meant to fill up on antipasti, though the temptation is to do just that, so inviting are all these little bowls and plates and platters spread across the festive board. And festive is the key word here, for the presence of antipasti on the table signifies an occasion, whether wedding or baptism, the celebration of a successful harvest, or simply a gathering of long-separated friends and family.

Pugliese restaurants pride themselves on their antipasti, vaunting the scope and variety of what they present. At Al Fornello, a restaurant on a shady hillside outside Ceglie Messápico that many consider one of Italy's best, I have counted as many as twenty-two separate dishes listed on the menu under what chef Dora Ricci calls *rusticcherie cegliese*—and that doesn't include the specials based on what she found in the market that morning. The antipasti range from a predictable, if first-rate, prosciutto with melon to freshly purged snails in a savory tomato sauce and deep-fried balls of goat's milk ricotta, the outside crisp and golden, the interior creamy and pale.

In Pugliese homes, antipasti are understandably more restrained than in restaurants. There will be not more than three or four of these little dishes, carefully chosen to balance flavors and textures, the simple with the complex, the raw with the cooked. One family favorite is *il benedetto,* the benediction, so-called because it includes eggs blessed by the priest in his annual pre-Easter visit to invoke the grace of the season on each home in his parish. The eggs are hard-boiled and sometimes served in their red-dyed shells along with fried artichokes, lettuce, radishes, capers, sliced oranges, and thin slices of soppressata, a local pork sausage, as an antipasto to precede the Easter feast.

Almost any part of the meal, almost any dish (except, of course, sweets), can be part—or all—of an antipasto, and almost anything on the antipasto table can—and does—show up in other parts of the meal. Tender chunks of octopus, grilled over the embers of an olive wood fire and dressed very simply with oil and lemon juice, chopped parsley, and a sprinkling of garlic, are deeply satisfying served hot as a main course—but left to cool to room temperature, then sliced thinly and mounded on a plate with a wedge of lemon, grilled octopus is a welcome antipasto. And the same is true of many other parts of the traditional antipasto—tiella, for instance, is served at home as a main course, but some restaurants send out a little oval dish with a portion as an antipasto. The only elements that won't appear elsewhere in a meal are the *sott'aceti* and *sott'olii,* vinegar- or oil-preserved vegetables like capers, green and black olives, strips of roasted eggplant, sun-dried tomatoes, sweet and hot peppers, artichoke hearts, and, best of all, dearest to the Pugliese heart and palate, lampascioni, the bitter bulbs of tassel hyacinth, that are boiled or roasted and then pickled in oil or brine.

An antipasto alla pugliese can be as simple as a slice of the dense Semolina Bread (page 190), toasted over wood embers, rubbed with garlic, drizzled with fresh olive oil, and then—the authentic touch—massaged with the cut half of a fresh, ripe tomato until the tomato pulp impregnates the toasted surface of the bread. Or it could be a lavish antipasto crudo, a presentation of fresh raw fish and shellfish artfully arranged on a great platter and brought to the table with fragrant lemon halves, cruets of thick Pugliese extra virgin olive oil, crisp sea salt, and a pepper mill.

Antipasto alla barese, as it's called in seafood restaurants in the great Adriatic port of Bari, almost always includes the following: sweetly fresh anchovies tasting directly, almost shockingly, of the sea, to be eaten, when very small, bones and all (and tiniest of all, transparent anchovy fry, no more than an inch long, their eyes like pin dots, eaten by the spoonful with olive oil and a few drops of lemon juice— a rare and delicious treat); baby cefalopods, thumb-sized squid and octopus in great variety—*seppioline, moscardini, calamaretti, polipetti,* tender and glowing on the plate like plump little pillows of violet-stained alabaster; iodine-rich, seaweed-flavored *ricci* (sea urchins) from the Adriatic south of Bari, their bottoms cracked open to reveal the dark blood-red roe that is dipped out with nubbins of bread; pale raw clams called *telline* and *vongole verace,* served on the halfshell; and raw oysters and black mussels from Taranto.

Raw seafood should be consumed with as much caution in Puglia, of course, as it is elsewhere in this troublesome world, but there are plenty of other dishes on the antipasto table. And just because they're called antipasti doesn't mean they can only be served at the beginning of a meal. Many of these are just as suitable as main courses on their own, whether for lunch or supper, while others are adaptable as snack food, to have on hand when hunger strikes.

In the following antipasto recipes, yields vary depending on whether the dish is served as part of a selection of appetizers or on its own.

marinated vegetables
VERDURE A SCAPECE

4 to 8 servings

At the Locanda del Gallo, east of Lecce, a selection of seasonal vegetables, grilled and marinated, makes a handsome presentation. The vegetables can be made a day or so ahead of time but should be brought to room temperature before serving.

---

2 Italian eggplants, about 1 pound

Salt

4 bell peppers, preferably red and yellow mixed

2 zucchini, about 1½ pounds

Extra virgin olive oil for brushing the vegetables

¼ cup extra virgin olive oil

¼ cup white wine vinegar

2 garlic cloves, chopped

2 oil-packed anchovy fillets, chopped

1½ tablespoons minced fresh mint or oregano

CUT eggplants into lengthwise slices about ½ inch thick. Place in a bowl and cover with water. Add ¼ cup salt for every 2 quarts water. Set a weighted plate in the bowl to hold the slices under water, and soak for 2 hours.

CUT each pepper in half lengthwise, removing and discarding the membranes and seeds. Slice the zucchini in diagonal slices about ½ inch thick.

WHEN ready to cook, prepare a medium-hot charcoal fire or preheat a gas grill or oven broiler. Remove the eggplant slices from the salt water and pat dry with paper towels. Brush the eggplant and zucchini slices lightly with olive oil and grill on each side for 10 to 18 minutes, or until the slices are dark brown on both sides. Remove from the grill and arrange on a deep platter.

PLACE the pepper halves skin side down on the grill or skin side up under the broiler. Cook until peppers are slightly blackened and the skin is starting to lift off and blister, about 5 or 6 minutes. Remove to the platter.

MIX the remaining ingredients together and pour over the *hot* vegetables. Cover immediately with aluminum foil and set aside at room temperature to marinate for several hours or overnight. Serve at room temperature.

sautéed black olives

OLIVE NERE SOFFRITTE

About 2 cups

Lightly frying black olives, then finishing them with an herby tomato sauce, lends an entirely different dimension to their flavor. Serve these with thick slices of country-style bread for mopping up the delicious juices—and with a reminder that olive pits may be left on the sides of the plate.

I pound small black brine-cured olives, such as Gaeta or Niçoise

2 garlic cloves, chopped

¼ cup extra virgin olive oil

2 drained canned plum tomatoes, coarsely chopped

I teaspoon dried crumbled oregano

I tablespoon minced flat-leaf parsley

I teaspoon salt or to taste

DRAIN the olives and rinse them in running water. Set aside.

OVER medium heat, sauté the garlic in the olive oil until it starts to soften. Do not let it brown. Add the olives and cook briefly, about 3 minutes, until softened. Add the tomatoes, oregano, parsley, and salt. Lower the heat and simmer for 15 to 20 minutes, basting the olives with the tomato sauce.

SERVE immediately.

roasted pepper rolls
P E P E R O N I   A R R O T O L A T I

16 rolls, about 8 to 16 servings

Stefano Tagliente, executive chef at Il Melograno, a gloriously simple retreat in the olive groves outside Monópoli, showed me how he prepares these filled and rolled red peppers. Lay each pepper strip on a sheet of plastic wrap, smooth the bread crumb stuffing over it, then use the wrap to roll it, jelly-roll fashion, into a tight package, twisting the ends to hold them. Steam the rolls on a rack over boiling water briefly, no more than a minute, to firm them, then removes the wrap and roasts the pepper rolls in the oven as described below. Home cooks are more apt to follow the simpler procedure in the recipe, but Tagliente's makes a neater presentation and avoids the use of toothpicks.

1½ tablespoons chopped capers

1½ tablespoons lightly toasted pine nuts

1½ tablespoons raisins, soaked in warm water for 15 minutes

2 boned and rinsed salted anchovies or 4 small oil-packed anchovy fillets, finely chopped

⅓ cup toasted bread crumbs

1 heaping tablespoon minced flat-leaf parsley

Salt and freshly ground black pepper to taste

1 tablespoon extra virgin olive oil

1 pound yellow and red bell peppers (4 large peppers), roasted (page 19), peeled, and each one sliced into 4 pieces

PREHEAT the oven to 425°F. Rub a little olive oil on a baking sheet.

IN a small bowl, combine the capers, pine nuts, drained raisins, anchovies, bread crumbs, and parsley. Add a little salt if necessary (there may be sufficient salt from the anchovies) and pepper to taste, and mix in the olive oil to make a loose paste.

LAY out the pepper slices, peeled side down. Spread a heaping teaspoon of the bread crumb mixture at the wide end of each slice, then roll the slice firmly toward the pointed end. Secure each slice with a toothpick and place on the baking sheet.

BAKE the rolled peppers for 15 minutes, or until they are warmed through and lightly toasted. Serve immediately or at room temperature.

sweet and sour onions
CIPOLLINE IN AGRODOLCE

4 to 8 servings

These little onions are as good served as an accompaniment to a meat course as they are as part of an antipasto.

---

1 pound small (pickling size) white or red onions (about 20 onions)

3 tablespoons extra virgin olive oil

2 bay leaves

2 tablespoons red wine vinegar

1 tablespoon sugar, or more to taste

Pinch of salt and a little freshly ground black pepper

TRIM the root and stem ends of the onions. Bring a pot of water to a rolling boil and drop the onions in. Lower the heat and cook for 5 to 7 minutes or until the onions are just softening. Drain immediately and peel.

MEANWHILE, in another saucepan, warm the olive oil with the bay leaves while the onions are cooking. Turn the peeled onions into the oil and cook very gently for about 5 minutes or until the onions just start to brown around the edges. Add the vinegar and sugar, raise the heat slightly, and cook, stirring frequently, until the vinegar-sugar mixture starts to caramelize, about 2 minutes. Remove from the heat and discard the bay leaves. Turn the onions gently to coat them thoroughly with the syrupy mixture. Season with salt and pepper. Set aside to cool and serve at room temperature.

grilled breaded mussels
COZZE ARRACANATE

4 to 8 servings

Passionate mussel-eaters, the Pugliese prepare these bivalves in dozens of ways. The black Mediterranean mussel, *Mytilus galloprovincialis,* is a different breed from our common Atlantic blue mussel, *M. edulis,* with a softer, more delicate flavor and a creamier texture. Atlantic mussels are perfectly fine to use in this dish, but the Mediterranean ones cultivated in Puget Sound are available by mail order (page 255) and in some seafood markets. To prepare mussels for cooking, see page 155.

2 pounds medium mussels (24 to 36), scrubbed and beards removed

Dry white wine, as necessary

2 tablespoons minced garlic

3 tablespoons minced flat-leaf parsley

$^{1}/_{2}$ teaspoon dried crumbled oregano

2 tablespoons freshly grated pecorino or Parmigiano-Reggiano, if desired

$^{1}/_{4}$ cup freshly grated bread crumbs

$^{1}/_{4}$ cup extra virgin olive oil

PREHEAT the oven to 425°F.

PREPARE the scrubbed mussels for cooking by rinsing under running water. Discard any that are gaping, keeping only those that are firmly closed; also discard any that are suspiciously heavy as they are probably packed with mud and sand.

PLACE the mussels in a pan with 2 to 3 tablespoons of water or dry white wine over medium-high heat and cook, stirring frequently, just until the mussels begin to open. (The mussels will continue cooking later.) With a slotted spoon remove the mussels to a bowl as they open. When all the mussels are removed, strain the liquid in the pot through a fine sieve or several layers of cheesecloth. Reserve the liquid. (You should have $^{1}/_{4}$ cup of liquid—if not, make up the difference with a little dry white wine or water.) Remove the mussels from their shells, reserving a half shell for each mussel. Set the half shells on a baking sheet and place a mussel in each one.

IN a small bowl, combine the garlic, parsley, oregano, grated cheese, and bread crumbs, then sprinkle the mixture over the mussels in a thin layer. Drizzle the olive oil and reserved strained mussel liquid over the bread crumbs.

BAKE the mussels for about 10 minutes or until the tops are brown and crisp. Serve piping hot or at room temperature. (Do not reheat as this will toughen the mussels.)

stuffed squid

SEPPIE RIPIENE

4 to 8 servings

These pretty little pockets of squid, their tops cut open to show the stuffing inside, are served at Gambrinus, an unassuming hole-in-the-wall trattoria on the Taranto waterfront across from where the fishing boats tie up. Nicla Granozio, an exuberant young cook from Puglia's other coast, the Adriatic near Bari, showed me how to make them. For best results buy the smallest, freshest calamari or squid you can find, with their tentacles still attached. Nicla doesn't use tomatoes or olives in her stuffing but other cooks do. If you leave out the tomatoes, you'll need to add a little more oil and/or milk to compensate.

In Puglia, these are sometimes served as a main course on a serving platter surrounded, in season, by a sauce of fresh green peas stewed in olive oil with a few fragments of sliced onion.

About 3 pounds whole, uncleaned squid (calamari) of even size (about 12 squid)

2 cups freshly grated bread crumbs

2 eggs, lightly beaten

3 garlic cloves

1 small onion, finely chopped

1/3 cup plus 3 tablespoons finely chopped flat-leaf parsley

2 to 3 tablespoons milk

6 tablespoons extra virgin olive oil

Salt and freshly ground black pepper to taste

1/2 cup freshly grated pecorino or Parmigiano-Reggiano

8 large green olives, pitted and coarsely chopped, optional

2 or 3 drained canned plum tomatoes, chopped, optional

1/2 cup dry white wine, or a little more if necessary

Lemon wedges, optional

PREPARE the squid: Rub the thin, purplish membrane from the outsides of the squid, being careful not to tear the bodies, or hoods, as you do so. (It isn't necessary to remove every scrap of this but the squid make a more attractive presentation without it.) Set the squid on a cutting board and cut a slit in the hood from the base of each squid to the top (leaving the tentacles attached at the base) to enable you to pull away the insides. Discard the innards, including the bony strip called the beak, then rinse the squid bodies carefully inside and out and set aside to drain. Using scissors or a sharp knife, cut away from the fanlike fins on either side of the squid body and the single very long tentacle. Chop these into small pieces.

IN a medium bowl, combine the chopped squid with the bread crumbs and eggs. Chop two of the garlic cloves with the onion, add ⅓ cup of the parsley, and add to the bread crumbs. Stir in the milk and 3 tablespoons of the oil and mix together briefly. Add salt and pepper, the cheese, and, if you wish, the olives and tomatoes. Using your hands, mix everything together very well. Stuff each squid hood *loosely* with the mixture.

MINCE the remaining clove of garlic and mix with the remaining 3 tablespoons of parsley. In a pan large enough to hold all the squid in one layer, heat the remaining 3 tablespoons of oil over medium heat and add the minced garlic and parsley. When the aromatics begin to sizzle, arrange the stuffed squid in the frying pan, open side down. Brown for about 3 or 4 minutes, then carefully turn and brown the other side. When brown on both sides, add the white wine to the pan, reduce the heat to a gentle simmer, and cook, covered, for about 30 minutes, or until the squid are tender; if the pan starts to look dry, add more wine.

SERVE immediately, with lemon wedges, if desired, and the small amount of sauce left in the pan spooned over the squid.

marinated fish with vinegar and mint
PESCIOLINI IN SCAPECE

4 to 6 servings

Scapece or escabeche, often made with sardines or other small, throw-away fish, is found all over the Mediterranean in one form or another as a way to preserve fish in vinegar for a short period of time. In the bustling fishing port of Gallípoli on Puglia's Ionian coast, the little fish, marinated in saffron vinegar, are sold at food festivals by street vendors called *scapecieri,* but home cooks make scapece with garlic and crushed mentuccia instead of the far more costly saffron.

Because sardines are so devilishly hard to find in this country, I have often made this with smelts instead. Smelts have an entirely different flavor but at least they are the right size. If you can find sardines, though—and they must be impeccably fresh, firm-textured, and with a clean briny fragrance—by all means use them instead.

Serve these with slices of crusty country-style bread, lightly toasted if you wish, for sopping up the juices.

---

4 or 5 garlic cloves, crushed

1 tablespoon chopped fresh mint

1 cup white wine vinegar

1 cup extra virgin olive oil

1/2 cup freshly grated bread crumbs

1 to 1 1/2 pounds small fish,

preferably sardines, but smelts may be used if necessary (the heads may be cut off but otherwise the fish should be left whole)

About 1/4 cup all-purpose flour

PLACE the garlic and mint in a small saucepan with the wine vinegar and set over medium-low heat. As soon as the vinegar starts to boil, lower the heat to well below the simmering point and leave the aromatics to steep with the vinegar while you proceed with the recipe.

IN about a tablespoon of the olive oil, toast the bread crumbs in a saucepan over medium-high heat until they are golden brown and crisp. Remove and set aside.

DREDGE the fish lightly in the flour. Sauté in half the remaining olive oil over medium-high heat, setting aside the fish to drain as they finish cooking. When all the fish have been fried, discard the oil and wipe out the pan. Add the remaining, clean oil to the pan and set over very low heat to warm. Layer the fish in a glass or ceramic dish (a soufflé dish is perfect for this), sprinkling each layer liberally with the toasted bread crumbs and distributing the garlic and mint from the vinegar infusion. The topmost layer of bread crumbs should completely cover the fish. Now combine the warm vinegar and warm clean oil and pour over the bread crumbs. Cover the dish and set aside for two to three days in a cool place (a refrigerator is fine) before serving.

mint omelet

FRITTATA DI MENTA

4 to 8 servings

The mint used in Puglia is wild mentuccia, closely akin to pennyroyal *(Mentha pulegium)* and with a subtler, less aggressive flavor than the kind of mint we usually grow in our gardens or find in our shops. The aim here is an omelet gently suffused with the aroma of mint rather than overpowered by it.

I small yellow onion, finely chopped

3 tablespoons extra virgin olive oil

I cup (loosely packed) fresh mint leaves

8 large eggs

3 tablespoons freshly grated Parmigiano-Reggiano

Salt and freshly ground black pepper to taste

GENTLY sauté the onion in 2 tablespoons olive oil in an ovenproof 10- to 12-inch skillet over medium-low heat until the onion is soft but not starting to brown—about 10 to 15 minutes. Away from the heat, add the mint to the onion and stir to combine well. Set aside to cool.

MIX the eggs in a bowl with a fork, then stir in the cheese, salt, and pepper. Stir the cooled onion-mint mixture into the eggs.

TURN on the broiler and adjust a rack so that the upper surface of the omelet will be about 6 inches from the heat source.

RETURN the skillet to medium-high heat. Add the remaining tablespoon of oil to the pan and swirl it over the bottom and sides. Turn the egg mixture into the pan. Cook, continually running a palette knife, narrow spatula, or cake icer around the edges of the pan to keep the eggs loose. From time to time, lift some of the cooked egg off the bottom of the pan to let uncooked egg run underneath. When the bottom of the frittata is set, remove from the stove top and run it under the broiler for 30 seconds or so, just long enough to glaze and brown the top.

CUT in wedges or small squares and serve immediately. Or set aside to cool to room temperature before serving.

octopus and potato salad
INSALATA DI POLPO E PATATE

4 to 8 servings

Each morning in fair weather, and sometimes in foul, elderly fishermen, retired from the commercial fleet but unable to turn their backs on the water, row their bright blue boats to the octopus grounds just outside the harbor of Monópoli and jig for octopus. Once caught, the octopus are tenderized by bashing them against the rocks and rinsing them in sea water, then are taken directly to the nearby market. Octopus this fresh may be eaten raw, or marinated in olive oil and grilled quickly over wood or charcoal embers.

Fresh octopus found here (try Italian- or Asian-owned fish markets) sometimes needs tenderizing; it's easiest to do this by dipping it three times in a large pan of boiling water, holding it under the water (with tongs) for 10 seconds each time; after this the octopus may be dressed with olive oil and grilled, then sliced for this salad. When I can't find fresh octopus, I have made this recipe most successfully, and a lot more easily, with already cooked steamed octopus from Japanese fish markets. Precooked octopus varies in tenderness; if it is tough, slice it thinly and steam over boiling water for up to 30 minutes until tender.

---

1 pound waxy (boiling) potatoes

1 pound cooked octopus tentacles, sliced crosswise ¼ to ½ inch thick

3 or 4 scallions, finely sliced (green and white)

2 tablespoons chopped flat-leaf parsley

½ cup extra virgin olive oil

3 tablespoons fresh lemon juice

1 garlic clove, finely chopped

Salt and freshly ground black pepper to taste

COOK the potatoes in a pan of rapidly boiling lightly salted water for 15 to 20 minutes or until they are thoroughly tender but not falling apart. Drain, and as soon as they can be handled, peel the potatoes and slice, while still warm, about ½ inch thick.

continues

MOUND the octopus slices attractively in the center of a platter and arrange the warm potato slices around the edge. Sprinkle with the scallions and parsley. Mix together the olive oil, lemon juice, garlic, salt, and pepper. Taste and adjust the seasoning, then pour the dressing over the octopus and still warm potatoes. Cover with a piece of foil and set aside in a cool place to marinate for several hours before serving.

NOTE: *When tomatoes are at their peak of ripeness they may be sliced and added to the salad at the moment of serving.*

meatless meatballs

POLPETTE DI LUPO

30 to 34 balls, about 6 servings

At Torre Cascine, a restaurant on the coast below Gallípoli, we were talking about la cucina povera and the dishes from that tradition that have recently become so fashionable. Spare, sparse, relying strictly on locally seasonal ingredients, foraged greens and mushrooms, dried beans and grains, and vegetables preserved in oil or vinegar, la cucina povera depended on labor and time, in the fields as much as in the kitchen. It took time to scavenge the meadows for all those tender bitter greens of the winter season, and it took time to clean them and prepare them. In today's world, time is the luxury, so cucina povera has become a symbol of those with wealth enough to have time to spare. "In fact," said Stefano, "la cucina povera today is really beef steak."

As prepared by Gianna Greco, the chef and owner of Torre Cascine, this is an old-fashioned cucina povera sort of dish. No, the polpette are *not* meatballs made from wolf *(lupo)* meat, nor from any kind of meat at all. (Perhaps they're called wolf balls because they keep the wolf from the door?) However that may be, they are a happy sign that meat is not necessary for an elegant table. Light in texture, delicate in flavor, these are especially good for summertime meals when meat seems excessive. I especially like this dish because it shows that the cooking of poor countryfolk can be just as refined and artistic as haute cuisine.

---

1 pound stale country-style bread, crusts removed

1½ cups milk

3 large eggs

½ cup grated pecorino or Parmigiano-Reggiano

2 tablespoons finely minced flat-leaf parsley

2 tablespoons finely minced basil

1 garlic clove, finely minced

Sea salt and freshly ground black pepper

1 cup extra virgin olive oil

Tomato Sauce (page 14), with fresh basil leaves torn and added

THICKLY slice the stale bread and soak the slices in milk until soaked through, then squeeze dry. Crumble and tear the soaked bread into

continues

smaller pieces, then process in the food processor, using quick pulses, to crumbs. This will yield about 4 cups soaked crumbs.

MIX the soaked bread crumbs in a bowl with the eggs, cheese, herbs, and garlic, adding salt and pepper as desired. Form into fat round balls about 2 inches in diameter. (It's easier to do this with wet hands.) Set aside on a rack or plate to dry for about 15 or 20 minutes.

IN a saucepan or deep skillet over medium-high heat, heat the oil to frying temperature (about 360°F.) and fry the bread balls until brown on all sides. Remove the balls as they brown and drain on a rack covered with paper towels.

HAVE the tomato sauce ready. Arrange the balls on a platter and spoon the sauce over them. Serve immediately, passing more grated cheese to garnish if you wish.

green-hearted meatball
POLPETTONE A CUORE VERDE

4 to 8 servings

The Ristorante Al Fornello, just outside the town of Ceglie Messápico, is justly famous for the variety and splendor of its antipasti. This and the following three recipes are almost always available at this fine restaurant.

Chef Dora Ricci's big fantasy meatball is similar to meat loaf but with a delicacy of texture and subtlety of flavor that comes from an astute combination of very simple ingredients. You could serve this warm as a main course, or at room temperature, thinly sliced, as an antipasto.

If you don't want to use veal, a combination of very lean ground beef and pork will do as well. Signora Ricci uses an aged pecorino cheese. Pecorino romano is too strong and sour-tasting, so if you can't find an aged Pugliese, Tuscan, or Sardinian pecorino, use freshly grated Parmigiano-Reggiano instead.

½ pound finely ground lean veal; or use half ground lean pork and half ground beef

1 cup plus 3 tablespoons freshly grated bread crumbs

1 cup freshly grated pecorino or Parmigiano-Reggiano

3 large eggs

½ teaspoon salt, or to taste

1 teaspoon freshly ground black pepper, or to taste

6 leaves fresh green chard, the smaller the better, stems removed

1 large carrot

3 tablespoons unbleached all-purpose flour

5 or 6 thin slices (about 2 ounces) caciocavallo, provolone, or other mild cheese

6 tablespoons extra virgin olive oil

2 fresh rosemary sprigs

1½ cups dry white wine

COMBINE the ground meat in a bowl with 1 cup of the bread crumbs, the grated cheese, eggs, salt, and pepper. Using your hands, mix together thoroughly.

BRING a large pot of water to a rolling boil and dip the chard leaves in it for a minute or so, until they are just wilted, then set aside. Add the car-

continues

rot to the boiling water and cook until barely al dente, about 10 minutes. Drain and, as soon as you can handle it, slice the carrot lengthwise in 5 or 6 slices.

COMBINE the flour with the remaining 3 tablespoons of bread crumbs and heavily dust a wooden work board with the mixture. Pat the ground meat into an 8-X-12-inch rectangle about ½ inch thick. Lay the chard leaves over the meat, leaving a border of about an inch on the short sides. Layer carrot slices over the chard, then cheese slices over the carrots. Now roll the meat, jelly-roll fashion, into a long thin sausage with the vegetables and cheese inside, packing the meat with your hands to make it as tight and firm as you can. As you roll the sausage, it will lengthen to about 16 inches. Cut the sausage in half crosswise, sealing the ends thoroughly with the meat mixture to prevent the cheese from oozing out during cooking. The outsides should be thoroughly dusted with the flour mixture; if necessary, add a little more to the board and roll the finished polpettone in it.

IN a frying pan large enough to hold the two meat rolls, heat the olive oil over medium-low heat. Add the rosemary and the polpettone and brown the meat on all sides, turning it carefully with wooden spoons or two spatulas. When the meat is thoroughly brown, remove and discard as much of the oil as you can. Pour half the wine over the top of the browned rolls, turn the heat down to medium-low, cover the pan, and cook for about 15 minutes. (If the wine evaporates during this time, add a little water to the pan.) Remove the cover, turn the meat rolls over, pour the remaining wine over them, cover again, and continue cooking for an additional 15 minutes.

TRANSFER the meat rolls to a cutting board. Return the skillet to medium-high heat and add ½ cup of water to the pan juices. Cook down, scraping up any brown bits, until you have 2 or 3 tablespoons of meat glaze. Strain to remove the rosemary leaves. Let the rolls cool to room temperature, then slice as thinly as possible and serve with the meat glaze drizzled over.

dora ricci's tiny meatballs

POLPETTINE

24 to 30 meatballs

When you sit down at the table at Al Fornello, a little plate of these tiny meatballs immediately appears before you. It's hard to believe that anything as easy as these could be so tasty, but the freshness of the preparation and the high quality of the simple ingredients guarantee lots of good flavor.

3/4 pound ground lean meat (veal, or a combination of veal and pork)

1 cup freshly grated bread crumbs

2 tablespoons grated pecorino

2 tablespoons minced flat-leaf parsley

1 garlic clove, finely minced

1 whole egg

Salt and freshly ground black pepper

1 cup extra virgin olive oil for frying

8 drained canned plum tomatoes

1 small white onion, peeled and very thinly sliced

2 tablespoons extra virgin olive oil

1 tablespoon slivered fresh herbs, such as basil, mint, or oregano, optional

IN order to keep the meatballs as light as possible, be careful not to over-mix them. Using your hands and working quickly, combine the meat, bread crumbs, grated cheese, parsley, garlic, egg, salt, and pepper in a bowl. The mixture should be homogeneous but not compact.

IN a pan appropriate for deep-frying, heat the olive oil to 360°F. While the oil is heating, form the meat mixture into little balls no more than about 3/4 inch in diameter. When the oil is hot, toss the meatballs in, a few at a time, and fry until brown on all sides. As they finish cooking, set aside to drain.

GENTLY stew the tomatoes and onion in 2 tablespoons of oil in a saucepan over medium heat, crushing the tomatoes with a fork as they cook, until most of the liquid has evaporated and the sauce is dense. Taste and add salt if necessary. Transfer the sauce to a food processor or food mill and process

continues

briefly, just long enough to make a smooth purée. Return to the pan in which the sauce was cooked, add the drained meatballs, and let them bubble gently over medium-low heat for 2 to 3 minutes to absorb the flavors. Just before serving, stir in the fresh herbs if you wish.

NOTE: *The meatballs may also be served without the sauce, passed on a plate with toothpicks for ease of handling.*

dora ricci's deep-fried ricotta balls
POLPETTE DI RICOTTA

24 to 30 balls

Fresh goat's milk ricotta and sheep's milk ricotta are available at some farmers' markets in this country or by mail order from Paula Lambert's Mozzarella Company in Dallas (page 256). In the absence of either milk ricotta, use the regular ricotta available in most markets, but you will have to boost the flavor considerably by increasing the quantities of grated Parmigiano-Reggiano and the aromatics.

1⅓ cups fresh goat's milk or sheep's milk ricotta

½ to ¾ cup freshly grated Parmigiano-Reggiano

2 tablespoons finely minced flat-leaf parsley

1 garlic clove, finely minced

Pinch of freshly grated nutmeg

2 eggs

Salt and freshly ground black pepper to taste

2 to 3 cups extra virgin olive oil for frying

⅔ cup freshly grated bread crumbs

IF the ricotta is coarse in texture, put it through a food mill to lighten it up. Then mix with the grated cheese, parsley, garlic, nutmeg and the *yolk* of 1 egg (reserving the white). Mix with a fork or wooden spoon to amalgamate all these ingredients thoroughly, then taste and add salt and pepper if desired. Form the ricotta mixture into balls about the size of small walnuts and set on a rack to dry slightly for about 15 minutes.

WHEN ready to cook, place the oil in a pan suitable for deep-frying and heat to about 360°F. The amount of oil you will need depends on the size of the pan, but it should be at least 2 inches deep.

IN a shallow bowl mix the egg white with the remaining whole egg, beating with a fork or wire whisk to break up thoroughly. Place the bread crumbs in another shallow bowl.

WHILE the oil is heating, dip each ricotta ball in the egg to coat it lightly, then roll it quickly in the bread crumbs. Drop the balls, a few at a time, in the hot oil and fry until golden brown. Remove with a slotted spoon and drain briefly on a rack, then serve immediately, crisp and hot.

savory fritters
PITTULE

50 to 60 fritters

Deep-frying in extra virgin olive oil is as routine in Puglia as it is in other parts of the Mediterranean where frying traditions are strong.

Italian-style 00 flour, a fine grind, is available from The King Arthur Flour Baker's Catalogue (page 256).

I teaspoon dry yeast

2¹/₂ cups very warm water

2¹/₂ cups unbleached all-purpose flour and I cup pastry flour, or 3¹/₂ cups Italian-style 00 flour

I teaspoon sea salt

I cup Pepper Relish (page 221) or ¹/₄ cup drained capers and ¹/₂ cup coarsely chopped pitted black olives

Extra virgin olive oil for deep-frying

I tablespoon drained capers

DISSOLVE the yeast in ¹/₂ cup of warm water in a large mixing bowl. After 15 minutes, add another cup of warm water and the flour, stirring with a wooden spoon or rubber spatula just enough to mix the dough without kneading it. Cover the bowl and set aside in a warm place to rise for 2 to 3 hours or until doubled in size.

WHEN the dough has risen, dissolve the salt in the remaining cup of warm water and add, mixing it into the dough with your hands. The dough will look very raggedy at first but gradually will form a more creamy texture, though still lumpy. Using your hand as a paddle, keep beating the dough until it is smooth and uniform in texture and you can feel the strands of gluten developing. If the dough is too liquid to handle, beat in up to another half cup of flour; it should not be at all like bread dough—rather more like a batter, dense and creamy in consistency. You should be able to gather the dough in one hand and squeeze it to form a very loose and amorphous ball of dough on top of your fist. If you can't do that, the dough is too liquid.

WHEN the dough has reached the right consistency, beat in the pepper relish, or the capers and olives, or one of the alternatives suggested below. Whatever you choose to flavor the fritter batter, beat it in thoroughly and then set aside, lightly covered with a cloth, to rest for about 15 minutes.

MEANWHILE, in a deep-frying pan, heat about 1 inch of oil to 360°F. Drop a tablespoon of drained capers in the hot oil to fry—they give a sweet spiciness to the oil. Have a bowl of water ready in which to dip your hands. Wet your hands and take up a little batter in your left hand (assuming you are right-handed). Make a fist, squeezing the dough up into a small, rather amorphous ball above your thumb. Take this in your right hand, which you will have dipped in water, and carefully drop it in the hot oil. Proceed with the rest of the batter: You can do up to a dozen pittule at once, depending on the size of your pan. As soon as they are golden-brown on one side, turn and brown on the other. Then remove and drain on paper towels spread on a cake rack. Serve immediately, while still crisp and hot.

VARIATIONS: *Any of the following may be added instead of the pepper relish or the caper-olive combination:*

Small pieces of steamed salt cod. Small cauliflower pieces, steamed until just tender, then lightly salted.

Combination of ¼ cup coarsely chopped pitted black olives, 2 boned anchovies or 4 oil-packed anchovy fillets, coarsely chopped, 1 tablespoon capers, coarsely chopped, 1 small onion, finely minced, and ¼ teaspoon crushed red pepper flakes.

NOTE: *If you prefer, rather than using your hands to drop the fritter batter into the hot oil, use two spoons, dipped each in the bowl of water each time before spooning out the batter.*

deep-fried savory tarts
PANZEROTTI

60 to 70 panzerotti

Deep-fried panzerotti are traditionally made in Bari for the feast of Sant'Antonio Abate (St. Anthony Abbot) on January 17, the day that marks the beginning of Carnival. But nowadays you're apt to find them whenever there's occasion for a festa. Like most Barese, my friend Pino Marchese likes hot panzerotti spread with ricotta forte, an almost painfully strong double-fermented cheese spread. But panzerotti are just as delightful on their own, especially made as small as possible in one-bite sizes. The stuffings vary, but the most popular is a mixture of onions, black olives, capers, anchovies, and tomatoes.

As an alternative to frying, panzerotti may be brushed with egg wash and baked in a preheated 375°F. oven for 15 minutes, until golden and puffed.

FOR THE DOUGH:

I teaspoon dried yeast dissolved in I cup warm water

6 to 8 cups unbleached all-purpose flour

I cup warm whole milk

3 tablespoons extra virgin olive oil

3 tablespoons dry white wine

I teaspoon salt, or to taste

FOR THE ONION-OLIVE STUFFING:

I pound yellow onions, halved and thinly sliced

3 tablespoons extra virgin olive oil

2 drained canned plum tomatoes, coarsely chopped

1/3 cup minced flat-leaf parsley

1/2 cup pitted black Kalamata olives (about 20 olives)

I tablespoon capers

4 oil-packed anchovy fillets, coarsely chopped

3 tablespoons freshly grated Parmigiano-Reggiano

Freshly ground black pepper to taste

FOR THE SPICY PORK STUFFING:

One I-inch slice stale country-style bread, crusts removed

1/2 pound very lean ground pork

I large egg

1/2 cup freshly grated Parmigiano-Reggiano

1/2 cup minced flat-leaf parsley

I teaspoon crushed red pepper flakes

I teaspoon freshly ground black pepper

1/2 teaspoon crumbled dried oregano

I teaspoon salt, or to taste

Extra virgin olive oil for deep-frying

MAKE the dough by stirring the dissolved yeast into about 2 cups of the flour. Gradually work in the milk, oil, wine, and salt, alternating with more flour, until you have used about 5 cups of flour. The dough should be very soft, but if it is too wet to knead by hand, add more flour. Sprinkle a cup of flour on a bread board and knead the dough for about 5 minutes until it is satiny and smooth. Place in a lightly oiled bowl, cover with a damp kitchen towel, and set aside in a warm place to rise for at least 1 hour until doubled in size.

WHILE the dough is rising make the stuffings (see directions below).

WHEN the dough has doubled, punch it down and form into 60 to 70 small walnut-sized balls. Set the balls on a lightly floured board, cover with a dampened cloth, and let rise 1 hour.

WORKING with a few pieces of dough at a time, roll out each ball on a lightly floured board to a thin 4-inch circle. Drop a tablespoon or more of stuffing on one side of the circle and fold over the other side, first running a damp finger around the edge. Seal the panzerotti by pressing on the rims with a fork. Set each one as it is finished on a rack. Leave the panzerotti to dry for at least 15 minutes after the last one is completed.

WHEN ready to cook, heat the oil in a deep-frying pan to a temperature of 360°F. Drop the panzerotti in the hot oil four or five at a time, and fry, turning as necessary, until both sides are golden brown, about 5 minutes. Remove and drain on a rack covered with paper towels. Serve immediately.

TO make the onion-olive stuffing, gently sauté the onions in the olive oil over medium-low heat until they are very soft but not brown, 10 to 12 minutes. Stir in the tomatoes and cook 5 minutes, or until the tomatoes are soft and dissolving. Away from the heat, stir in the remaining ingredients.

TO make the spicy pork stuffing, cover the stale bread slice with warm water and immediately squeeze all the water out and tear the bread into small pieces. Combine all the ingredients with the soaked bread in a small bowl, kneading well with the hands to mix.

soups

*A*part from the various kinds of fish soups, which are often lavish, main-course affairs with a multitude of ingredients and complex, vivid flavors, soup does not play a major role on Pugliese tables. Whether in the form of zuppa, minestra, or minestrone, soup tends to be a winter dish, often based on legumes or wild vegetables, and with unmistakable links to the kitchens of poor countryfolk.

Some of the most satisfying Pugliese dishes are these mostly vegetable (though by no means vegetarian) soups. And they are a good example of how simple, even humble ingredients, carefully selected and thoughtfully combined, can produce miracles to grace the most sophisticated table. Sometimes the vegetables used are totally unfamiliar, unobtainable even in other parts of Italy, like *cardonciedd',* wild cardoons that are hard enough to find in Puglia and spiny, sticky things to clean when you do come across them. But cardonciedd' in brodo is a hauntingly fragrant and soothing preparation when the wild thistles are ripe and ready, and should you be in the northern Tavoliere at that time of the year, seek out this soup. Other soups, like the Summer Minestrone (page 52), are made of vegetables commonly found in our supermarkets, so familiar that it seems a wonder they could be made to taste so special.

Like most Pugliese cooking, nothing in these recipes is cast in stone, and in fact most of them change subtly from one kitchen to another. The idea behind them is quite simply that—an *idea* of a thing, rather than a precise reproduction. Those who live in Puglia in the wintertime, for instance, can make a minestra with wild fennel and cicorielle foraged from dormant fields, but the rest of us can use the concept of the *minestra maritata* instead, a rather brilliant idea, layers of vegetables combined and baked together to meld the flavors, using what we find in our own markets.

soup with winter greens and meatballs
ZUPPA CON POLPETTINE

6 to 8 servings

A rich meat broth is a prerequisite for this soup, which is often served as a first course for the Christmas feast, especially in the Salento, at the bottom of the Pugliese heel.

---

1 pound very lean ground beef or veal

3 eggs

1 cup fresh bread crumbs

1/4 cup freshly grated pecorino or Parmigiano-Reggiano

1/4 cup minced flat-leaf parsley

1 garlic clove, finely minced

Salt and freshly ground black pepper to taste

1/2 cup plus 2 tablespoons extra virgin olive oil

6 cups Meat Broth (page 16)

2 bunches escarole, chard, or other winter greens

About 1/4 cup flour

1 pound stale bread

IN a small bowl, mix together the ground meat, 1 egg, the bread crumbs, grated cheese, parsley, garlic, a pinch of salt, and black pepper. Form into meatballs, about the size of a walnut. Heat 2 tablespoons of the oil in a sauté pan over medium heat and brown the meatballs a few at a time.

BRING the broth slowly to a simmer in a 2- to 3-quart saucepan over medium-low heat. Wash the escarole in several changes of water, then sliver the leaves and add the slivers to the meat broth to simmer for 7 to 10 minutes or until the greens are tender. Add the meatballs to the stock and continue to simmer until the meatballs are thoroughly cooked, about 10 minutes longer.

WHILE the meatballs are simmering, place the flour on a soup plate. In another soup plate, beat the remaining 2 eggs. Remove the crusts from the stale bread and cut it into cubes no larger than 3/4 inch. Roll the cubes in the flour, then in the beaten eggs. In a small sauté pan, heat the remaining 1/2 cup olive oil over medium-high heat and fry the bread cubes until they are golden brown on all sides. When they are done, drain on paper towels.

TO serve, put a few bread cubes and a few little meatballs in each plate, then pour the simmering broth over.

IF you wish, pass a bowl with more grated cheese to be added at the table.

summer minestrone
ZUPPA DI VERDURA STUFATA

6 to 8 servings

Stufata means a cooking technique similar to a braise, in which the ingredients are cooked in little or no water; the juices from the vegetables themselves serve to give the soup its requisite "soupiness." This makes a very thick soup that should be served immediately, otherwise the vegetables absorb the small amount of liquid and it becomes more like a ciambotta (page 86), still delicious but no longer really a soup.

---

1 pound eggplant (1 or 2 small eggplants)

Sea salt

1 large or 2 medium potatoes

1 medium carrot

2 medium red or yellow bell peppers

¼ cup extra virgin olive oil, plus a little more for garnish

1 medium onion, coarsely chopped

1 stalk celery, chopped in 1-inch lengths

½ pound (1 bunch) fresh green or red chard, thinly sliced

½ pound green beans, sliced in 1-inch lengths

5 to 6 ripe red tomatoes, peeled and coarsely chopped

2 medium zucchini, cubed

½ cup coarsely chopped flat-leaf parsley

3 or 4 sprigs fresh oregano

1 bay leaf

1 sprig fresh rosemary

1 small dried hot red chile pepper, if desired

CUT the eggplant in 1-inch cubes. Place the cubes in a colander, sprinkling them liberally with salt. Weight the eggplant with a can set on a small plate and set the colander in the sink to drain for at least 1 hour. Then rinse the cubes thoroughly and pat dry with paper towels.

CUT the potatoes and carrot into cubes the same size as the eggplant. Cut the peppers in half lengthwise, discard the seeds and inner white membranes, and slice thinly.

ADD the oil to a big heavy saucepan or rondeau large enough to hold all the vegetables and place over medium-high heat. Quickly sauté the eggplant and potato cubes for about 5 minutes, or until they just start to brown along the edges. Stir in the onion and celery, lower the heat to medium-low, and continue cooking and stirring until the onion softens and starts to turn golden. Add the carrot, chard, green beans, and peppers and stir to combine everything well.

ADD ½ cup hot water to the vegetables in the pan, cover, and cook together for about 5 minutes, then stir in the chopped tomatoes, zucchini, and the aromatics, together with the hot pepper if desired. Add a pinch of salt, cover tightly, and cook for 30 minutes, adding a very little water from time to time if necessary. Remove oregano sprigs, bay leaf, and rosemary sprig before serving. Garnish each serving with a thin drizzle of olive oil.

bread soup
PANCOTTO

6 to 8 servings

The name means simply cooked bread, and like so many similar soups all over Italy the key ingredient is slightly stale bread. In Italian, the bread, once it's no longer fresh, is called *pane raffermo,* meaning bread that has firmed up—a nicer terminology than our "stale bread" with its negative connotation of bread that is no longer any good.

Ideally, pancotto should be flavored with lots of wild herbs and greens like borage, wild fennel, wild chicory, and rocket or arugula, but if you can't find these herbs, use a handful of fresh rosemary, thyme, basil, sage, arugula, and/or parsley, combined and chopped.

The vegetables can be varied with the season—add a handful of fresh fava beans in springtime, a few cauliflower florets in the fall, or bright cubes of butternut squash in winter.

About ¹/₂ cup chopped fresh wild or garden herbs (see above)

2 zucchini, quartered and cut in chunks

¹/₂ pound fresh green beans, broken in short lengths

1 pound small new potatoes, preferably white ones, their skins rubbed off, or larger potatoes, peeled and cut in chunks

2 ripe red tomatoes, peeled and coarsely chopped, or 1¹/₂ cups drained canned tomatoes

1 garlic clove, peeled and crushed with the flat blade of a knife

¹/₂ cup chopped white onion

Salt

Two 1-inch-thick slices slightly stale country-style bread

¹/₂ small dried hot red chile pepper

Freshly ground black pepper to taste

¹/₂ cup extra virgin olive oil or olio santo (see page 247)

IN a stockpot or soup kettle place the herbs, zucchini, green beans, potatoes, tomatoes, garlic, and onion and cover with water to a depth of one inch. Add salt to taste and bring to a simmer over high heat, then turn the

heat down to medium-low, cover the pot, and cook until the potatoes are tender, 20 to 30 minutes.

CUT the crusts off the bread slices and soak briefly in water, then squeeze the bread to get rid of all the water. Tear and crumble the soaked bread and add to the simmering soup along with the chile pepper. Cook, stirring with a wooden spoon, until the bread has thoroughly broken down and thickened the soup, about 10 minutes longer. Taste and adjust the seasoning, adding more salt if necessary and pepper if desired.

SERVE the soup immediately, with a good dollop of olive oil or olio santo and a little sprinkle of freshly chopped green herbs atop each serving. You may also pass a bowl of freshly grated pecorino or Parmigiano-Reggiano.

chick-pea soup
MINESTRA DI CICERCHIE

6 servings

Cicerchie are small dried beans that look like miniature broad beans or fave, but they are said to be an older, more primitive form of chick-peas. They have long been associated with la cucina povera. Until recently, cicerchie had almost disappeared in Italy except in a few pockets of rural Umbria, the Campagna outside Rome, and in Puglia. Like many similar foods, they have been rediscovered and lent a certain costly chicness by restaurant chefs. It's not likely that you'll find cicerchie in this country, but the soup is just as tasty made with *ceci* (chick-peas), *fagioli* (dried beans of any sort), or *fave secche* (dried broad beans).

Like most bean soups in Puglia, this one may also be served over slices of stale country-style bread, lightly toasted and brushed with a little garlic if you wish.

---

8 ounces (1 cup) dried chick-peas or other dried legumes

1 garlic clove

1 medium yellow onion, cut in half

3 or 4 ripe tomatoes, peeled and seeded, or 2 cups drained canned tomatoes

1 stalk celery, including the top green leaves

1 bay leaf

1 small dried hot red chile pepper

Salt and freshly ground black pepper to taste

A little extra virgin olive oil

A little finely minced flat-leaf parsley

PUT the chick-peas in a bowl, cover with cool water, and set aside to soak for 6 to 8 hours or overnight. Then drain and place in a soup kettle with fresh cold water to cover to a depth of one inch. Put the kettle on medium-low heat and when the water commences to boil, lower the heat, cover the kettle, and simmer until the chick-peas are half-cooked—about 45 minutes to 1 hour, depending on the age of the beans. Add simmering water from time to time, if needed.

WHEN you judge the chick-peas to be half-cooked, coarsely chop the garlic, onion halves, tomatoes, and celery and add to the pot, along with the bay leaf, chile pepper, salt, and pepper. Continue cooking, adding boiling water as necessary, until the chick-peas are tender. Remove the bay leaf and chile pepper.

SERVE immediately, garnished with the olive oil and parsley.

VARIATIONS: *Brown 1 coarsely chopped red onion over medium heat in 2 tablespoons olive oil. Add 1 teaspoon red wine vinegar and pass.*

Sauté 2 ounces diced pancetta (or bacon that has been blanched 2 minutes in boiling water) in 1 teaspoon olive oil until crisp. Scatter the bacon over the minestra just before serving.

pea soup with croutons
CECAMARITI

6 to 8 servings

Cecamariti is what this was called at the Ristorante Bruna, just 10 minutes outside Lecce in the town of San Donato, and Claudia Bacile told me that it means a dish thrown together with whatever's at hand to placate a hungry husband. At the Ristorante Acaya, on the other hand, in a village of the same name on the *other* side of Lecce, the exact same dish was called *muersi,* meaning little morsels—though whether it was morsels of peas or of fried bread wasn't clear.

Whatever it's called, this is a real peasant dish, the kind that can be easily transported out to the fields, or that will fill the farmer up in the morning before he leaves the house so he can pass the rest of the day with just a little piece of bread and cheese to keep him going. A pure dish of the Salento, the southeasternmost tip of Puglia, it's proof positive of the goodness of simple ingredients when they're combined as intelligently as they are here.

Leftover cooked greens, such as dandelion greens or broccoli rabe, are often stirred in at the last minute before serving, along with the fried bread.

---

1 pound whole dried peas, soaked overnight (see note)

1 yellow onion, diced

4 or 5 small very ripe tomatoes, peeled and diced, or 1 cup drained canned tomatoes, chopped

1 stalk celery, diced

1 bunch flat-leaf parsley, chopped, to make 1/2 to 3/4 cup

1 small dried hot red chile pepper, coarsely chopped

Sea salt and freshly ground black pepper to taste

4 or 5 slices country-style bread

1/2 cup plus a little more extra virgin olive oil

DRAIN the peas and put in a heavy pan. Add fresh water to cover to a depth of 1 inch—about 4 cups of water. (Cooks in the Salento use a handsome terra-cotta *pignatta* for this, but any heavy, lidded pot will do.) Set the pot over medium-low heat and when the liquid begins to simmer, lower the heat and cover the pan. After about 1 hour of simmering (half an hour for split peas—see below), stir in the diced vegetables, parsley, and chile pepper. Cook 5 minutes, then taste and add salt and pepper as desired.

COVER the pan again and continue simmering another hour or longer, until the peas are very tender and have started to dissolve into a mush—time depends on the age and size of the peas, and split peas will take a good deal less than whole ones. Add a very little boiling water from time to time if the peas become too thick.

WHEN the peas are thoroughly cooked, purée the contents of the pan, using a food mill or an immersion mixer. You should have a thick purée that is fairly smooth but with some discernible bits of peas and vegetables in it. Return the purée to the rinsed-out pan and keep hot while you prepare the bread.

CUT the bread slices into large croutons about 1 inch square, discarding the crusts. In a frying pan over medium heat, heat ½ cup of the olive oil until it is just below smoking. Add the bread pieces and fry until crisp and golden brown on all sides. Remove and drain on a rack covered with paper towels.

TRANSFER the peas to a heated serving dish, stir in the bread cubes, and serve immediately, drizzled with the olive oil left in the pan after sautéing the bread pieces—or add fresh olive oil if desired.

NOTE: *Whole dried green peas are used in the Salento, but they're not always easy to find here. I've made the soup very successfully with split peas instead, though the cooking time for the peas may be reduced by half.*

cardoon soup,
CARDONCIEDD' IN BRODO

4 to 6 servings

In February, when spiny clumps of wild cardoons dot the fields and hedgerows of the Masseria Cirillo in the rolling grasslands south of Foggia, Gigliola Bacile uses the wild greens to make a robust soup that is hearty enough for a main course at supper. Traditionally, the soup was made with lamb or mutton broth, with bits of the meat adding sustenance; this lighter version uses vegetable broth, and just a little chopped ham at the end. This, with the beaten-egg *stracciatelle* (rags), gives the soup extra body.

Wild cardoons require laborious cleaning to rid them of their spines and tough filaments, but, as far as I can tell, they are unobtainable in America anyway. Garden-grown cardoons can be found in ethnic or health-food markets and are a fine substitute when you can get them; use only the thick ribs, stripping away the leaves and chopping the ribs in short lengths. Elizabeth Schneider, in her excellent *Uncommon Fruits and Vegetables,* says that cardoons should be precooked in a vast amount of boiling water for 15 to 30 minutes, until tender, then drained and used in the recipe.

Since artichokes and cardoons are closely related and have a similar flavor, I have also made this soup very successfully with artichoke hearts—once, indeed, with canned artichoke hearts.

---

2 garlic cloves, finely chopped

1 medium onion, coarsely chopped

2 tablespoons extra virgin olive oil

2 stalks celery, including green tops, coarsely chopped

1/4 cup finely chopped flat-leaf parsley

1 cup canned chopped tomatoes

4 cups light Chicken Broth (page 17) or Vegetable Broth (page 18)

Salt to taste

2 pounds cardoons, cleaned and trimmed, or 2 pounds artichokes, trimmed to hearts and quartered

1 small dried hot red chile pepper, optional

1 cup very flavorful baked ham or mortadella sausage cubes

1 egg for every 2 people served

IN a heavy soup kettle over medium-low heat, sauté the garlic and onion very gently in the oil until they are soft but not brown. Add the celery and parsley and continue cooking another 5 minutes or until the celery starts to soften. Stir in the chopped tomatoes, mixing well. Then add the stock. Cover the pan and bring the soup to a boil. Taste, adding salt if desired, then cover again and leave the soup to simmer gently for 15 minutes.

COARSELY chop the trimmed cardoons or artichoke hearts and add to the soup. Cover again and simmer about 45 minutes. Add the hot red pepper, if desired, and the ham and let cook another 5 minutes, or just long enough to develop the flavors. The soup may be prepared ahead of time up to this point.

BEAT the eggs in a small bowl. Bring the soup to a very slow simmer and slowly pour the beaten eggs into it, stirring them into the soup with a fork. The eggs will cook and scramble into stracciatelle (rags), which is what they're supposed to do. Remove from the heat and serve immediately.

VARIATION: *If you want to make a more traditional version of this old-fashioned soup, first make a lamb broth, using very meaty bones—breast of lamb, if you can get it, is an excellent cut for broth—along with the usual flavorings (onion, garlic, carrot, parsley, and herbs if you like). Strain and degrease the broth and use it in place of the chicken or vegetable broth in the recipe. Pick the meat off the soup bones, chop it fine, and add to the soup in place of the ham.*

winter vegetable soup
MINESTRA MARITATA ALLA FOGGIANA

6 to 8 servings

When icy blasts from the Daunian mountains sweep across the wintry plains of the Tavoliere around Foggia, the countryfolk huddle inside next to smoky fires, venturing forth only to scavenge whatever scraps are left from summer's abundance. A little of this, a little of that, a pinch of something else, go into the layers that make up a proper maritata. But don't make the mistake of thinking you can just throw any old leftovers together. Each of these greens is carefully, separately, cooked, then layered and dressed with little squares of pancetta and a grating of pecorino before the final bath of rich meat broth and a quick turn in a hot oven to marry the flavors—whence, apparently, the name maritata.

Since the usual ingredients of the maritata—including wild fennel, wild chicory, and other wild greens—are not easy to obtain in this country, I have adapted the concept with greens that can be found here. You could even use Asian greens, such as tatsoi and bok choy. If you wish to make a vegetarian version, simply leave out the bacon and use vegetable stock instead of meat stock. A maritata can be infinitely varied, depending on what's in the market. Cauliflower might make one of the layers, for instance, or even thinly sliced potatoes. Some cooks like to increase the soup's warming potential with a few sprinkles of crushed red pepper flakes, and it's often served in a deep soup plate over a toasted crust of bread that's been rubbed with garlic and drizzled with olive oil.

½ pound pancetta or slab bacon, cut into ¼-inch dice

2½ to 3 cups Meat Broth (page 16)

I bunch (I pound) escarole, rinsed

I bunch (I pound) red or green chard, rinsed

I bunch (I pound) dandelion greens, broccoli rabe, spinach, or turnip greens, or whatever is available, rinsed

4 to 5 tablespoons extra virgin olive oil

2 medium yellow onions, coarsely chopped

I bulb fennel, coarsely chopped

I bunch celery hearts, coarsely chopped

¾ cup freshly grated pecorino or Parmigiano-Reggiano

½ cup freshly grated bread crumbs

Salt and freshly ground black pepper

IF you are using slab bacon, immerse the diced bacon in a pan of rapidly boiling water and blanch for 2 minutes to get rid of the excessively smoky flavor. Add the pancetta or blanched bacon squares to the meat stock in a saucepan and bring to a simmer very slowly over low heat. Once the stock reaches the simmering point, turn the heat down very low, so that the stock remains hot without actually cooking.

PLACE the rinsed and still wet escarole in a large pot and cook until tender but still al dente. If necessary, add just a little water to the liquid clinging to the leaves to keep them from burning. When done, remove from the pot, chop coarsely, and set aside. Add the chard to the liquid remaining in the pot, cook until al dente, remove, chop, and set aside. Now add the final bunch of greens and proceed as for others. As you do this, you'll build up a few tablespoons of flavored vegetable stock in the bottom of the pot.

HEAT 2 tablespoons of the oil in a sauté pan over medium-high heat. Add the onions and cook for about 10 minutes, stirring frequently. Adjust the heat so that the onions soften and turn golden but do not become brown. Using a slotted spoon, remove the onions from the pan, leaving most of the oil behind, and set aside. Add another tablespoon of oil to the pan and sauté the fennel until soft and golden. Remove, drain, and set aside. Finally, adding yet another tablespoon of oil if necessary, gently cook the chopped celery till soft and golden, drain, and set aside.

PREHEAT the oven to 425°F.

LAYER the cooked escarole in the bottom of an ovenproof soup pot, preferably an earthenware casserole. Arrange a few squares of the

continues

pancetta or bacon over the top and sprinkle with a tablespoon of grated cheese. Top with the sautéed onions, add more pancetta and cheese, and continue in this manner, layering the vegetables in the pot—chard, fennel, dandelion or other greens, celery—interspersed with pancetta and cheese. Taste and add salt and pepper as necessary. Make a thick layer of cheese on the topmost layer of vegetables and sprinkle with the bread crumbs. Use the oil remaining in the pan to drizzle over the top, or add a fresh tablespoonful if necessary.

ADD any juices left from the greens pot to the almost simmering stock and pour it over the layers in the soup pot. The liquid should just come to the topmost layer of vegetables. Place the pot in the preheated oven and bake for 45 minutes, checking from time to time. If the top gets too brown, turn the heat down to 325°F. and continue cooking.

Ubiquitous Fish Soup

NOT JUST IN PUGLIA, but all around the Mediterranean, each tiny fishing port, each major coastal city, claims a version of fish soup—and not just *a* version, but *the* version—unique, close to perfect, the best, putting all others to shame, indeed, truth to tell, the original from which all others are derived and of which they are but pale imitations. Thus we have in Puglia alone, zuppa di pesce brindisina, gallipolina, barese, tarantina, nardina (from Nardò, just north of Gallípoli), not to mention zuppe di cozze (mussels), zuppe di vongole (clams), zuppe di frutta di mare (assorted shellfish), and zuppa di baccalà (salt cod).

The curious thing is that most of these fish and seafood soups are prepared in a very similar fashion and share a good many characteristics, among them the almost universal presence of garlic, onions, tomatoes, and parsley. Almost always they start with a soffritto, gently sautéing garlic and onions in olive oil, then adding tomatoes and parsley, and then the seafood—and this is the most important part—*in the order in which it should cook.* That means calamari, squid, or octopus first; then the fish; then the shrimp or other crustaceans; and finally, the clams, mussels, or scallops.

But each and every one of these fish and seafood soups also has a distinguishing touch, a *tocco,* that makes it unique. It might be the addition of celery and lots more garlic, as in Brindisi, or a touch of fresh basil at the end, as in Taranto, or a few spoonfuls of vinegar to boost the flavor, as in Nardò, or the individual touch of an inspired home or restaurant cook adding a spoonful of capers or a bit of lemon peel or a dried hot red chile pepper to the basic soup.

One fish soup, however, is indisputably unique—*zuppa di pesce fuggito,* detailed by the late Luigi Sada, Puglia's great food historian, who found the recipe among the papers of a seventeenth-century Barese physician named Sebastiano Mola. The name of the dish alone, Sada says, is an expression of the melancholic irony of the Barese poor—fish soup from which the fish has fled *(fuggito),* leaving behind only seaweed-covered rocks from which to extract the flavor.

Here's my translation of Sada's transcription of the seventeenth-century recipe:

If you want to make a fake fish sauce, take a rotolo [about 1 kilo] of seashells or rocks with seaweed [alga] and put them in a cooking pot with five carafes [each one about 700 grams] of water and let it boil slowly, skimming off any scum that rises to the surface; when you've skimmed it well, put in the white part of celery, a grain of basil, a clean onion, four heads black pepper, a rotolo of tomatoes, a misurella [100 grams] of oil, raise the heat and cook everything together. Strain the broth and keep it hot. Boil a rotolo of vermicelli and place on a serving dish with the boiling sauce of pesce scappato [escaped fish].

white fish soup

ZUPPA DI PESCE BIANCA

6 servings

A fish soup that does not call for tomatoes! This one is a good deal more refined than most Pugliese fish soups, a dish you'd be more likely to find in upscale restaurants than in home kitchens or humble fishermen's trattorie. Spice it up, if you wish, by adding a little dried hot red chile peperoncino, either whole or in flakes.

In the course of testing this recipe, I discovered by accident something that would probably shock my Pugliese friends deeply: This tart soup is delicious cold and deeply refreshing during the dog days of summer.

2¼ pounds boneless, firm-textured white fish (cod, hake, haddock, halibut)

Sea salt

4 cups Fish Broth (page 15)

⅓ cup minced flat-leaf parsley

6 small bay leaves

2 tablespoons white wine vinegar

1 lemon, very thinly sliced—at least 6 slices

2 garlic cloves, crushed and coarsely chopped

1 teaspoon black peppercorns

6 small sprigs flat-leaf parsley

Best quality extra virgin olive oil

PREPARE the fish by cutting into 2-inch pieces. Set on a cake rack and sprinkle lightly with the sea salt. Leave for at least 10 minutes, no more than 30 minutes, in order to firm up the texture.

BRING the fish broth to a very gentle simmer in a stockpot over low heat. Add minced parsley, bay leaves, vinegar, lemon slices, garlic, and peppercorns. Cover the pot and simmer and infuse for about 10 minutes.

ADD the fish pieces to the pot and continue simmering very gently until the fish is cooked through, about 5 minutes. Remove the bay leaves.

SERVE immediately, making sure that each plate has, in addition to the fish and broth, a slice of lemon, a few black peppercorns, and a small bay leaf. Float a parsley sprig on the top of each serving and pass a cruet of fine olive oil for garnishing.

fish soup
ZUPPA DI PESCE

6 servings

This is a basic fish soup, which may be changed and elaborated in dozens of different ways. You might, for instance, add other kinds of fish (but never strongly flavored fish like salmon, mackerel, or tuna, which would dominate the dish), or shellfish such as clams or shrimps. Or you might use different aromatics, depending on what's available, perhaps a little basil when it's fresh from the garden, some crushed dried red chile pepper, or a handful of chopped black olives if you have them on hand. The point is to use the recipe as a model rather than a hard-and-fast rule.

2¹/₄ pounds boneless fish (halibut, haddock, monkfish, snapper, or the like)

Sea salt

1 dozen large mussels, prepared for cooking (page 155)

¹/₂ cup dry white wine

1 medium onion, chopped

1 garlic clove, chopped with the onion

2 tablespoons extra virgin olive oil

7 or 8 ripe red tomatoes, peeled, seeded, and chopped, or 4 cups canned whole tomatoes, chopped

2 bay leaves

1 teaspoon minced fresh oregano, or ¹/₂ teaspoon dried

1 tablespoon capers, rinsed, drained, and coarsely chopped

¹/₄ cup finely minced flat-leaf parsley

Freshly ground black pepper

CUT the fish into 2-inch pieces and set on a cake rack. Sprinkle lightly with sea salt and leave for at least 10 or at most 30 minutes. This will firm up the fish for cooking.

RINSE the scrubbed, debearded mussels, discarding any that are gaping or have broken shells. Place in a large pan with the white wine and set over medium-high heat. Cook, shaking the pan vigorously from time to time, until the mussels have all opened, 8 to 10 minutes. Discard any that

continues

fail to open by the end of this time. Remove the mussels from the pan and set aside. Strain the pan juices through a double layer of cheesecloth to get rid of any grit. Reserve the juices.

IN the same or a similar pan, sauté the onion and garlic in the olive oil over medium-low heat until the vegetables are soft and golden but not yet turning brown, about 10 minutes. Add the tomatoes and the strained juices from the mussels, along with the bay leaves and the oregano. Cover the pan and cook for 5 or 6 minutes, then uncover it and add 2 cups of water. As soon as the water has returned to a simmer, add the fish pieces and continue cooking for 10 to 15 minutes, adding the capers and the mussels for the last 5 minutes of cooking. (Note that if you are using very firm-textured fish, such as monkfish, it will need longer cooking than, for instance, haddock.)

WHEN the soup is done, remove the bay leaves, stir in the parsley and black pepper, and serve immediately.

LIKE most fish soups, this is traditionally served over slices of thick country-style bread, either fried in olive oil or toasted over wood embers or in an oven broiler and drizzled with olive oil. Each slice is set in the bottom of a soup bowl, then the hot soup poured over the top.

fish soup from brindisi
ZUPPA DI PESCE ALLA BRINDISINA

The more kinds of fish you can use, the better this extravaganza of a soup will be. It comes from Adriatic Brindisi where a pillar still marks the eastern end of the Appian Way (the other end was in Rome) and the spot from where Caesar's minions once sailed to conquer the East.

With the Mediterranean increasingly unreliable as a resource, because of pollution and overfishing alike, more and more of what's in the market is coming from as far away as Australia and New Zealand. With seafood worth its weight in gold, it's hard to imagine there was a time not so long ago when fish was considered the food of the poor.

Make the Brindisi version exactly as you did the Fish Soup, except use as many different kinds of firm-textured white-fleshed fish as you can find and omit the mussels. Then, to the initial sauté of onion and garlic, add a small heart of celery, chopped, and ½ cup white wine. Omit the oregano, but add plenty of freshly ground black pepper. Rub a clove of garlic over the slices of toasted bread before drizzling on the olive oil.

fish soup from nardò
ZUPPA DI PESCE DI NARDÒ

Make the Fish Soup with a variety of fish and a dozen or so mussels, then, at the moment the fish is added to the pot, stir in about ¼ cup white or red wine vinegar and continue as directed.

mussel soup from taranto
ZUPPA DI COZZE ALLA TARANTINA

Taranto is on the opposite coast from Brindisi, the Ionian, in the great bay that forms the high arch of Italy's foot. Since mussels have been cultivated here since ancient times in Taranto's lagoonlike Mar Piccolo, it's not surprising that mussels are featured in the local soup. The main difference from the brindisina version, then, is in the addition of lots of mussels—far more mussels, in fact, than fish, and a little chopped fresh basil at the very end. For 6 people, 40 to 60 mussels should be plenty, used with no more than a pound of boneless fish fillet.

seafood soup
ZUPPA DI FRUTTI DI MARE

6 servings

Frutti di mare are fruits of the sea, hence lots of different kinds of shellfish. You may, if you wish, make this with mussels alone, or with clams alone, or you may add to the basic mixture a pound of peeled shrimp or calamari cut in little rings, adjusting cooking times accordingly. Scallops come in their shells in Puglia, and they make a very pretty addition to the soup; in this country, unshucked scallops are seasonally available in some markets; if they're still in their shells, you'll need a pound or more of them.

1½ pounds small clams (Manila or mahogany) in the shell

1½ pounds mussels

½ to ¾ pound shucked scallops, or medium (26 count) shrimp, or sliced calamari rings

¼ cup plus 3 tablespoons extra virgin olive oil

2 garlic cloves, sliced

½ cup dry white wine

1 can (32 ounces) whole tomatoes, drained and chopped

Salt and freshly ground black pepper

¼ cup finely minced flat-leaf parsley

Six 1-inch-thick slices of country-style bread

SCRUB and rinse the clams and mussels under running water, pulling away the beards from the mussels and discarding any mussels or clams with broken or gaping shells. Rinse shucked scallops; scrub scallops in shells. Squid or calamari rings need simply be rinsed rapidly under running water.

IN a large soup kettle or saucepan, heat 3 tablespoons of the olive oil over medium-low heat and add the garlic. Cook gently, stirring occasionally, until the garlic is soft but not brown. If you are using shrimp, calamari, or shelled scallops, add them now, raise the heat to medium-high, and cook quickly. After about 5 to 7 minutes, when the shrimp are pink or when the other seafood has lost its translucent sheen, remove from the pan with a slotted spoon and set aside. Add the clams, mussels, and scallops in shells, if using, to the pan, along with the white wine, cover the pan, and cook, shaking the pan vigorously from time to time, until all the shells are opened. This should take about 10 minutes. Any mussels, clams, or scallops that are still tightly closed at the end of this time should be discarded. Remove the shellfish from the pan and set aside.

IF the shellfish released any trace of grit into the pan juices, strain the juices through a double layer of cheesecloth, rinse out the cooking pot, and return the strained juices to the pot.

ADD the tomatoes to the pan juices together with a pinch of salt and several grinds of black pepper and let stew over medium heat for 15 to 20 minutes, or until the mixture has thickened somewhat. Return all the seafood to the pan, along with half the parsley, and stir to mix well. Continue cooking for an additional 5 minutes, or just long enough to reheat the shellfish and marry the flavors.

WHILE the seafood is reheating, fry the bread slices in the remaining ¼ cup olive oil over medium heat until they are crisp and golden on each side. (If you prefer less oil, you may toast the bread slices on a grill or under a broiler and drizzle a little oil over each one.) Set a slice of fried or toasted bread in the middle of each soup plate and ladle the shellfish and their sauce over. Sprinkle with the remaining parsley and serve immediately.

fish soup with salt cod
ZUPPA DI BACCALÀ

6 to 8 servings

This recipe comes from a delightful book called *La checine de nononne,* or *Grand-mother's Kitchen,* by Giovanni Panza, a Barese dignitary who collected his memories of eighty years of wonderful eating in his home town. It may seem odd, in a region with such a long and varied coastline, where the markets are ordinarily teeming with fresh seafood of all varieties, to include a recipe for dried salt fish from the Atlantic. But the use of salt cod is typical throughout the Catholic Mediterranean where the association of fish with fasting was so strong that even when bad winter weather meant fresh fish was unavailable, it was unthinkable not to have fish in some form on the table. But salt cod is not just "some form" of fish. Recipes like this one, developed over the centuries by gifted home cooks and great chefs, have brought dignity to this symbol of fasting and poverty.

If you've never worked with salt cod, buy the largest pieces of dried fish that you can find, preferably a whole side, rather than the bits and pieces that come in wooden boxes from Nova Scotia. You may have to go to a Greek, Italian, or Portuguese neighborhood fishmonger or market to find whole sides of salt cod, but it's well worth the effort. The dried fish must be soaked for at least 24 hours before cooking in order to reconstitute the flesh. In Italy, this is done for you by the shopkeeper, who usually has a basin of fish with constantly running water from which you make your selection. To soak the fish, put it in a basin or sink, fill the sink at least halfway with water, enough to fully immerse the piece of fish (which may be cut in half if it's too long), and adjust the stopper so that the water can run constantly without either spilling over or running out. Or, simply immerse the fish in a plastic laundry tub of cool water, changing the water every couple of hours, until the flesh has softened and no longer tastes sharply saline. Some people suggest soaking the fish for two or even three days, but oversoaking will leave you with a bland, uninteresting piece of fish.

2 pounds boneless salt cod

1 medium white onion, sliced

3 stalks celery, thinly sliced on the diagonal

2 tablespoons extra virgin olive oil

1/2 cup finely minced flat-leaf parsley

1/2 cup pitted green or black olives

1/2 cup golden raisins, plumped in warm water

1 cup drained canned tomatoes, chopped

1/2 cup juice from the tomatoes

Salt, if desired, and freshly ground black pepper

Slices of bread, toasted and drizzled with olive oil

CUT the cod in 1-inch pieces, or ask the fishmonger to do this for you. Place the pieces in a basin and add water to cover to a depth of several inches. Soak for 24 hours, changing the water at least three times during this period, then drain the cod and set aside.

IN a soup kettle over medium-low heat, gently sauté the onion and celery in the olive oil until soft and golden but not yet brown. Add the parsley, olives, and raisins and cook, stirring frequently, until the aromas begin to rise, about 5 minutes. Add the tomatoes, tomato juice, and the fish and cook, covered, for about 15 minutes, or until the pieces of cod are cooked all the way through. Add salt and pepper, if desired.

SERVE immediately over toasted bread, garnishing the soup with more olive oil.

pasta

*b*enedetto Cavalieri is a pasta-maker, though the term hardly does justice to this wiry, energetic, deeply cultured man who seems to count most of the population of the city of Lecce as cherished friends. The pasta factory that bears his name was established nearly eighty years ago by his grandfather, in the small town of Maglie just south of Lecce. Recently the present Benedetto's son Andrea, a teenager, has begun working at the *fabbrica* during summer holidays with the intent, on all sides, of taking over from his father when the time is right.

Although it's surprisingly hard to find in its home region, Cavalieri pasta, widely recognized in the rest of

Italy for its high quality and fresh, wheaten flavor, has recently become available in the United States (see page 255). The pasta is made by what pasta-producers call *il metodo delicato,* the delicate method, which uses less heat, both in the formation of the dough and in the drying of the shaped pasta, than more conventional industrial methods. Lower heat means a longer drying time (twenty-four to forty hours, depending on the size and shape of the pasta form—conventional methods take a tenth of that time) but the slower process retains the nutty flavor of hard durum wheat, mostly grown in the vast, rolling plains of the Tavoliere around Foggia in northern Puglia.

To borrow a term from the late Pugliese food historian Luigi Sada, Puglia is a country of pastivores. Many people, they say, eat pasta morning, noon, and night. I have no statistics for the morning part, but as for the noontime and the evening, my personal anecdotal research revealed that very few meals take place in Puglia without at least one, and often more, plates of pasta. It matters not whether it's an elegant dinner party in Lecce or lunch in a humble countryside trattoria in the rolling uplands of the Murge; it can be homemade hard wheat pasta or some of the best manufactured pasta in Italy; it can be dressed with complex sauces of fish or meat—the spaghetti and meatballs beloved of Italo-American cooks has its origins here in Bari—or the simplest of peasant sauces, olive oil, garlic, a little hot pepper, perhaps some sautéed bread crumbs in lieu of cheese.

Traditionally, much of the pasta in Puglia was handmade from hard wheat flour and water, nothing more. This creates a very hard paste that requires skill and a certain amount of muscle power to work to the smooth silken texture of a good pasta dough. Even the best home cook sometimes sneaks in an egg when no one's looking to help the dough adhere, but the occasional pasta recipes that actually call for eggs in the dough, Pugliese cooks say, are imports from the Abruzzi to the north, and not from the home region at all. Nowadays, like so many home-based traditions, handmade hard wheat pasta is disappearing from the lives of women who have too many other tasks. But every Pugliese town has at least one pasta-maker to supply local tables with the fresh product.

Besides, there are a great number of recipes in the Pugliese tradition that call for high-quality machine-made pasta—spaghetti, macaroni, vermicelli, bucatini, tubettini, penne, and so on—like the pastas made by Benedetto Cavalieri and a few others like him. On page 255, you'll find a list of recommended brands of these pastas, together with their U.S. suppliers.

penne with cauliflower
PENNE CON CAVOLFIORE

6 servings

A fine example of how humble ingredients from the vegetable garden that supplies much of the food on the tables of country families can be combined in a dish that is almost elegant, without betraying the simplicity of its origins.

½ cup olive oil

1 garlic clove, crushed

2 pounds tomatoes, peeled, seeded, and chopped, or 4 cups canned whole tomatoes, drained and chopped

1 medium cauliflower, broken into florets

Salt to taste

1 pound penne

½ cup finely chopped flat-leaf parsley

Freshly ground black pepper to taste

Freshly grated pecorino or Parmigiano-Reggiano to taste

IN a saucepan over medium heat, warm the olive oil and add the garlic clove. Cook briefly until the garlic starts to soften and turn color. (Do not let the garlic brown, as it will give an acrid taste to the sauce.) Add the tomatoes and cook, stirring, until the tomato pieces begin to soften. Now add the cauliflower pieces and stir to mix well. Add about ½ cup of very hot water, cover the pan, lower the heat to medium-low, and cook gently for about 30 minutes, or until the cauliflower is very tender.

MEANWHILE, bring a large pan of salted water to a rolling boil and add the penne, timing them to finish cooking at the same time as the cauliflower. They should take no more than 8 to 10 minutes to cook. As soon as the penne are done, drain them and add to the pan with the cauliflower. Sprinkle with parsley, plenty of black pepper, and grated pecorino to taste. Serve immediately.

VARIATION: *Toss a handful of unflavored bread crumbs, gently sautéed in 1 tablespoon olive oil on the pasta in place of the cheese.*

penne with artichokes
PENNE AI CARCIOFI

6 servings

Artichokes, they say, grow best close to the sea, so it's not surprising that the best artichokes in Puglia (and many would agree, the best in Italy) are grown in the broad coastal plain that extends from Bari south toward Brindisi, where the salt-kissed winter rains sweeping in off the Adriatic are quickly followed by sunshine that, even in February, is intense with warmth. Not surprising, either, that the people of this region have developed a whole repertoire of artichoke dishes, among which a favorite is this artichoke sauce to serve with penne or another short, stubby, tubular pasta shape.

½ lemon

4 or 5 artichokes (enough to make 3 cups, sliced)

1 medium onion, minced

2 ounces pancetta (unsmoked bacon), diced

2 tablespoons extra virgin olive oil

Salt to taste

1 cup dry white wine

1 pound penne or similar pasta

2 eggs

2 tablespoons grated Parmigiano-Reggiano or pecorino

FILL a bowl with clean, cool water and squeeze the juice of the lemon into it, setting the rind aside. Clean the artichokes by cutting the stems back to about 1 inch and breaking away the tough outer leaves until about ¾ of each inner leaf is tender. As you work, constantly rub the cut surfaces with the reserved lemon half to keep them from blackening. Use kitchen shears or a sharp knife to cut off the tough remaining tops of the leaves. If you are using ordinary American artichokes, you will have to remove the choke: Cut the artichoke in half lengthwise and use a spoon (a serrated grapefruit spoon is fine for this) to scrape away every bit of the prickly spines or choke situated just above the heart of the artichoke. Then slice the trimmed artichoke quite thinly, dropping the slices in the bowl of water acidulated with the lemon juice. Clean and slice the remaining artichokes.

IN a saucepan over medium-low heat, gently stew the onion and pancetta in the olive oil until the onion is soft, but not brown—about 10 minutes. Drain the artichokes and add to the pan, stir to mix well, cover, and leave to stew for another 10 minutes.

MEANWHILE, bring a kettle of water to the boil. Add a pinch of salt to the artichokes, and then the wine, a little at a time, mixing well after each addition and adding more as the wine evaporates. When all the wine has evaporated, add boiling water just to cover the vegetables, cover, and cook for 30 minutes, or until the water has been fully absorbed by the artichokes and the vegetables are tender. Remove from the heat and set aside until ready to cook the pasta.

BRING a large pot of lightly salted water to a rolling boil and add the pasta. Cook, uncovered, until al dente, about 8 to 10 minutes.

WHILE the pasta is cooking, return the artichoke pan to low heat to warm up. Beat the eggs in a small bowl and beat in the grated cheese. As soon as the artichokes are hot, remove from the heat and slowly add the egg mixture, stirring constantly with a wooden spoon. The heat from the artichokes should thicken the eggs to a sauce consistency; don't put the pan back on heat because you don't want to scramble the eggs.

HAVE ready a heated bowl in which to serve the pasta. Drain the pasta when it's done, turn into the bowl and immediately pour on the artichoke sauce, mixing quickly so that the hot pasta will further thicken the eggs.

SERVE immediately, passing more grated cheese if you wish.

spaghetti with green olive sauce
SPAGHETTI ALLE OLIVE VERDE

4 to 6 servings

Gigliola Bacile was raised in the beautiful baroque southern city of Lecce, and it was there, she says, that she learned to dress spaghetti with chopped green olives. Her secret? She starts her soffritto with just a little extra virgin olive oil, and adds more fresh raw oil (olio crudo) at the end.

---

6 tablespoons extra virgin olive oil

¾ cup freshly grated bread crumbs

3 salted anchovies or 6 oil-packed anchovy fillets

3 garlic cloves

½ small dried hot red chile pepper, crumbled, or ¼ teaspoon crushed red pepper flakes

1 cup coarsely chopped pitted green olives (about 1 pound whole olives)

Salt to taste

1 pound spaghetti

PUT a teaspoon of the olive oil in a small saucepan and toast the bread crumbs in the oil over medium heat for a few minutes, until they are golden brown and crisp. Remove from the heat and set aside. If you are using salted anchovies, rinse them under running water to rid them of salt, strip away the bones, and chop coarsely; if using anchovy fillets, simply chop them.

IN 3 tablespoons of the remaining oil, sauté the garlic cloves over medium heat until they are brown. Add the chopped anchovies and, using a fork, stir and crush them into the oil. Crumble the chile pepper into the oil. Remove the garlic cloves and discard. Stir the olives into the oil and let cook for about 3 minutes, just long enough to mix the flavors. Set aside.

BRING a large pot of lightly salted water to a rolling boil. Drop in the spaghetti and cook until done—10 to 12 minutes. As the pasta finishes cooking, reheat the olive sauce. Drain the pasta and turn into a heated serving bowl. Add the remaining olive oil and the toasted bread crumbs to the olive sauce and toss with the pasta. Serve immediately.

spaghetti with oven-roasted tomatoes
PASTA CON POMODORI AL FORNO

6 servings

This recipe comes from my landlord and friend Pino Marchese. He makes this in the summertime when Puglia's pride, big plump Sammarzano plum tomatoes, weighing nearly a pound each, are at their peak. Whatever tomatoes you use, make sure they are absolutely ripe, juicy, and full of flavor—this is one recipe where canned tomatoes simply won't work. Pino uses spaghetti, but linguine, vermicelli, or bucatini will do as well.

---

8 large very ripe tomatoes	$1/2$ cup extra virgin olive oil
Coarse sea salt to taste	1 pound thin spaghetti or linguine
4 garlic cloves, coarsely chopped	Freshly ground black pepper
$1/2$ cup minced flat-leaf parsley	$1/2$ cup shredded basil leaves
$1/2$ cup freshly grated bread crumbs	Freshly grated Parmigiano-Reggiano or pecorino, optional

PREHEAT the oven to 425°F.

SLICE each tomato in half and set, cut side up, in a lightly oiled oven dish that will hold all the tomatoes in one layer. Sprinkle the halves with salt, garlic, and parsley.

TOAST the bread crumbs in a frying pan over medium heat until they are light golden-brown. Sprinkle the bread crumbs over the tomato halves and drizzle all the olive oil over them. Place the dish in the preheated oven and roast for 30 to 45 minutes, or until they are very soft and juicy.

MEANWHILE, bring a large pot of salted water to a rolling boil, timing it so the pasta will finish when the tomatoes are ready. Add the pasta and cook, partially covered, until the pasta is done, about 10 minutes depending on its size and shape. Drain the pasta well and turn it into a heated bowl. Scrape in the cooked tomatoes fresh from the oven, together with any juices. Mix furiously, taste, and add more salt if necessary, an abundance of ground black pepper, the basil, and, for those who wish, a handful of grated Parmigiano-Reggiano or pecorino.

midsummer eve's pasta

VERMICELLI ALLA SANGIOVANNELLO

4 to 6 servings

In years past, on the night of June 24, the Feast of St. John or San Giovanni, true Baresi celebrated midsummer's eve by taking their tables outside and dining in the streets or on overhanging balconies from which they could call to each other and carry on conversations and flirtations. "True" Baresi are denizens of the old town, living in the crowded warren of narrow streets and alleys and overarching white-washed walls that still curls like a North African medina around the harbor's edge beside the beautiful twelfth-century church of the city's protector, St. Nicholas of Myra, now of Bari. (Even among themselves, the Baresi have a reputation for thievery so it's not at all surprising that they seem to have entered Christian history in the year 1087, when a group of Barese businessmen of the time stole into the Greek city of Myra on Turkey's Aegean coast and made off with the relics of the local saint, Nicholas, whom they later set up as the patron of Bari. And, yes, he was the original Santa Claus.)

On this, the longest (or almost) night of the year, the traditional dish served is vermicelli, spaghetti, or penne with a simple sauce of oil, garlic, anchovies, and tomatoes. Some add capers, some hot chile peppers and parsley, some olives, either black or green, but the basic idea is a quick, fresh, simple dish that celebrates the flavors of summer.

---

3 salted anchovies or 6 oil-packed anchovy fillets

1 garlic clove, chopped

⅓ cup extra virgin olive oil

1 pound fresh red ripe tomatoes, peeled and chopped

Freshly ground black pepper to taste

½ small dried hot red chile pepper or ¼ teaspoon crushed red pepper flakes, optional

1 tablespoon capers

⅓ cup pitted and chopped black or green olives

⅔ cup finely chopped flat-leaf parsley leaves

Salt to taste

1 pound spaghetti, vermicelli, or penne

IF you are using salted anchovies, rinse them thoroughly under running water and strip away their bones. Then chop them coarsely. (If you are using oil-packed anchovy fillets, simply chop them.)

IN a large saucepan over medium-low heat, gently sweat the garlic in the oil. When the garlic is soft, add the anchovies and cook, stirring with a fork and pressing the anchovies to dissolve them in the oil. Add the chopped tomatoes and cook just long enough to soften them and release their juices. Add black pepper and, if you wish, the pepper flakes, and cook a few minutes more to blend the flavors. Stir in any or all of the other possible ingredients—capers, olives, and parsley, reserving a little parsley for a garnish.

BRING a large pot of lightly salted water to a rolling boil. Drop in the pasta and cook until almost done—about 10 minutes. Drain the pasta and turn it into the pan with the sauce. Stir to mix well and let the pasta finish cooking in the sauce, another 2 minutes. Turn into a heated serving bowl, garnish with parsley, and serve immediately.

oven-baked penne with eggplant
PASTA AL FORNO CON MELANZANE

8 servings

The directions I've given for this flavorful dish are those a Pugliese cook would follow, but it is possible to cut down on the amount of oil by baking the eggplant slices rather than frying them. To do so, set the oven at 450°F. Rinse and dry the salted eggplant slices as described below. Lightly oil a baking sheet and lay the slices in a single layer on the sheet. Using a pastry brush, lightly brush the top of each slice with a little oil. Set in the preheated oven for about 15 minutes, or until they are golden brown on both sides. (They will brown on both sides without turning.) Remove from the oven and proceed with the recipe.

---

2 pounds eggplant, sliced about ¼ inch thick

Sea salt

¾ cup extra virgin olive oil (less if using method above)

1 pound penne or other short, stubby pasta

1½ cups Tomato Sauce (page 14)

1½ pounds ripe plum tomatoes, sliced about ¼ inch thick

½ cup unseasoned bread crumbs

Salt and freshly ground black pepper to taste

⅓ cup grated pecorino

4 or 5 coarsely chopped sprigs fresh basil

STACK the eggplant slices in a colander, sprinkling each slice with sea salt. Weight the slices (a can of tomatoes set on a small plate makes a good weight) and set the colander in the sink so the juices run free. Leave for at least 1 hour, then rinse the slices thoroughly and pat dry with paper towels.

HEAT the olive oil in a sauté pan over medium-high and sauté the dried eggplant slices on both sides until they are golden brown. (Or, to use less oil, follow the directions in the headnote.) Reserve the oil in the pan to use in the rest of the recipe.

BRING a pot of lightly salted water to a rolling boil, add the pasta, and cook until it is not quite done—about 5 minutes. Drain the pasta and immediately toss with about 1 cup of the tomato sauce.

SET the oven at 375°F.

USE about a tablespoon of the reserved oil to grease the bottom and sides of a glass or ceramic oven dish—a 2½- to 3-quart soufflé dish will be fine. Layer half the tomato slices over the bottom and sprinkle with half the bread crumbs, plus salt and pepper to taste. Spread half the sauced pasta on top, then half the eggplant slices in a layer. Drizzle about ¼ cup of tomato sauce over the eggplant and sprinkle with half the grated cheese and half the chopped basil. Now add in layers the remaining pasta, the remaining eggplant, the remaining tomato sauce, the remaining cheese, and the remaining basil. Top with the remaining sliced tomatoes and bread crumbs. Drizzle ¼ cup of the reserved oil over the top and place the dish in the oven. Bake for 1 hour. Remove from the oven and set aside to rest for at least ½ hour before serving.

spaghetti with fish and vegetables
CIAMBOTTA*

6 servings

The Terra di Bari includes the bustling fishing ports of Molfetta and Mola di Bari as well as Bari itself. In this region, ciambotta is the name given to a rich mixture of fish and vegetables cooked together. This is traditionally made with the *fragaglia*, the smallest fish in the daily catch, that aren't worth using for anything else. Since this kind of fish is often difficult to find in American markets, I have adapted the recipe to use larger fish, but if you find a good source of small (no more than 5 or 6 inches long) fish, cook them as directed, then extract them, remove the flesh from the bones, discard the bones and skin, and return the fish to the sauce for another 5 minutes or so, just long enough to meld the flavors.

This is sometimes served as a fish soup, over slices of toasted, garlic-rubbed bread, but more often it's mixed with pasta.

---

3 garlic cloves, crushed and coarsely chopped

1 medium onion, coarsely chopped

3 tablespoons extra virgin olive oil, plus more to garnish the dish

1 small bunch flat-leaf parsley, coarsely chopped (about ½ cup)

About 1 pound fresh very ripe tomatoes, peeled, seeded, and chopped, or 2 cans canned tomatoes, chopped

1 green pepper, cored and thinly sliced

1 small dried hot red chile pepper or ½ teaspoon crushed red pepper flakes, if desired

1 teaspoon salt or to taste

1½ cups Fish Broth (page 15)

½ cup dry white wine

Freshly ground black pepper to taste

1½ pounds white fish steaks, such as haddock, halibut, cod, or snapper

1 pound spaghetti, perciatelli, or fusilli

Olio santo for garnish (page 247)

---

* The word ciambotta turns up over and over again in southern Italy. Before I spent time in the Terra di Bari, ciambotta meant to me a mixture of summer vegetables cooked with potatoes as in the recipe on page 136 from Lecce. Pino Marchese, who is from Bari, says ciambotta is a mixture of mostly fish; his wife, Anna Longano, who comes from Monópoli, just thirty kilometers south of Bari, insists it's mostly vegetables. Apparently it's a dialect term for any kind of mixture.

IN a very large saucepan over medium-low heat, gently sauté the garlic and onion in the oil until the vegetables soften, about 10 minutes. Do not let them brown. Set aside a few tablespoons of the parsley for garnish and stir the rest into the vegetables in the pan. Add the tomatoes, green pepper, chile pepper, if using, and salt, stirring to mix well. Cover the pan and cook on low heat for about 20 minutes or until the tomatoes have softened and begun to dissolve into a sauce.

(IF you are using small fish—you'll need about 3 pounds—add them at this point, together with 2 cups of water. Cover the pan and cook for about 30 minutes, or until the fish are very well done and have lent all their flavor to the sauce. Otherwise proceed with the recipe as below.)

ADD the fish broth and wine to the vegetables and bring to a simmer. Taste and adjust the seasoning, adding more salt if necessary and lots of ground pepper. Now add the fish steaks, spooning the sauce over them. Cook the fish steaks for about 15 minutes, or until they are cooked through. Remove them with a slotted spoon when they are done and set aside.

IF the sauce seems too liquid, raise the heat slightly and boil, uncovered, until it is thick enough to coat the pasta. While the sauce is reducing, remove and discard any skin and bones from small fish or steaks. Flake the fish flesh and when the sauce is sufficiently reduced, return the fish to it. Cook over gentle heat, uncovered, for about 5 minutes or just long enough to meld the flavors. (If the sauce is too thick, thin it with a little of the boiling pasta water.) Set aside, but keep warm while you make the pasta.

BRING a large pan of salted water to a rolling boil and add the pasta all at once. Cook, partially covered, until the pasta is almost done—cooking time depends on the size and shape of the pasta, but spaghetti should take about 7 or 8 minutes. Drain the pasta and stir it into the sauce. Return the saucepan to gentle heat for 3 to 5 minutes to let the pasta absorb a little of the sauce.

SERVE immediately, garnishing each plate with a drizzle of chili oil and a sprinkle of reserved parsley.

VARIATION: *When the cooks of Bari tire of pasta (which even they sometimes do), they stir about 2 cups of almost—but not quite—thoroughly cooked chick-peas into the sauce. This, too, can be served over slices of toasted, garlic-rubbed bread.*

spaghetti with clams or mussels
SPAGHETTI CON DATTERI

4 to 6 servings

The harvest of datteri, small bivalves with elegantly burnished brown shells that look, in fact, like fresh dates (hence the name), is forbidden in Italy. The reason? The method of collecting this exquisitely sweet, succulent mollusk destroys, of necessity, the bedrock of the coast within which they grow and flourish.

Since datteri, even if they weren't forbidden fruit, are impossible to get in America, make this pasta sauce with Manila clams or mussels. The utter simplicity of the sauce is the best way to show off the finest of the fruits of the sea, especially if you take care that the other ingredients (the pasta, the oil, the tomatoes) are also the very best you can obtain.

---

2 pounds Manila clams or small mussels

4 garlic cloves, coarsely chopped

1/2 cup extra virgin olive oil

I pound ripe, very sweet cherry tomatoes, halved, or 2 cups canned tomatoes, drained and coarsely chopped

Sea salt to taste

I pound spaghetti or spaghettini

1/4 cup finely minced flat-leaf parsley

Freshly ground black pepper to taste

IF the clams or mussels seem very gritty, they may be purged by immersing them in 1/2 cup of sea salt dissolved in 2 quarts of fresh water and left to sit overnight. (This is not always necessary.)

NEXT day, drain the mollusks and scrub well under running water. If using clams, discard any that are not tightly closed; if using mussels, discard any that are gaping open. Trim the mussels of their beards (see page 155 for detailed instructions on cleaning mussels).

IN a saucepan or skillet large enough to hold all the ingredients, gently sauté the garlic in the olive oil over medium-low heat until it is soft but not brown. Add the halved or chopped tomatoes to the pan. Raise the heat

slightly and cook the tomatoes until they soften and give off their juices, about 10 minutes.

MEANWHILE, bring a pot of lightly salted water to a rolling boil, drop in the pasta, and cook for about 7 to 10 minutes.

NOW drop the cleaned mollusks into the pan containing the tomatoes and cook, stirring and tossing, until all the shells have opened, about 10 to 15 minutes. Discard any that refuse to open at the end of this time.

DRAIN the pasta and add to the saucepan, stirring and tossing to mix well with the mollusks and tomatoes. Let cook for about 3 minutes so that the pasta absorbs some of the juices in the pan. Add the parsley, give a few turns of the pepper mill, and toss to mix well.

SERVE immediately, passing a pepper mill to grind over the top of each serving.

pasta with mussels and beans
TUBETTINI CON FAGIOLI E COZZE

8 servings

I came across the funky little restaurant called Gambrinus on the fishermen's docks in Taranto's Città Vecchia one blustery day in early December when this combination of pasta, beans, and mussels seemed just about perfect. The oldest part of Taranto, the Città Vecchia is perched on an isthmus between two great harbors, the Mar Grande and the Mar Piccolo. Although the Mar Piccolo is a branch of the Ionian Sea, it is almost enclosed and its brackish waters are fed by *citri,* underwater springs of fresh water. This makes the Mar Piccolo a perfect place for the cultivation of mussels and oysters, which in fact has been going on here since ancient times when Taranto was a flourishing capital of Magna Graecia.

The mussels grown and used in Taranto, naturally, are Mediterranean black mussels, now being cultivated in the Pacific Northwest (see page 255). But if you can't get black mussels, Atlantic blue mussels, the kind commonly available from fishmongers, will be just as satisfying.

---

1 cup dried white cannellini beans, soaked overnight

1 small carrot, coarsely chopped

1 stalk celery, including leafy top, coarsely chopped

4 pounds mussels

1/4 cup dry white wine

4 garlic cloves, coarsely chopped

1/4 cup extra virgin olive oil

5 plum tomatoes, peeled, seeded, and chopped, or 1 cup canned whole tomatoes, drained and chopped

1/2 pound tubetti or penne

Handful of minced flat-leaf parsley

2 or 3 leafy sprigs fresh basil

Salt and freshly ground black pepper to taste

DRAIN the beans and place in a large, heavy saucepan over medium heat with the chopped carrot and celery. Add 2 cups of fresh water and bring to the boil, then turn the heat down to simmer, cover the pot, and cook until the beans are tender—45 minutes to 1 hour. Check the water level from time to time and add more boiling water as it cooks down—the beans should always be just covered with boiling liquid.

SCRUB the mussels in running water and cut away their beards. Discard any mussels with gaping shells or any that feel suspiciously heavy, an indication that they're full of mud. Place the mussels in a pan with the wine and set over high heat. Cook, stirring frequently, until all of the mussels have opened. Remove from the heat and set aside to cool. Strain the liquid in the bottom of the pan carefully through several layers of cheesecloth and set aside.

WHEN the mussels are cool enough to handle, remove the flesh and discard the shells. (The mussels may be cooked ahead of time and they, and their liquid, kept refrigerated until ready to use.)

WHEN ready to proceed, gently sauté the garlic in the oil in a soup kettle or saucepan set over medium-low heat. When the garlic is soft but not brown, add the tomatoes and cook for about 10 minutes, or until the tomatoes are soft and starting to disintegrate. Stir in the cooked beans with their liquid and simmer gently while the pasta cooks.

BRING a large pot of salted water to a rolling boil and drop in the pasta. Cook, partially covered, until the pasta is almost done, about 10 minutes. Drain and mix with the beans; add the strained mussel liquid. The consistency should be saucy rather than soupy—if there is too much liquid, raise the heat and cook down briefly. Gently stir in the mussels and cook over low heat for about 5 minutes, or until the mussels are thoroughly heated and the flavors have melded. Stir in the parsley, basil leaves, salt to taste (the mussel liquid may be quite salty), plenty of black pepper, and serve immediately.

vermicelli with salt cod and tomatoes
VIERMICEDDI CU LU BACCALÀ

4 to 6 servings

This sumptuous dish from the Salento is traditionally served on Christmas Eve. Throughout Catholic Europe, Christmas Eve is a time to eat fish. This is a relic from centuries past when the Christmas feast, like all calendar feasts, was preceded by a ritual period of fasting, in this case the three-week fast of Advent. Advent is scarcely observed at all in the modern Christian world—to our loss, I think, for there's something deeply satisfying in the idea that a feast is not so much a right as a privilege that must be earned.

See page 72 for information on salt cod, an ill-esteemed (unjustly, to my mind) fish.

---

1 pound boneless fillet of salt cod

3 tablespoons extra virgin olive oil

2 garlic cloves, chopped

1 fat leek, cleaned and thinly sliced

¼ cup finely chopped flat-leaf parsley, plus a few more tablespoons for a garnish, if desired

3 or 4 ripe red tomatoes, peeled, seeded, and chopped, to make 2 cups, or 2 cups canned tomatoes, chopped

1 small dried hot red chile pepper

Freshly ground black pepper to taste

1 tablespoon salt for the pasta water plus more salt if desired

1 pound vermicelli, spaghetti, or spaghettini

12 to 24 pitted black olives, chopped, if desired

CUT the salt cod in smaller pieces and put to soak in abundant water for about 24 hours, changing the water two or three times during this period. When the cod is fully refreshed, drain it and dry the pieces with paper towel. Cut them into 1-inch chunks.

IN a saucepan large enough to hold the sauce and the pasta, heat the olive oil over medium-low heat and gently sauté the garlic for 5 to 7 minutes or until it is soft. Add the pieces of salt cod and raise the heat slightly to cook the cod on all sides until it has lost its translucent look. Scatter the leek and parsley over the top of the fish and continue cooking until the vegetables have become very soft, about 10 minutes. Add the tomatoes, together with the chile pepper, pepper, and stir to mix well. Cook, uncovered, for about 10 minutes to reduce and thicken the tomato juices. (The recipe may be prepared ahead of time to this point.)

WHEN ready to proceed, bring a large pot of lightly salted water to a rolling boil. Drop in the pasta and cook until half done—that is, until the pasta has lost its stiffness but is still far from cooked through, about 7 minutes. Meanwhile, reheat the sauce if necessary to the simmering point. Drain the pasta and turn it into the pot with the sauce, stirring to mix everything together very well. Return to medium-low heat and continue cooking, covered, until the pasta is thoroughly cooked. Turn into a heated serving bowl and garnish, if desired, with the black olives and more chopped parsley.

st. joseph's day pasta
LASAGNETTE DI SAN GIUSEPPE

4 to 6 servings

An old tradition links the feast of San Giuseppe (St. Joseph) on March 19 with mid-Lenten festivals, a brief but joyful holiday, reminding us that we're halfway to Easter but still within the constraints of the Lenten fast. Pino Marchese, who spent his childhood in Bari's old town, says they used to make big bonfires *(falò)* for San Giuseppe in the main piazzas of the old town, using discarded furniture, broken-up chairs, even the heavy wooden gates that swung back to admit people to the family courtyard. Of course, no one very much observes the Lenten fast these days, but San Giuseppe continues to be celebrated in Bari with this dish.

Lasagnette are not like what we call lasagna pasta. Rather they are inch-wide strips of curly-edged ribbon pasta, but similar shapes will also do. If you can't find anything similar, use the widest tagliatelle or fettuccine available.

---

³/₄ cup blanched almonds	1 small onion, finely chopped
¹/₂ cup extra virgin olive oil	1¹/₂ cups Tomato Sauce (page 14)
2 cups unseasoned bread crumbs	6 or 8 leaves fresh basil, torn to shreds
8 salt-packed anchovy fillets, rinsed and chopped	Salt to taste
Freshly ground black pepper to taste	1 pound lasagnette or similar inch-wide pasta ribbons
1 garlic clove, finely chopped	

IN a small frying pan over medium heat, gently toast the almonds in a teaspoon of the olive oil until they are golden brown. Remove the almonds to a cutting board and chop them as fine as you can. In the oil remaining in the pan (adding a little more if necessary), toast the bread crumbs until they are golden brown and very crisp. Combine the bread crumbs with the almonds in a small bowl.

ADD 2 tablespoons of oil to the frying pan. Over medium-low heat, stir in the anchovies and crush into the oil with a fork. Mix the anchovies and oil with the bread crumbs, add lots of black pepper, and set aside.

ADD the remaining oil to the frying pan and gently sweat the garlic and onion over medium-low heat until they are soft but not brown. Add the tomato sauce and cook for about 3 or 4 minutes, or just long enough to mix the flavors. Add the basil and set aside.

BRING a pot of lightly salted water to a rolling boil, drop in the pasta, and cook until al dente—about 10 to 12 minutes. Drain and dress with the tomato sauce and half the bread crumb mixture. Sprinkle the remaining crumb mixture over the top and serve immediately.

VARIATION: *An old-fashioned recipe I came across called for boned fresh mackerel to be used in place of anchovies. The mackerel, cut in small pieces, is fried in olive oil. Then the pasta is mixed with the tomato sauce, sprinkled with the bread crumbs and almonds, and finally topped with the fried bits of fish. If you use mackerel, add salt to the tomato sauce, to make up for the salt in the anchovies.*

pounded wheat berries and greens
CRANU PESTATU E FOJE

6 to 8 servings

To make cranu pestatu (or grano pestato, as it's called in Italian), whole wheat berries are first soaked in water, then drained and pounded with a pestle or *stompatura* in a *stompu,* a deep stone mortar (the words' origins are Greek, suggesting the antiquity of the polishing process). The purpose? To husk the grain and rid it of the thin pellicule or glume that surrounds it.

This is an ancient food that probably goes back to the very origins of wheat cultivation in the Mediterranean—and thus to the origins of human culture and cuisine. The original Mediterranean wheat was a type of glumed grain, like farro, an old-fashioned strain of wheat.

Soaked overnight, then drained and steamed very slowly in fresh water until the grains are soft and tender, grano pestato can be served like pasta with a little tomato sauce and grated cheese. But it is also delicious cooked with vegetables or legumes: At Il Poeta Contadino, a restaurant in Alberobello, the capital of the trulli country, grano pestato is an elegant dish mixed with lots of green vegetables cut in the smallest of dice and cooked to a creamy consistency.

Grano pestato is, alas, almost impossible to find outside Puglia; if you go there, it's one of the products you should seek out and bring back. This dish can be made with the wheat berries available in any well-stocked health-food store, or with farro. If you use wheat berries, however, they will require longer soaking and cooking to reach a creamy texture.

I cup grano pestato or farro or whole wheat berries

I ounce sliced pancetta or lean bacon

I medium onion, finely chopped

I tablespoon extra virgin olive oil

2 cups diced green vegetables, such as celery, escarole, chard, zucchini, spinach, or chicory

I teaspoon minced fresh marjoram

I tablespoon Tomato Sauce (page 14), or I teaspoon tomato concentrate dissolved in I tablespoon hot water

Sea salt to taste

Freshly grated pecorino or Parmigiano-Reggiano for garnish

IF using wheat berries, soak the grains in water to cover to a depth of 1 inch for 12 hours or overnight. When ready to cook, drain thoroughly. (This may not be necessary with farro.)

IF you are using bacon, blanch it for 2 to 3 minutes in a pan of rapidly boiling water to rid it of some of the smoky flavor. Drain and cut the bacon, or the pancetta, in small cardons. In a saucepan or stockpot large enough to hold all the ingredients, gently sauté the pancetta or bacon and the onion in the oil over medium heat until the onion pieces start to brown. Add the drained wheat and stir to mix well. Add about 2 cups of boiling water, or enough to cover the grain to a depth of 1 inch. Bring to a boil, lower the heat to medium-low, cover the pan, and cook very slowly, adding *boiling* water from time to time as the grain absorbs the water in the pan. (It is difficult to give precise times or measurements for this, as so much depends on the age of the grain and whether you are using grano pestato, farro, or wheat berries.)

CHECK the grain from time to time and when the kernels start to get tender, add any or all of the diced vegetables. Stir in the marjoram and the tomato sauce or diluted concentrate. Taste and add salt if necessary or desired. Continue cooking over low heat until the vegetables are cooked and the grain is very tender. Serve immediately, passing grated cheese to sprinkle on top if you wish.

Handmade Pasta

THE ladies in the kitchen in Lecce were making orecchiette, little ears of pasta that in fact look more like little hats, the kind a contadino might wear out in the fields to protect himself from the sun and the rain, round disks with a bump in the middle pushed up by a stout thumb, about the trickiest pasta shape I've ever made.

The durum wheat flour, creamy yellow in color, gritty and grainy in texture, had been heaped in a pyramid in the middle of a pasta board. Italians call this flour semola but in America it's called semolina—confusingly because in Italian semolina means this kind of flour ground again to a finer texture. Durum wheat semola is the flour required by Italian law for all commercial pasta, whether made by huge enterprises like Barilla, the largest-selling pasta-maker in Italy, or by small, artisanal, old-fashioned firms like Benedetto Cavalieri (see page 255). Because semola is made from the vitreous grains of durum wheat, it is reputed to be a difficult flour to work by hand, and it's not generally used to make pasta at home—except in Puglia, and even there fewer and fewer women find the time for the task of pasta-making.

To my great surprise I found that the durum wheat semola, which was as gritty as fine cornmeal, was actually a very pleasant flour to work with, making up into a silken dough that was easy to handle. Certainly the results, in terms of flavor and texture, are well worth the effort. But that is always true of handmade pasta, no matter what kind of flour it's made with. Kneading and rolling the dough by hand always seems to give results that are inimitable any other way.

We had gathered in Claudia Bacile's home kitchen to make orecchiette— Adriana Bozzi-Colonna, Silvana Camisa, and I. Adriana had brought the flour, freshly milled and aromatic, with more of the bran left in it than a normal, store-bought semola would have. She made a well in the flour pyramid and, while Silvana slowly dribbled salted water into the well, Adriana worked the flour together, kneading water and semola to make a very raggedy paste. More water was added, about two cups in all, and Adriana worked and beat and turned the dough. For pasta made in the traditional manner, no eggs are added, though even Pugliese cooks may add an egg to make handling easier.

Once the dough was thoroughly kneaded, punched and turned and punched and turned again, once it had achieved that satiny texture of good pasta dough, it was set aside to rest briefly. Then we proceeded to make the orecchiette, rolling lumps of dough into long serpents not more than an inch thick, then cutting off small pieces, no bigger than a thumbnail, which were dragged (*strascinate* is the word) with a blunt-ended knife across a rough old wooden bread board to give them an uneven texture that would capture the sauce. (When I did this at home in Maine, I used a clean wooden shingle to achieve the same effect.) Once dragged out like this, each orecchietta is reversed over the thumb to give it a hump in the middle.

Fortunately, although the good cooks of Puglia dispute me on this, there are commercially made and packaged orecchiette available and you can sometimes find them imported from Italy. One good brand, good because the orecchiette have the proper dragged surface, is Il Trullo: Sapori di Puglia.

Here are some other pasta shapes traditionally made in Pugliese kitchens:

CHIANCARELLE. Smaller orecchiette, named for the flat limestone slabs that are overlayed to make the roofs of Pugliese trulli.

POCIACCHE. Larger orecchiette.

TROCCOLI. Made in the northern region around Foggia, the center for durum wheat production, and in the mountains of the Gargano peninsula, these long, thin noodles, square in section, like spaghetti alla chitarra from the Abruzzi, are made with a special wooden rolling pin that has carved cutting edges. These often have an egg added.

PESTAZZULE; STACCHJODDI. Little disks like orecchiette but without the concave bump in the middle.

MIGNUICCHIE. Little gnocchi made of semolone, very coarsely ground durum wheat.

FENESCÈCCHIE (CAGGHIUBBI IN BRINDISI). A sort of macaroni, made by rolling a disk of pasta around a metal rod like a knitting needle.

SAGNE INCANNULATE. Typical of the Salento, long strands of pasta, half an inch to an inch wide, that are twisted around thin canes for very slow drying.

As with orecchiette, most of the following pasta recipes, except ciceri e tria, may be easily adapted to use with commercially made dried pasta. They are included here in this section, however, because they are traditionally made with homemade semolina pasta.

chick-peas and handmade pasta
CICERI E TRIA

6 servings as a main course; 8 servings as a first course

Ciceri are chick-peas and tria is an old-fashioned word, derived from an Arabic original, for pasta—further evidence of an Arab connection in the spread of pasta traditions in Italy. This is a dish right out of the cucina povera of the Salento. Hard to believe that anything so simple could be so tasty, but it's the added inventive fillip of fried pasta as a garnish that makes all the difference. When I made this back home for a vegetarian friend, she insisted that the fried pasta was actually bacon!

Ciceri e tria is *always* prepared with homemade semolina pasta. Could you make it with commercial pasta, I asked Concetta Cantoro, since she makes the best ciceri e tria I've ever tasted. She looked aghast and drew herself up to her full five feet: "Absolutely not!" she said. "Then it's just pasta e ceci."

3/4 pound (about 2 cups) dried chick-peas (garbanzos)

2 garlic cloves, crushed

1 small yellow onion, cut in quarters

2 bay leaves

1 stalk celery, chopped

1 teaspoon sea salt

2/3 cup warm water

2 cups semolina (Italian semola) for pasta

Extra virgin olive oil for deep-frying

1 small dried hot red chile pepper

PUT the chick-peas in a bowl and cover with cool water to a depth of about 1 inch. Set aside to soak overnight.

NEXT day, drain the chick-peas, place them in a deep saucepan, and cover with fresh water to a depth of 1 inch. Add 1 of the garlic cloves, the onion, bay leaves, and celery to the pan and bring to a boil over medium heat. Lower the heat, cover the pan, and simmer very gently for 1 to 2 hours, or until the chick-peas are very tender—time depends on their age and size. Add *boiling* water from time to time as the chick-peas absorb what is in the pan. There should always be about 1 inch of water over them; as they cook, the liquid will become thicker and more soupy.

WHILE the chick-peas cook, make the pasta. Dissolve 1 teaspoon salt in about ⅔ cup very warm water. Put the semolina in a mixing bowl and slowly turn the salted water into the flour, a little at a time, gradually mixing until most of the water has been thoroughly incorporated. (You may need a little more warm water or a little more semolina, depending on ambient temperature and humidity.) Knead the pasta in the bowl for a few minutes. As you knead, you'll feel the semolina granules begin to soften and relax. Once the dough is well amalgamated, turn it out onto a board. If the dough feels stiff, brush a little water on the board with your fingers; if, on the other hand, the dough feels loose and wet, scatter 1 tablespoon or so more semolina on the board. Continue kneading on the board until the dough has reached a soft, silky texture, then set it aside, covered with a cloth, to rest for about 30 minutes.

USING half the pasta at a time, roll it out on a very lightly floured board into the thinnest possible sheet. (If you are using an Atlas or Imperia pasta maker, roll the dough out to the #5 opening.) Cut the sheet into long noodle strips about ½ inch wide (more or less, but more is better than less). Drape the pasta over a rack or a chair back covered with a clean dish towel and leave to dry slightly—15 to 30 minutes is plenty.

TO a saucepan or deep-frying pan about 10 inches in diameter, add olive oil to a depth of 1 inch. Add the remaining crushed garlic clove and the chile pepper, broken in two, and set over medium heat. As the oil warms, the garlic will start to brown. Before the garlic is fully brown, remove it and discard. Adding a few strips at a time, rapidly fry about a third of the pasta in the hot infused oil until crisp and brown. Remove and set aside to drain on paper towels.

BY now the chick-peas should be very soft. Remove the bay leaves, raise the heat under the chick-peas to medium-high, adding more boiling water if necessary to keep them covered to a depth of 1 inch. Gently stir the remaining pasta into the chick-peas and let cook until the pasta is done— about 5 to 7 minutes. When the pasta is al dente, remove from the heat, and serve immediately, without draining, garnishing each bowl with a generous handful of fried pasta.

orecchiette with broccoli rabe
ORECCHIETTE CON CIME DI RAPE

4 generous servings

Cime di rape, or turnip tops, are the greens sold in American produce markets as broccoli di rape or broccoli rabe. This magnificent vegetable is both delicious, with a bitter bite that is extraordinarily pleasing, and nutritious, with all the remarkable properties of the cabbage family—loaded with antioxidants and other healthy things. If you are unable to find broccoli rabe, you may substitute ordinary broccoli, but the dish will lack the complex flavors that come from the combination of bitter broccoli rabe, sweet garlic, oil, salty anchovies, and pungent chili peppers.

HOMEMADE SEMOLINA PASTA
  MADE WITH:

$2^1/_4$ cups semolina

1 cup water

$1^1/_2$ teaspoons sea salt;

(or use 1 pound packaged
  orecchiette)

$^1/_2$ cup extra virgin olive oil

2 garlic cloves, sliced

6 anchovy fillets, boned and
  coarsely chopped

1 small dried hot red chile pepper,
  coarsely chopped, or $^1/_2$ teaspoon
  red pepper flakes

1 pound (2 bunches) broccoli rabe

Sea salt and freshly ground black
  pepper to taste

MAKE the pasta dough as in the recipe for ciceri e tria (see page 100). Divide the dough into 8 more or less equal portions. Roll each portion into a long snake not more than 1 inch thick, then cut the snake into smaller, thumbnail-sized pieces, similar to small gnocchi. Using the thick side of a table knife, drag each of these across a rough wooden surface to elongate it and give it a rough texture on one side. You may leave them as they are for strascinate or stacchjoddi, or turn each one gently over your thumb to make a little hat for orecchiette.

THIS will make about 50 orecchiette, or enough for 4 generous servings. Set the finished pasta aside on a lightly floured cloth to dry for about 30 minutes.

WHILE the pasta is drying, prepare the sauce: Put the oil in a saucepan over medium heat and add the garlic slices. When they begin to soften and turn color (don't let them brown), add the anchovies. Cook over medium heat, crushing the anchovy fillets into the oil with the back of a fork to make a coarse paste. When all the anchovy fillets are mashed into the oil, add the hot pepper. Stir to mix well and set aside in a warm place until ready to use.

CLEAN the broccoli rabe, discarding any yellow, old, or tough outer leaves and the thick stems. Coarsely chop the leaves and thinner stems leaving the little flower clusters intact. Bring a large pot of lightly salted water to a rolling boil, drop in the broccoli rabe pieces, and boil, uncovered, for about 3 minutes.

ADD the pasta to the water in which the broccoli is cooking and boil until the pasta is just tender—about 7 to 9 minutes. Drain in a colander, transfer to a heated bowl, and toss with the anchovy-garlic sauce. Or, if the pan in which the sauce cooked is large enough, turn the drained broccoli and pasta into the sauce and cook briefly, just long enough to impregnate the pasta with the flavors of the sauce. Taste and add salt if necessary (the anchovies may give it sufficient salt) and lots of black pepper. Serve immediately.

NOTE: *If you use commercially made orecchiette, the overall cooking time will be longer; add the orecchiette with the broccoli and cook both together for about 15 minutes, or until the pasta is al dente.*

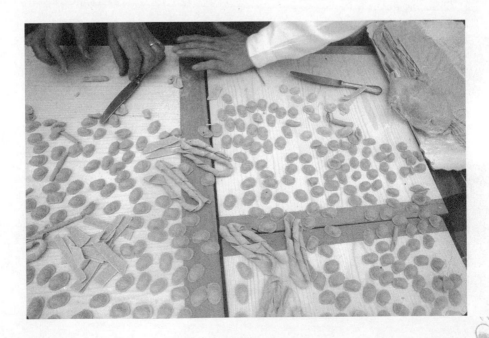

pasta with meatballs
STACCHJODDI E PALPÈTTA

4 servings as a main course; 6 to 8 servings as a first course

Who says spaghetti and meatballs isn't "really" an Italian dish? From Puglia, this hearty preparation was transported to America and turned into the very symbol of Italian-American cooking. Here's how they make stacchjoddi e palpètta back in the old country. Stacchjoddi are similar to the little ears of orecchiette but flatter and without that tricky thumb-bump. But this sauce is also delicious with commercial dried pasta, whether orecchiette, penne, small shells, or a similar shape. In Puglia, a spoonful of very strong double-fermented cheese, ricotta forte, is often melted into the sauce at the end.

HOMEMADE SEMOLINA PASTA
    MADE WITH:

2$^{1}/_{4}$ cups semolina

I cup water

I$^{1}/_{2}$ teaspoons sea salt;

(or use I pound dried orecchiette
    or penne)

$^{1}/_{2}$ pound stale, coarse, country-
    style bread

I pound ground lean veal and lean
    pork

I large egg

$^{1}/_{4}$ cup grated pecorino, plus more
    grated cheese for garnish

I garlic clove, finely minced

$^{1}/_{4}$ cup minced flat-leaf parsley

Salt and freshly ground black
    pepper

$^{1}/_{2}$ cup fresh basil leaves

2$^{1}/_{2}$ cups Tomato Sauce (page 14)

2 tablespoons extra virgin olive oil

I small white or yellow onion,
    finely chopped

I cup dry white wine

TO make fresh pasta dough, follow the directions in the recipe for ciceri e tria, page 100. Shape the pasta according to the directions for orecchiette, pages 102–103, but leave the pasta shapes flat, without the thumb-bump that turns them into orecchiette. Set aside on a lightly floured towel to dry for 30 minutes while you make the sauce.

IMMERSE the bread in a bowl of cool water and when it is thoroughly soaked, squeeze it dry and tear into small pieces to make about 2 cups

soaked bread crumbs. Using your hands, mix the bread with the ground meat in a bowl. Add the egg, cheese, garlic, and parsley and mix well, adding salt as desired and lots of pepper. Form the mixture into small meatballs about the size of a walnut.

CHOP the basil leaves and set aside 1 tablespoon to be used as a garnish. Stir the remainder into the tomato sauce.

IN a sauté pan, heat the olive oil over medium heat and brown the meatballs on all sides, removing them and setting aside as they brown. Add the onion to the pan, lower the heat, and sauté the onion gently until the pieces are soft but not brown. Return the meatballs to the pan together with the wine, raise the heat slightly, and cook until the wine has reduced to about half. Now stir in the tomato sauce and cook gently just long enough to thicken the sauce, about 10 to 15 minutes. The sauce should nap the meatballs, with sufficient "juice" to dress the pasta. If the sauce gets too thick, add a small amount of boiling water. Taste and adjust the seasoning.

WHILE the sauce is cooking, bring a large pot of lightly salted water to the boil. Add the pasta and cook until al dente—about 7 to 10 minutes for homemade pasta, 12 to 15 minutes for commercial pasta. Drain, turn into a heated bowl, and dress with the sauce, reserving a few meatballs to garnish the top along with the reserved chopped basil. Serve immediately, passing additional grated cheese.

butcher's sauce for pasta
RAGÙ DEL MACELLAIO

6 servings as a main course; 8 servings as a first course

A hearty ragù like this may be served with any of the homemade semolina pastas described, but it's a traditional accompaniment to laganari or troccoli, long, thin, square pastas like the famous Abruzzese pasta alla chitarra. The wooden rolling pins with regular sharp ridges that you sometimes see in shops in Italian neighborhoods are specially made for cutting this kind of pasta, which, unlike the other semolina pastas, has an egg added to strengthen it. The meaty sauce is also fine served with a first-rate commercial pasta.

All over Italy stews and sauces are made from mixtures of a variety of meats—pork and veal, or chicken, rabbit, and lamb, or a selection of game. However, there is no need to go to desperate lengths to acquire small amounts of a variety of meats for this sauce. The dish is just as good, possibly even better, made with pork, beef, veal, or lamb alone. (If you make it with lamb alone, and increase the amount of red pepper to give it a definite piquant heat, it will become *ragù del pastore*, shepherd's sauce, instead of sauce from the butcher.)

I large onion, halved and thinly
  sliced

¼ cup extra virgin olive oil

½ pound lean veal or pork

½ pound lean lamb

I cup dry red or white wine

I pound very ripe red tomatoes,
  peeled, seeded, and chopped,
  mixed with 2 tablespoons tomato
  purée; or 2 cups canned
  tomatoes, chopped (one
  28-ounce can)

I small dried hot red chile pepper
  or ½ teaspoon crushed red
  pepper flakes, if desired

5 or 6 whole cloves

Salt and freshly ground black
  pepper to taste

2 bay leaves

HOMEMADE SEMOLINA PASTA
  MADE WITH:

2½ cups semolina

I large egg

I cup water

1½ teaspoons sea salt;

(or use I pound packaged pasta)

IN a saucepan large enough to hold all the ingredients, gently sauté the onion slices in the oil over medium-low heat until the onion is very soft and starting to turn golden.

WHILE the onion is cooking, use kitchen shears to snip the meat into very small pieces. Add the snips of meat to the onion, raising the heat slightly, and cook, stirring continually, until the meat is brown on all sides and the liquid it gives off has evaporated. Add about a third of the wine, stirring to scrape up any brown bits from the bottom of the pan, and cook slowly; when the wine has almost fully evaporated, add another third, stirring repeatedly, and then the final third. By the time the final addition of wine has almost completely evaporated, the meat should be quite soft.

ADD the chopped tomatoes, chile pepper, cloves, and a little salt and stir to mix well. Lower the heat so that the sauce bubbles gently, add the bay leaves and several grinds of black pepper, and cover the pot. Leave on gentle heat for 2 to 2½ hours, from time to time adding, if necessary, a little boiling water to keep the sauce from becoming too thick.

MEANWHILE, make fresh pasta, following the directions in the recipe for ciceri e tria (page 100), but adding the egg, lightly beaten, with the water. Cut the rolled-out pasta with a ridged rolling pin (available in shops in Italian neighborhoods) or put through the pasta machine to make narrow strips. Set aside on a lightly floured towel to dry for 30 minutes while the sauce cooks.

WHEN the sauce is done, taste and adjust the seasoning. Remove and discard the bay leaves and cloves.

BRING a large pot of lightly salted water to the boil. Add the pasta and cook until al dente—about 5 to 7 minutes for homemade pasta, 10 to 12 minutes for commercial pasta. Put a ladleful of the sauce in the bottom of a heated serving bowl. Drain the pasta and turn it into the sauce, mixing well, then add more sauce on top. Serve immediately, passing additional sauce and a little grated cheese if desired.

from field and garden

PUGLIA'S VEGETABLE TRADITIONS

*t*he people of Puglia love vegetables so much they even eat them for dessert. This is no joke: The course that ends a Pugliese meal, whether feast or family supper, is called, variously, *verdura cruda,* meaning raw vegetables, or *sopratavola,* in the sense of an addendum to the table, or the meal. This sopratavola could be as simple as a plate of raw fennel cut in quarters, but for a feast it will be a great platter heaped with an abundance of crisp, raw, seasonal things—heads of fennel and celery, sweet red-tinged carrots, raw favas or broad beans, raw peas, the tender chicory called *catalogna,* fresh cucumbers (both long, skinny ones and little round ones called *cocomeri* that look like baby watermelons), peppery radishes, little heads of romaine lettuce, all this to be sliced and dipped in salt with perhaps a few timely fruits added for variety—oranges in winter, cherries and green almonds in spring, figs at the height of summer, pears in the waning days of the year.

Puglia's great historian, Luigi Sada, who died last year after a lifetime spent tracking the foods and foodways of his beloved region, traced this tradition of raw vegetables at the end of the meal way back, to the prescriptions of Archestratus, the Mediterranean's first recorded food writer, and to the glory days of Magna Graecia when Puglia was a lively cultural outpost of overseas Greece. Even the sober Romans, Sada pointed out, concluded their *secundae mensae* with raw lettuce, prescribed by their medicine men to dissipate the evil fumes of wine.

I would be hard put to find a genuine vegetarian among my Pugliese acquaintances, although Pythagorean doctrines had a certain strength in the region. Still, most people seem to see meat as a *contorno,* or accompaniment, to vegetables rather than the other way round, and many Pugliese vegetable dishes are in a category one could call "almost-vegetarian," meaning that small amounts of meat (often in the form of preserved pork, bacon, ham, or sausage) or meat broth are used in the preparation. Thus these dishes are very easy to adapt to vegetarian constraints— you simply omit the meat and increase the amount of olive oil a little to compensate, or use a rich vegetable stock rather than meat broth when necessary.

And what vegetables (and fruits) there are in Puglia! This is one of the great garden areas of Italy, a paradise producing in successive and magnificent profusion artichokes, celery, fennel, cherries, table grapes, fava beans, citrus fruits, tomatoes, broccoli rabe, potatoes, cauliflower, zucchini, onions, eggplant, and sweet peppers for the national, and indeed the European, table. Beyond the industrial cores of Bari, Brindisi, and Taranto, Puglia is in its deepest essence green and agrestic, in the words of an Italian guidebook, "really one immense and incredible farm that feeds the fruit and vegetable markets of all Italy and sends its products to half of Europe."

With vegetables like these, least is often considered best in the kitchen, whether we're talking about actual cooking time or the complexity of a production. Like most Mediterranean people, the Pugliese like their vegetables either raw or cooked, not located in some indecisive place between. Vegetables are often prepared in the simplest way possible, steamed and served with a drizzle of good olive oil. But some complex dishes are dear to the Pugliese cook's heart, notably the multilayered preparations called tielle that have an ancient history throughout the Mediterranean, and I would include in this category dishes like ciambotta that, like the Provençale ratatouille it so resembles, are not so much layered as combined, but combined thoughtfully and with great attention to the cooking requirements of each separate ingredient.

Anyone who wants to delve more deeply into the Pugliese vegetable tradition could do no better than to pass the time in a market like the one that takes place every day but Sunday in Monópoli. The sheer visual pleasure of textures, shapes, and vibrantly glowing colors (lemons and clementines set like costly ornaments against their deep dark leaves) may give way to frustration for cooks who can't get to a stove—but there's enough to satisfy, from asparagus to prickly pears to cauliflower, for those who'll eat them raw.

Apparent in the Monópoli market too is another strong link between the food of Puglia and the food of Greece, whether ancient or modern. That's the obvious appeal of wild vegetables, especially wild greens. *"Roba proprio campestra, signora,"* says the vegetable vendor, "real stuff from the fields," as she displays a sack of beautifully cleaned, bittersweet cicorielle, like tiny dandelion greens with their softly dented leaves.

Anthropologists speak of hunter-gatherer cultures as if they existed only in ancient times and far-off places, but the Pugliese are still happily immersed in that foraging culture, even if it is just to supplement the products of gardens and supermarkets. The phenomenon is not limited, on the one hand, to poor countryfolk with no other source of greens, or on the other to romantic hippies trying to get back to the old ways. Everyone in Puglia, it seems, gets a yearning for these atavistic vegetables on a regular schedule, and the markets are full of them, each in their season, lampascioni and cicorielle in dead of winter, pencil-thin (no, as thin as twisted twine) wild asparagus and feathery poppy greens as spring begins to warm up the earth, and wild fennel at summer's height.

Farm dooryards always have a rosemary bush and perhaps a bay (laurel) tree at hand, but wild herbs are also foraged and used in cooking, as they are throughout the Mediterranean—especially varieties of wild mint, wild thyme, and the many members of the oregano/marjoram family. Available year round, herbs, except for oregano, tend to be used fresh far more often than dried. The buds of wild capers *(Capparis spinosa),* found in early summer either growing in crannied walls or fresh in markets, are salted or pickled in vinegar for the pantry cupboard. And several kinds of mushrooms are found here, the most sought after being a kind of pale oyster mushroom, both wild and cultivated, that is called, like wild cardoons, cardonciedde or cardoncelle.

Lampascioni or *cipollotti selvatichi* (wild onions) have been mentioned frequently but a fuller explanation is in order, as these are so important on the Pugliese table. They are the bulbs of a wild hyacinth, the botanical name of which is *Muscari.* There are at least two types of Muscari—*M. racemosum,* the variety native to Puglia and, not surprisingly, highly prized there; and *M. comosum,* which is both wild and cultivated in other parts of the Mediterranean and the source, suspicious shoppers darkly claim, for the lampascioni that have proliferated in Pugliese markets in recent years—most of them, they say, from Morocco. In English the wild flowers are called tassel hyacinth, from the tiny, tassellike blossom they produce, a lovely dark velvety purple in color. Only the bulbs are eaten. They have a bitter but pleasing flavor, and are never, to my knowledge, eaten raw.

You might find fresh lampascioni, if you're lucky, in Greek greengrocers', where they're called, naturally, by their Greek name, *volvi*. Pickled in oil or brine and put up in jars, the little bulbs are also occasionally available in Greek and Italian markets.

Prepare fresh lampascioni as you would an onion, slicing off the sprouting top and the base roots and peeling away one or more layers of the outside skin. Cut a shallow cross in the root end and toss them into a bowl of salted water to soak for up to twenty-four hours to get rid of the bitterness. (Other cooks suggest half-cooking the bulbs, then discarding the water and adding fresh water to continue the cooking.) After cooking, drain them, set on a plate with the root ends down and squashed gently, then dress while still hot with salt, pepper, extra virgin olive oil, and vinegar. Lampascioni may also be grilled over charcoal or wood embers, and in the Foggia region, they are sometimes combined in a tiella with mushrooms and potatoes.

In the recipes that follow, I have used only vegetables that are available in America. There are many others, common in Puglia and are often hard to find here, that gardeners, especially those who live in a warm, dry climate similar to Puglia's, may want to try from seed.

CIPOLLA PORRAIA (ALLIUM AMPELOPRASUM, ALSO CALLED SPONSALE). I don't know any seed source for this currently, but if you go to Puglia, seeds are perfectly legal to bring back. Long, thin, and blanched for five or six inches before the green tops begin, these look like skinny leeks (or fat scallions), but their flavor is sweeter than leeks' and more substantial than scallions'. Too tough to eat raw, they may be braised like leeks in water, oil, or a little vinegar.

CARDE, CARDOONS. These artichoke family vegetables were once prevalent in American gardens where they provided a nice vegetable alternative throughout the cold months. They look a bit like artichokes while growing, but it's only the pale stalks that are eaten, the green leaf parts being stripped away. They can be boiled and served with a vinaigrette, or braised with onions and garlic, or used in a soup like the one on page 60. Seeds are available from specialty mail order seed catalogs.

FAVE, BROAD BEANS. Another old European vegetable that was once much more prevalent in our gardens than it has been in recent years. The growing interest in Mediterranean food, however, has brought increased attention to this vegetable. One reason for their disfavor may be the peculiar belief of restaurant chefs in this country that favas must be shelled and then the outer husk of each individual bean must be peeled. This is just nonsense. A broad bean (fava) that needs its inner skin peeled is a broad bean that's too old to be eaten.

The exception to this rule is dried fava beans. Here the Pugliese are way ahead of us with their *fave sgusciate,* dried beans from which that outer skin has been peeled so that they cook down to a thick purée. If you can find these, and they're sold at several of the sources listed on page 255, they are the best to use for any Pugliese recipe that calls for dried fave. If you cannot find them, you will have to use ordinary dried favas, which are often available in Portuguese, Spanish, and Italian markets. Dried favas should be soaked, after which it's an easy matter to slip the outside skin away before cooking. If this is not done, the dried beans will never dissolve into a purée.

Fresh broad beans, increasingly available in good farmers' markets, should have bright green, fleshy pods, no more than about ³/₄ of an inch wide and well filled out with beans. Broad beans are easy to grow, even in cool climates, and most catalog seed suppliers have two or three varieties. They may be cooked like fresh peas, lightly steamed and dressed with olive oil.

TOMATOES. Pugliese cooks have access to many more tomato varieties than we do. One such is a cherry tomato called *pomodoro a pendula,* hanging tomato. Great clusters of these brilliant crimson tomatoes are suspended, like shiny red Christmas ornaments, outside the shops of small-town greengrocers throughout the winter, adding their color to the season. The whole tomato vine is pulled up and turned upside down to dry slightly, then the individual tomatoes are intricately strung together with twine to make a bright tumbling garland of fruit. To my astonishment, if they're stored in a cool dry pantry they will keep through the winter, growing drier, of course, but still full of flavor even at Easter. The farmers' markets that have blessed so many of our towns and cities in recent years are often repositories of varieties like Brandywine and ox-heart, old heirloom tomatoes that have almost disappeared from high-speed commerce. In season, any of these varieties are perfectly acceptable to use in Pugliese recipes, just so long as they are ripened on the vine and full of juice and flavor. Pugliese cooks also, when the season of the year is not cooperative, turn to canned tomatoes in various forms—whole, chopped, in purée, or concentrated. Good-quality canned tomatoes are perfectly acceptable to use as a substitute for fresh in most recipes.

dried fava beans with bitter greens
FAVE E CICORIA OR 'NCAPRIATA

6 servings as a main course; 8 servings as a first course

Fava beans are one of the ancient, fundamental foods of Puglia. This classic combination of sweetly satisfying puréed beans with bitter greens dressed in oil is irresistible. It's no wonder that, purely as a symbol, fave e cicoria, or 'ncapriata, has captured the imagination of restaurant chefs. Dried fava beans are not easy to find in America, and as for wild greens, they are almost impossible unless you're willing to go out in the early springtime with a kitchen knife to harvest dandelion greens—a good substitute for wild Pugliese cicoriella as long as you make sure you are harvesting from an area that has not been treated with weed-killers or pesticides. You can also find wild greens in season in some farmers' markets. Otherwise, shop your produce vendor for farmed bitter greens like dandelions or various chicories. They won't have that nervous edgy quality of wild ones, but they will do.

Fava purée is not always served with cicorielle, or not with cicorielle alone. You could serve it with turnip tops, broccoli rabe, collards, or other bitter greens. Chinese broccoli, prepared as in this recipe, is a wonderfully pungent foil for the sweet bean purée, or *macco*.

'Ncapriata is a splendid vegetarian main course, or it might be a first course to precede a meat or fish dish, or even as part or all of an antipasto. The following is the simplest, most basic way of preparing the beans and greens, although I should note that some cooks always add a peeled potato cut in chunks to the pot to cook with the beans and dissolve into the purée.

½ pound dried peeled fava beans
   (*fave sgusciate*), or 1 pound whole
   (unpeeled) dried fava beans
Salt to taste
½ cup extra virgin olive oil

1 pound bitter greens (wild
   dandelion greens, broccoli rabe,
   collards, Chinese broccoli, turnip
   greens, or other)

SOAK the fave overnight, then drain and if using unpeeled fave, pull the outer skin away. Place the peeled fave in, preferably, a terra-cotta cooking vessel that is higher than it is broad—like an old-fashioned bean pot, though a Pugliese *pignatta* is the ideal form. Add fresh water to cover the beans, cover the vessel, and place over a rather high flame to come to a boil. (Of course a terra-cotta cooking vessel should never be set on an electric burner, so if you have an electric stove, put the beans in a heavy soup or stock kettle instead.) As the beans start to boil they will give up foam, which should be skimmed off with a spoon. Once the foam ceases to rise, add a good pinch of salt, and, as the beans cook down, stir them thoroughly with a long-handled wooden spoon. The beans will gradually dissolve into the cooking liquid; keep a kettle of water simmering on the back of the stove and, if necessary, add boiling water from time to time to keep the beans from scorching. The beans should take about 1 hour to cook—you will need to stir them constantly during the last 10 or 15 minutes. When they are completely dissolved, without any lumps, they should have the consistency of clotted cream. Using the wooden spoon, beat in ¼ cup of the olive oil and taste, adding salt if necessary.

WHILE the beans are cooking, clean the greens thoroughly in several changes of water. Place them in a large kettle and boil them in the water clinging to their leaves until they are thoroughly cooked and tender. (You may have to add a very little boiling water from time to time.) Drain in a colander, turn into a bowl, and dress the hot greens with the remaining ¼ cup of olive oil and salt to taste. Toss to mix well.

PILE the fava purée on one side of the plate, the greens on the other, and serve with lots of thick slices of country-style bread, fried in olive oil if you wish, or toasted and drizzled with olive oil. Eat the greens and purée together, accompanied by the crisp bread.

NOTE: *Paola Pettini served me a fava purée beautifully mounded on a heavy antique platter, surrounded by the following garnishes: red onions, slivered rather thickly and steeped in vinegar; whole small green peppers (rather like poblanos, spicy but not burning hot) deep-fried in olive oil (page 132); black olives sautéed in oil and mixed with a little Tomato Sauce (page 14); the quintessential steamed chicory greens, dressed in oil. The whole plate was topped with a scattering of thick bread crumbs sautéed in oil until they were crisp and crunchy.*

fava beans and artichokes
FAVE E CARCIOFI AL TEGAME

4 servings

There's a certain period of the year, usually in April, when the end of the artichoke season overlaps with the beginning of the fava season and Pugliese cooks seize the opportunity to prepare this dish.

---

2 pounds fresh young fava beans

1 lemon

4 medium artichokes

1/3 cup extra virgin olive oil

1 medium yellow onion, coarsely chopped

1 garlic clove, chopped with the onion

Salt and freshly ground black pepper

SHELL the fava beans, discarding the soft pods.

SQUEEZE the juice of half the lemon into a bowl of cool water. Trim the artichokes, cutting off the tops and bending back the tough outer leaves until you get down to the softer paler part beneath. Rub the cut surfaces with the other half of the lemon as you work to keep them from blackening. Cut the artichokes in half lengthwise and scrape away the prickly choke in the center. Slice the artichokes lengthwise about 1/4 inch thick and toss the slices into the bowl of acidulated water.

HEAT the olive oil over medium-low heat and add the onion and garlic. Sweat the vegetables in the oil until they are soft and starting to turn golden; do not let them brown. Add the fava beans to the pan and stir to mix well. Drain the artichokes but do not rinse them. Add to the pan and mix well, so that artichokes, beans, and onions are distributed fairly evenly throughout. Add about 1/2 cup of water, raise the heat to medium-high, and bring the liquid to a rolling boil. Let the liquid in the pan cook quite briskly until the vegetables are tender. If necessary, add a little *boiling* water to the pan from time to time. The vegetables should be done in 15 to 20 minutes. Adjust seasoning.

SERVE immediately or cool to slightly warmer than room temperature.

artichokes with eggs
CARCIOFI ALL'UOVA

4 servings

This simple dish makes a fine light supper, with just a salad to accompany it, but it would do equally well as a first course. Try it with zucchini, too, omitting the initial blanching. The difference between this and a frittata is in the proportions—more vegetable than egg, rather than vice versa.

---

1 lemon

4 artichokes, cleaned and trimmed as described in the preceding recipe (about 2 cups)

1 garlic clove

½ minced flat-leaf parsley

2 to 3 tablespoons extra virgin olive oil

2 eggs

¼ cup grated pecorino or Parmigiano-Reggiano

Salt and freshly ground black pepper to taste

USE half the lemon to rub the cut surfaces of the artichokes as you prepare them. Squeeze the juice of the other half into a bowl of water and as the artichokes are prepared, toss them into the acidulated water. When all the artichokes are prepared, cut them into smaller pieces. Transfer the artichokes with their water to a saucepan, bring to a boil, and boil for about 5 minutes, or until they are somewhat softened but not tender all the way through. Drain and set aside.

COARSELY chop the garlic clove with the parsley. Heat the oil in a frying pan over medium-low heat and add the garlic-parsley mixture. Sauté briefly, 2 to 3 minutes, then add the drained artichoke pieces. Continue cooking until the artichokes are thoroughly tender, adding a very little water, no more than 1 tablespoon, if necessary.

BEAT the eggs in a small bowl with the grated cheese. When the artichokes are done, remove from the heat and, stirring continuously, mix in the eggs. Reduce the heat to low. Return the pan to the heat and continue cooking, stirring carefully and continuously, until the eggs are just set. Remove from the heat and stir in salt and pepper to taste. Serve immediately.

braised baby fennel
FENECCHIEDDE

6 servings

In Bari this dish is a favorite for Christmas Eve, a time of year when the fronds of new fennel poke up, acid green against the red Pugliese earth. Fennel is most often served as a *frutta verde* or sopratavola, a vegetable eaten plain at the end of the meal. Cooked in this manner, it takes on an entirely new dimension. *Fenecchiedde* are the small plants left in the fields after the larger, more productive bulbs have been transplanted for blanching. Since you won't be able to get these in the United States unless you are a fennel-grower (or have an obliging supplier in a local farmers' market), use the smallest, most tightly compact bulbs you can find.

About 1 dozen very small fennel
bulbs, or 4 to 6 larger bulbs,
quartered

¼ cup extra virgin olive oil

3 garlic cloves

6 salted anchovy fillets, prepared as
on page 9, or 8 oil-packed
anchovy fillets, coarsely chopped

½ small dried hot red chile pepper,
chopped

Freshly ground black pepper to
taste, if desired

BRING a pot of water to a rolling boil and drop in the whole fennel bulbs or quarters. Return to the boil and cook, uncovered, for about 10 minutes, until the fennel is tender. Drain and set aside.

IN a frying pan large enough to hold all the fennel, heat the oil over medium-low heat and add the garlic, anchovies, and chile pepper. Cook gently until the garlic has softened, mashing the anchovy bits into the oil to make a paste. Add the fennel and continue cooking, stirring to coat the fennel with the garlicky, peppery oil. Cook together, stirring occasionally, for an additional 5 minutes. Serve hot, or let cool to slightly warmer than room temperature.

fresh green peas
PISELLI

4 servings

This is a classic dish that you'll find all over Italy, or at least from Rome south, when peas are in season. The peas you select should be as fresh as possible, preferably harvested that morning from your own garden. If you have access to equally fresh young tender fava beans, they may also be prepared in this fashion. If you must use bacon instead of pancetta, blanch it first in boiling water for a couple of minutes to rid it of its smoky flavor, which otherwise will dominate the dish.

3 tablespoons extra virgin olive oil

1 medium onion, thinly sliced

2 ounces pancetta or blanched lean bacon, cut in small dice or lardons

$^3/_4$ pound *shelled* peas (about 2$^1/_2$ pounds peas in their pods)

Salt to taste

PUT the oil in a saucepan, preferably one made of terra-cotta, over medium-low heat and add the onion and pancetta. Cook slowly, stirring frequently, until the onion is thoroughly softened and the bits of pancetta start to take color and release their fat. Add the shelled peas and mix well. Let the peas cook for a few minutes to absorb the flavors of the other ingredients, then add 1 cup of boiling water. Cover the pan, lower the heat, and cook for about 20 minutes, or until the peas are very soft. Remove the cover, turn the heat up slightly and boil rapidly to reduce the pan juices to a syrupy liquid that coats the peas. Serve immediately.

NOTE: *In all its simplicity, this is often served as a first course or starter, but at the beginning of pea season, when the desire for their fresh, green sweetness is most acute, this could be served in quantity as a main course, accompanied only by slices of bread for sopping up the juices.*

braised broccoli rabe
BROCCOLI DI RAPE STUFATI

4 to 6 servings

Broccoli di rape or cime di rape (also called, in America, broccoli rabe or rapini) is a staple of wintertime markets and tables. It can be part of an antipasto selection, or a contorno—that is, a vegetable to accompany a main course of fish or meat. It's often used to sauce homemade pasta like orecchiette (page 102). And it can be served on its own, with nothing but toasted bread with olive oil to scoop it up. Like most of the brassicas, this is a vegetable rich in vitamins and antioxidants; it is not a vegetable that takes kindly to undercooking.

To select broccoli rabe, which is available in the produce sections of well-stocked supermarkets, look for bunches with deep green leaves and flowers that are still tightly furled. To prepare the vegetable for cooking, discard any coarse, yellowing, or wilted leaves. Cut away tough stems, leaving the flowers with their stalks and the tender young side leaves.

¼ cup extra virgin olive oil

I garlic clove, crushed with the flat blade of a knife

½ small dried hot red chile pepper

3 bunches broccoli rabe, prepared as above

Salt to taste

¼ cup very small black (Niçoise-type) olives, pitted

IN a deep saucepan large enough to hold all the broccoli rabe, heat the olive oil over medium heat. Chop the garlic coarsely and add it with the chile pepper to the oil. Cook briefly, just until the garlic starts to soften, about 3 to 5 minutes.

WHILE the garlic is cooking, wash the broccoli rabe thoroughly. Add it to the saucepan with the water clinging to its leaves. Cover the pan tightly and cook the broccoli rabe for 20 to 30 minutes, or until it is very tender and just a few spoonfuls of savory water remain in the bottom of the pan. (There should be plenty of water for cooking clinging to the leaves, but check the pan from time to time and have a little boiling water ready to add if necessary.) When the broccoli is tender, stir it well to mix it with its sauce and add a little salt and a handful of the smallest black olives you can find, stir again, and serve immediately.

ACCOMPANY the broccoli rabe, if you wish, with slices of bread fried in olive oil or toasted and drizzled with olive oil. Or top with sautéed bread crumbs.

VARIATION: *This is a standard way of preparing greens, whether wild or culti-vated. Poppy leaves, for instance, called paparina, are great favorites in Puglia served this way; dandelion greens, beet greens, chard, or Chinese flowering broc-coli, just to give a few examples, may be prepared in a similar fashion, adjusting cooking times for the tenderness of the vegetables.*

summertime bread and tomato salad
CIALDA PUGLIESE

6 servings

This is a wonderfully refreshing, rustic summer salad that immediately recalls Tuscan panzanella and Andalucian gazpacho.

Pugliese cooks use round, melonlike fruits grown locally and called cocomeri that have a definite cucumber flavor. (In other parts of Italy, cocomero refers to watermelon—and these do look like a smaller, paler, jade green version of the more familiar fruit.) American cooks will make do with cucumbers themselves. Around Grumo Áppula, southwest of Bari, they add a little hot red chile pepper to the mixture and call it crépamariti.

The point of this salad is the bread. If you have made Friselle (page 209) this is a perfect use for them. Otherwise, cut thick slices from a rather stale country-style loaf and toast them slowly in the oven until they are golden brown and as hard as Holland rusks.

---

2 very large, very ripe tomatoes (about 1 pound), seeded and coarsely chopped

2 medium cucumbers, peeled, seeded, and coarsely chopped

1 red onion, halved and finely chopped

½ cup extra virgin olive oil

Salt and freshly ground black pepper to taste

1 small dried hot red chile pepper, if desired, chopped

6 slices of stale country-style bread, toasted as above, or 6 Friselle (page 209)

¼ cup aged red wine vinegar or sherry vinegar

A small handful of coarsely torn basil leaves

COMBINE the chopped tomatoes, cucumbers, and onion and toss with your hands to mix well. Add the olive oil, a generous pinch of salt, black pepper to taste, and the chopped red pepper. Stir to mix well and set aside, covered with a towel, for 30 minutes to 1 hour to let the flavors develop.

IF using bread, prepare it while the vegetables are steeping. Preheat the oven to 350°F. Slice the bread about ¾ inch thick and arrange the slices on a cookie sheet. Toast in the oven for about 30 minutes, turning once, until the slices are golden brown on both sides and firm all the way through.

WHEN ready to serve, dip the bread slices or the friselle quickly in a bowl of water just to dampen them, drain them well, and arrange them on a platter.

JUST before serving, pour ¼ cup ice water and the vinegar into the bowl of vegetables and mix well. Pile the soupy salad on the platter of bread, making sure that each slice is well covered. Garnish with basil leaves and serve immediately.

eggplant parmesan
PARMIGIANA DI MELANZANE

6 servings

Despite its name, this southern Italian dish has nothing to do with Parma except possibly the use of Parmigiano-Reggiano cheese between the layers of eggplant. *Parmigiana di melanzane,* often mistakenly called *melanzane alla parmigiana,* was one of the great dishes that immigrants from Puglia and other parts of the Italian South brought with them to the United States. It has become a staple of old-fashioned Italian-American restaurants where, as with most immigrant foods, it got decked out with an abundance and richness that is absent from the appealing simplicity of the original.

This may seem like a complicated preparation, but much of it can be made ahead of time and, indeed, since the dish is more often eaten at room temperature than it is hot from the oven, the whole thing can be, and often is, prepared in the morning to serve at dinner that evening. Originally, it went in the oven after the bread had come out. It is often made with zucchini instead of eggplant, and, in wintertime, with artichokes, sliced and fried. This is the simplest, most everyday version of the dish.

I medium eggplant, weighing at least I pound

Sea salt

½ pound mozzarella (see page II)

I large egg

½ to ¾ cup all-purpose flour

Extra virgin olive oil

2 cups Tomato Sauce (page I4)

⅔ cup freshly grated Parmigiano-Reggiano

I teaspoon crumbled dried basil

Freshly ground black pepper to taste

Handful of fresh basil leaves

PEEL the eggplant and slice crosswise in slices about ½ inch thick. Stack the slices in a colander, sprinkling layers generously with salt, set a weight on top (a can of tomatoes on a plate will do very well), and leave to stand for 1 hour; then rinse the slices well in running water and dry them with paper towels.

MEANWHILE, grate the mozzarella on the large holes of a cheese grater and set aside. Beat the egg with a fork in a soup plate with 2 tablespoons of water. Place the flour in another soup plate.

ADD olive oil to a frying pan to a depth of ½ inch and heat on a medium burner to frying temperature (360°F., when a little cube of bread quickly turns golden and crisp). Lightly dip each dried slice of eggplant in flour and then in beaten egg, and fry the slices, turning them once, until they are golden brown on both sides. Drain the fried eggplant slices on a cake rack covered with paper towels.

HEAT the oven to 425°F.

PUT a couple of spoonfuls of warm tomato sauce in the bottom of a 2-quart ceramic or earthenware oven dish and layer the eggplant slices in the dish, scattering over each layer an abundance of grated Parmigiano-Reggiano, more tomato sauce, a handful of grated mozzarella, and a sprinkle of dried basil and black pepper. On the topmost layer of eggplant, spread an abundance of tomato sauce and a scattering of grated Parmi-giano-Reggiano. Bake, uncovered, in the preheated oven for 45 minutes. Sprinkle with fresh basil. The eggplant can be eaten hot, but is best at room temperature.

meatballs for eggplant parmesan

For special occasions, Pugliese cooks may garnish the tomato sauce with tiny meat-balls, and add slices of hard-boiled egg and mortadella sausage to the layers. To me, the egg and sausage seem to be too much, but the meatballs add a little substance to what is a very simple dish. Here's how to make them:

½ cup unseasoned bread crumbs	¼ cup finely minced flat-leaf parsley
½ pound finely ground lean veal or pork, or veal and pork mixed together	2 tablespoons finely minced basil, if desired
¼ cup freshly grated Parmigiano-Reggiano	Salt and freshly ground black pepper to taste
Yolk of 1 large egg	2 tablespoons extra virgin olive oil

THOROUGHLY combine the bread crumbs with all the other ingredients except the olive oil. Dampen your hands with a little water and form the mixture into small meatballs about the size of marbles. Heat the olive oil in a sauté pan over medium heat and quickly brown the meatballs all over. Distribute the meatballs over each layer of eggplant slices in the dish.

artichoke parmesan
PARMIGIANA DI CARCIOFI

6 to 8 servings

This is how a parmigiana was traditionally done in the wintertime when eggplant was not in season.

These layered, baked dishes, whether simple like a parmigiana or elaborately complex like some of the Pugliese tielle, or the rice timballi from Sicily and Naples, are so characteristic of the Italian South that they might be called a determining factor in the cuisine. If that's true, then a parmigiana is simply a rustic country version of the urbane and sophisticated tiella, which is itself, I'm convinced, a bourgeois version of the eminently aristocratic timballo.

½ cup unbleached all-purpose flour

Salt

About 1¼ cups extra virgin olive oil

6 or 8 large artichokes

1 lemon, cut in half

½ pound fresh mozzarella, thinly sliced

⅓ cup freshly grated Parmigiano-Reggiano

1½ cups Tomato Sauce (page 14)

Freshly ground black pepper, optional

MAKE a batter: Put the flour in a bowl with a pinch of salt and, using a fork, gradually beat in about ¼ cup of water. Beat in 2 tablespoons of the olive oil, then add more water until the batter is the consistency of heavy cream. (Some cooks beat in 1 tablespoon dry white wine along with the olive oil to give the batter more flavor.) Set the batter aside to rest while you prepare the artichokes.

TRIM the stems of the artichokes, cut away the pointed tops, and break off the leaves until you reach the tender part. Constantly rub the cut surfaces with a lemon half to keep them from darkening. Slice each artichoke in half lengthwise and, using a pointed grapefruit spoon, scoop out the prickly choke. Cut the cleaned artichokes in vertical slices about ¼ inch thick. Squeeze the remaining lemon half into a bowl of cool water and toss the slices in the acidulated water.

PUT about 1 inch of olive oil in the bottom of a skillet or frying pan over medium-high heat. When the oil is at frying temperature (about 350°F.), working rapidly, dip the artichoke slices in the batter and fry until crisp and golden. Remove the artichoke pieces as they finish cooking and drain on paper towels.

THE recipe may be prepared ahead of time up to this point. When ready to proceed, heat the oven to 425°F.

LIGHTLY oil the bottom and sides of a rectangular terra-cotta or glass oven dish. Arrange half the fried artichoke slices over the bottom of the dish, covering with thin slices of mozzarella and a sprinkling of half the grated Parmigiano-Reggiano. Dot with half the tomato sauce, adding salt and pepper if desired. Arrange the remaining ingredients in a second layer, finishing with tomato sauce and grated cheese.

PLACE in the oven and bake for 30 minutes.

MAY be served hot but is best at room temperature.

herbed broiled eggplant with capers and olives

MELANZANE ALLA GRIGLIA

4 servings

You'll need to use what are called Italian or Japanese eggplants, or small eggplants that are longer than they are round, for this simple but rather elegant dish.

---

4 small, slender eggplants

Salt and freshly ground black pepper to taste

¼ cup pitted black olives

¼ cup capers

1 tablespoon minced fresh mint, preferably pennyroyal

1 tablespoon minced fresh basil

2 tablespoons freshly grated pecorino or Parmigiano-Reggiano

½ cup extra virgin olive oil

CUT each eggplant in half lengthwise and sprinkle the cut side liberally with salt. Turn upside down on a rack or draining board and leave for 30 minutes to 1 hour. Rinse thoroughly to get rid of the salt and pat dry with paper towels.

PREHEAT the broiler.

USING a small paring knife, make a series of diagonal cuts on the surface of each eggplant half to make a grid. Cut into the flesh but not through to the skin.

CHOP together the olives, capers, mint, and basil to make a coarse paste. Add pepper and grated cheese, mix well, and taste, adding salt if it seems necessary. Push this mixture into the cuts in the surface of the eggplants. Set the stuffed eggplants, cut sides up, on a grill rack. Pour a few spoonfuls of oil over each and set the rack under the broiler about 4 inches from the heat source. Broil until the tops of the eggplants are crisp and bubbling, or about 30 minutes, checking from time to time to make sure the eggplants are not burning. When done they should be crisp and brown on top. Cool to room temperature before serving.

baked eggplant halves stuffed with olives, capers, and tomatoes
MELANZANE RIPIENI AL FORNO

4 servings

A more elaborate treatment, these eggplant halves are filling enough to make a main-course lunch or supper dish.

---

4 small, slender eggplants

Sea salt

1/4 cup extra virgin olive oil, plus more for deep-frying

1 cup very small bread cubes, cut from a stale loaf

25 pitted black olives, coarsely chopped

1 pound ripe plum tomatoes, peeled, seeded, and diced

1 tablespoon chopped capers

1 garlic clove, finely chopped

1/2 cup chopped flat-leaf parsley

1/4 cup plus 2 tablespoons freshly grated pecorino or Parmigiano-Reggiano

1/2 cup Tomato Sauce (page 14)

CUT the eggplants in half lengthwise, sprinkle the cut surfaces liberally with salt, and set aside to drain for at least 30 minutes or up to an hour. Rinse the eggplants to rid them of the salt and dry with paper towels.

USING a small paring knife, carefully cut out the insides of each eggplant half, leaving a shell about 1/4 to 1/2 inch thick. Coarsely chop the flesh and set aside. Fill a deep sauté pan with olive oil to a depth of at least 1 inch, heat the oil to frying temperature (360°F.) over medium-high, and when it is hot, deep-fry the eggplant halves, turning to brown on all sides. Remove and set aside to drain on paper towels.

PREHEAT the oven to 400°F.

MIX the chopped eggplant with the bread cubes, olives, tomatoes, capers, garlic, and parsley. Stir in 1/4 cup of the grated cheese and 2 tablespoons of olive oil. Use this mixture to fill the eggplant halves loosely. Set them in a baking dish, drizzle with the tomato sauce, and sprinkle with the remaining 2 tablespoons grated cheese. Bake for 1 hour. As with most eggplant dishes, this may be served at any temperature from oven-hot to room-warm.

mushroom-style eggplant
MELANZANE A FUNGHETTO

6 servings

Why this should be called "mushroom-style" is anyone's guess, but it's often suggested that mushrooms are prepared in a similar manner, hence the name. But so are zucchini, and sweet peppers, and even green beans, so. . . .

Whatever. This dish is often served to accompany a fava purée in summertime, but it's also very good on its own. And as noted, you can prepare many other vegetables in a similar fashion.

---

2 small eggplants (1 pound total), cut in cubes

Sea salt

1/3 cup extra virgin olive oil

2 garlic cloves, chopped

1 bunch flat-leaf parsley leaves, chopped

4 or 5 small ripe plum tomatoes, peeled, seeded, and diced

2 or 3 tablespoons chopped fresh basil

PUT the eggplant cubes in a colander and toss with several tablespoons of salt until the cubes are well coated. Set a plate on top, weight it, and leave to drain for 30 minutes to 1 hour. Rinse thoroughly and dry with paper towels.

IN a large skillet, heat the oil over medium-low. Add the garlic and parsley and stir over the heat for about 2 minutes, then add half the eggplant cubes, raise the heat to medium-high, and cook, stirring vigorously, until the eggplant cubes have browned on all sides. Remove the cubes and brown the remaining eggplant. Return all the eggplant cubes to the pan, stir in the tomatoes and basil, and cook an additional 5 minutes. Taste, and add salt if necessary. May be served immediately or at room temperature.

a simple dish of sautéed
sweet peppers
PEPERONATA

6 to 8 servings

This is similar to the preceding recipe, but it features red and yellow peppers. Bell peppers are fine to use for this, but if you can find more adventurous types—Hungarian wax peppers, or somewhat hotter cascabells, or Italian-style *corno di toro* (all available from U.S. seed suppliers)—the dish will be even more interesting and flavorful.

---

2 garlic cloves, thinly sliced

I yellow onion, halved and thinly sliced

2 to 3 tablespoons extra virgin olive oil

2 pounds peppers, preferably red, yellow, and green, seeded and cut in lengthwise strips

I hot fresh chile pepper, if desired, cut in lengthwise strips

2 ripe medium plum tomatoes, peeled, seeded, and chopped

1/3 cup finely chopped flat-leaf parsley

Salt and freshly ground black pepper to taste

GENTLY sweat the garlic and onion in the oil over medium-low heat for about 5 to 7 minutes, until they are soft. Add the pepper strips (both sweet and hot), raise the heat to medium, cover the pan, and cook the peppers for about 30 minutes, or until they are thoroughly soft. Check from time to time to make sure they are not burning. If they are, lower the heat and add 1 tablespoon water.

WHEN the peppers are soft, add the chopped tomatoes, parsley, a pinch of salt, and a little black pepper. Stir to mix well, cover again, and cook an additional 20 minutes. Serve immediately.

fried whole green peppers to garnish a fava purée
PEPERONI FRITTI

6 servings

The peppers used for this are somewhere between sweet and hot, not as bland as ordinary bell peppers, without the kick of, for instance, jalapeños, but still with plenty of zip to let you know they're really peppers. If you can get them, the best peppers to use for this are Anaheims (also called New Mexico) or poblanos. If bell peppers are the only ones available, you might want to spice them up with the addition of a few jalapeños or serranos. Whatever you use, note that the peppers should be green.

---

2 pounds whole small green peppers

Extra virgin olive oil for deep-frying

Sea salt

WASH the peppers very well and dry thoroughly.

PLACE olive oil to a depth of about 1 to 1½ inches in a skillet and set over medium-high heat. When the oil is hot but still well below smoking temperature, at about 320°F., drop the peppers into the pan and fry, turning several times, until they are soft. Remove from the pan, drain thoroughly, sprinkle with a little sea salt, and serve immediately.

crisp-baked zucchini and potatoes
ZUCCHINI E PATATE IN TEGAME

6 servings

Don't be limited to zucchini alone for this dish—any kind of squash will do, including yellow summer squash, pattypan, and hard winter squash like butternut, acorn, or even the big end-of-the-season Hubbard squash and West Indian pumpkin. Adjust the cooking time if necessary for the firmer squashes.

3 medium zucchini, sliced about $1/2$ inch thick

3 medium potatoes, peeled and sliced about $1/4$ inch thick

$1/4$ cup extra virgin olive oil

1 large yellow onion, coarsely chopped

$1/2$ cup minced flat-leaf parsley

Big pinch of crumbled dried oregano

Sea salt and freshly ground black pepper to taste

$1/4$ cup bread crumbs from a country-style loaf

PREHEAT the oven to 425°F.

IN a terra-cotta or glass oven dish combine all the ingredients except the bread crumbs. Toss to mix well and coat the vegetables with the oil. Spread in the oven dish and add about $1/4$ cup boiling water. Sprinkle the vegetables with bread crumbs. Place in the oven and bake, uncovered, for 50 to 60 minutes, or until the potatoes are cooked through.

SERVE hot or at room temperature.

baked rice with vegetables

T I E L L A

6 to 8 servings

The ubiquitous Pugliese tiella is a structured, layered dish of several ingredients—see the discussion on pages 6 and 7. This one was made for me by Totó Marchese's grandmother, Nonna Stella Longano. Many recipes call for arborio rice in a tiella, but Nonna Stella uses a long-grain rice *"che non scuosce mai,"* that doesn't break apart when cooked. The closest U.S. alternative, I've found, is Carolina long-grain rice. Another tip from Nonna Stella: Have all your ingredients ready and laid out before you start to assemble the dish.

---

8 ounces (1¼ cups) Carolina long-grain rice

3 fresh lemon halves

1½ pounds yellow-fleshed potatoes (such as yellow Finns or Yukon gold)

4 large globe artichokes—about 2 pounds in all

2 garlic cloves, finely minced

¾ cup finely chopped flat-leaf parsley

1 tablespoon dried oregano

About ½ cup extra virgin olive oil

About 1 cup dry bread crumbs

1½ medium white or yellow onions, thinly sliced

1 cup canned, drained, chopped tomatoes

¾ cup freshly grated pecorino or Parmigiano-Reggiano

Salt as desired

PUT the rice to soak in water to cover to a depth of 1 inch for 30 minutes while you prepare the rest of the ingredients.

PREPARE two bowls of acidulated water, using the juice of half a lemon for each bowl and filling the bowls with cool water. Peel the potatoes, slice about ⅛ inch thick, and add to one of the bowls to keep them from discoloring. Trim the artichokes of all their hard leaves, rubbing the cut surfaces with the remaining lemon half to keep them from blackening. Slice the artichokes in half lengthwise and, using a grapefruit spoon or a small sharp knife, scrape away the prickly choke; trim off the sharp points of the internal leaves. Slice the artichokes lengthwise into approximately ¼-inch-thick slices and put them in the second bowl of acidulated water.

WHEN you're ready to assemble the tiella, heat the oven to 375°F. Toss the garlic, parsley, and oregano together and set aside. Smear a little oil around the bottom and sides of a ceramic, glass, or earthenware oven dish about 8 to 10 inches in diameter, or an 11-×-8 rectangular dish. Sprinkle 2 tablespoons of bread crumbs over the bottom of the dish and drizzle 1 tablespoon of oil over the bread crumbs.

DRAIN the potato slices in a colander and divide roughly in two portions. Layer one portion over the bottom of the dish. (The bottom should be covered with only a slight overlap among the slices.) Distribute about a third of the onion slices over the potatoes and sprinkle with a third of the herb mixture. Dab about ¼ cup of the chopped tomatoes over the top, then sprinkle with ¼ cup of the grated cheese, a pinch of salt, 2 tablespoons of bread crumbs, and 1 tablespoon of oil.

DRAIN the rice, squeezing to rid it of as much water as possible, and divide roughly in two portions. Distribute one portion over the top in a thin layer, not covering the potatoes entirely.

DRAIN the artichoke slices in a colander and layer them on top of the rice. Use the remaining rice to top the artichokes. On top of this layer of rice, distribute another ¼ cup of tomatoes, a third of the onion slices, and a third of the herb mixture. Sprinkle as above with ¼ cup of grated cheese, a pinch of salt, 2 tablespoons of bread crumbs, and 1 tablespoon of oil.

FOR the final layer, use the remaining sliced potatoes, dressing with the remaining ½ cup of tomatoes plus the remaining onion and the herb mixture. Sprinkle with a pinch of salt, ¼ cup of grated cheese, ½ cup of bread crumbs (to make a thicker layer than the previous ones) and drizzle it with about ⅓ cup of olive oil.

BRING a kettle of water to a boil and add boiling water to the tiella to come about halfway up the container, a depth of about 1½ inches. Place in the oven and bake for 1 hour.

SERVE hot from the oven or at room temperature.

a braise of fresh summer vegetables
CIAMBOTTA DI VERDURE

8 to 10 servings

This is the vegetable version of the much-disputed dish called ciambotta (see page 86). Serve it as a first course, as a contorno with grilled meat or fish, or on its own as a vegetarian main course.

Concetta Cantoro told me the proportions of a good ciambotta should always be more, a good deal more, potatoes than any other ingredient—"and maybe," she mused, "more potatoes than all the rest put together." When I asked her what the word means, she said, *"Un insieme di qualcosa"*—a togetherness of somethings, a phrase I really like.

---

2 small eggplants

Sea salt

4 medium yellow-fleshed potatoes (yellow Finns, or Yukon Gold), about 2 pounds in all

2 medium zucchini

1 yellow or red bell pepper

1 green bell pepper

1/2 cup extra virgin olive oil

1 medium white onion, cut in half and thinly sliced

4 very ripe plum tomatoes, peeled, seeded, and coarsely chopped, or 1 cup canned tomatoes, chopped

Freshly ground black pepper

CUT the eggplants into 3/4-inch dice and layer in a colander with salt. Weight the eggplant and set aside for 1 hour, then rinse the cubes well in running water, drain, and dry well with paper towels.

PEEL the potatoes and cube the same size as the eggplant. Put the potato cubes in a bowl and cover with water to prevent discoloration while you prepare the rest of the vegetables. Cube the zucchini and slice the peppers lengthwise, discarding the core and seeds.

DRAIN and dry the potato cubes with paper towels. Add 1/4 cup of the oil to a frying pan over medium-low heat and gently sauté the potato cubes and onion slices, stirring frequently, until the onions are soft and the potatoes are starting to brown, about 20 minutes. Stir in the tomatoes and let cook an additional 5 to 10 minutes, or until the tomatoes have dissolved somewhat to form a sauce for the potatoes. The potatoes should be tender but not falling apart.

IN another, larger frying pan, sauté the zucchini, peppers, and eggplant in the remaining ¼ cup oil over medium-low heat, stirring frequently, until the vegetables are tender and starting to brown, about 15 minutes. Now combine the potato–tomato mixture with the other vegetables, add salt and pepper to taste, and stir gently with a wooden spoon to mix. Continue cooking over medium-low heat for an additional 15 minutes to blend the flavors well. Taste and add more salt and pepper if desired.

THE ciambotta may be served immediately, but more often it's set aside to cool to room temperature before serving.

NOTE: *Some cooks add a handful of grated pecorino at the very end before setting the dish aside to cool.*

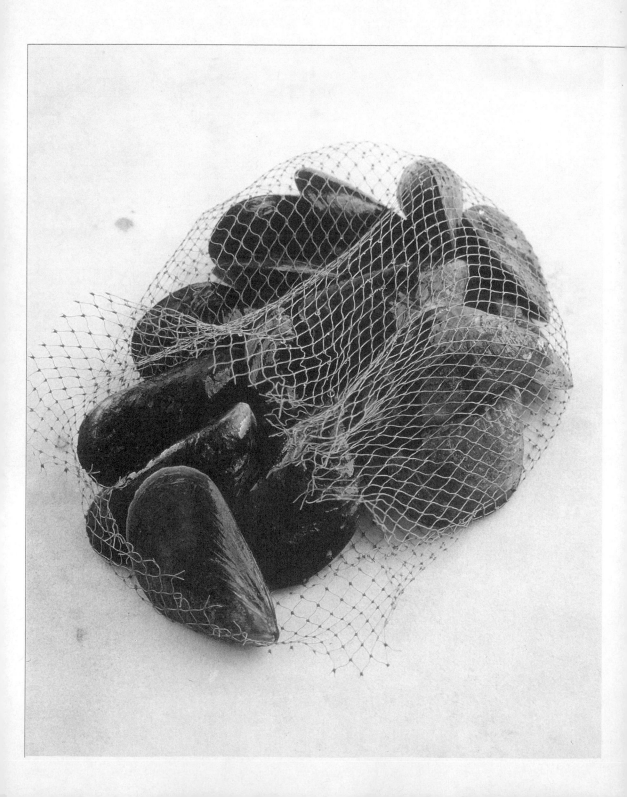

between two seas

*i*t is the sea, first and last, that epitomizes Puglia, a luminous presence from almost any perspective. Wherever you are, it seems, even deep in the interior, climb a tower or a hilltop and there it lies, Ionian or Adriatic, etched in the distance a deeper blue than the blue of the sky, somber at times and at others sparkling with sunlight—you could, it seems, reach out and touch it. Stretching from the Gargano Peninsula out along the heel of Italy to Santa Maria di Léuca (where St. Peter landed on his way to Rome) and then up the arch past Taranto, a coastline like this, more than four hundred miles long, alternating flat sandy dunes with rocky heights and protected harbors, means an incredible richness of resource, even today when the Mediterranean suffers from pollution and overfishing. So it is not surprising that the products of the sea have always dominated Pugliese tables, rich and poor alike.

"Oc-topus!" sings a vendor in Monópoli's morning market. *"I've* got octopus, *fresh* octopus! Here, lady," he cries as I hesitate by his stall, "you wanna try?" And before I can move on he thrusts at me a blob of raw octopus, glistening damp and pale as alabaster. Challenged, I take it in my mouth and the tang of its flavor, fresh and briny as the sea itself, sends a shock through my taste buds. For the first, perhaps the only, time in my life I eat raw octopus for breakfast.

In a market like this one, just a stone's throw from the docks where the blue-painted fishing boats tie up and fishermen mend their nets, compare their catch, and share a coffee or a glass of wine after the day's labors, the variety is both constant and as changing as the vendors' cries: octopus, squid, and cuttlefish, silvery mottled mackerel, sardines and anchovies, spiny sea urchins to be cracked open by the vendor and the orange roe eaten raw on the spot, fat eels, pink shrimps and prawns and other less familiar crustaceans, black and shining clumps of mussels, half a dozen kinds of clams in pale terra-cotta colors, oysters fresh from the oyster beds of Taranto, and then the bigger fish from deeper waters, increasingly rare and increasingly expensive—red mullet, nacreous dentex and daurade, homely St. Peter's fish (John Dory in English), rose-colored bream, and monkfish, called *rana pescatrice,* the fishing frog, or *coda di rospo,* toad's tail, names that belie the prestige of its firm white flesh. And always in the market there are wicker baskets full of *pesciolini piccoli,* little throwaway fish from which fine cooks derive fish soups of extravagant flavors and dimensions. Always, too, there is salt cod (baccalà), sitting in its bath of water, already plumped up and ready to take home and cook. And more and more often these days Norwegian salmon, steaks and fillets glowing their familiar flamingo pink.

Some of these fish will be unfamiliar to North Americans, but fish is fish, I always think. So long as it's the freshest and cleanest you can find, it's the preparation that matters. Haddock, halibut, cod, and snapper are all acceptable substitutes for the larger Mediterranean fish like bream and dentex and daurade. Monkfish is available from most good fish vendors, mussels and clams are almost the same on whatever sea bed they lie, and Norwegian salmon is universal. Moreover, local and regional fish, like wolffish, blackfish, ling cod, black bass and striped bass (whether wild or farmed), all the drums and groupers, tilefish, mahimahi, shark, and so on are all adaptable to Pugliese cooking styles, since their solid flavors stand up well to the vigorous aromas of the Pugliese kitchen.

Of course, some fish commonly available in Puglia are almost unobtainable in America—that fresh octopus from the Monópoli market is the most obvious, but I include a recipe for it anyway, as a curiosity. And, as noted, I've had great success using monkfish in the preparation. Both sardines and anchovies are very hard, though not impossible, to find here, but I've included recipes for both, with recommendations for some substitutions.

Some of the most interesting Pugliese ways with seafood are in the form of pasta sauces and fish soups, and those appear in earlier chapters of this book. Buying whole fish is not always easy, even in coastal zones, but many recipes for whole fish can be adapted for fish steaks or thick fillets. More than any other item on the table or in the kitchen, fish depends for its quality on freshness. In many parts of the country, fresh fish may very well mean frozen, but if the fish has been thoughtfully handled and frozen at sea, it can be fully as good as and often better than so-called fresh fish. Perhaps the most important advice a writer can give on the subject of fish has nothing to do with recipes and varieties, and everything to do with finding the finest seafood vendor available to you. Surprisingly, that often turns out to be the manager of the seafood section in a local supermarket, though it might also be a fishmonger in an ethnic neighborhood market, whether Italian, Greek, Portuguese, or Japanese.

salt-baked snapper

PESCE ARROSTO IN SALE

6 to 8 servings

I was taken aback when a vendor in the Monópoli market told me that his favorite way to cook fish at home was to roast it in salt, a method I knew only from fancy restaurants in other parts of the world. "Completely cover it with salt and then put in a very hot oven *(al massimo)* for fifteen to twenty minutes. That's all," he said. Later, Gianna Greco, a gifted cook with a fine country restaurant at Torre Casciani on the coast south of Gallípoli, confirmed this. And naturally you must use sea salt to cover it, she said.

Wherever it originated, salt-baked fish has become widely, wildly, and deservedly popular in recent years for its simplicity of execution and its fresh, direct, and uncomplicated flavor. That flavor, of course, depends entirely on the quality of the fish itself. You will need a whole fish for this, head, tail, bones, everything but the innards, which the fishmonger will clean out for you. And don't stint on quality—only the best will do. A whole snapper would be my choice here, though the preparation is also fine with a whole salmon, or any other whole fish, although flat fish like sole and halibut will not be successful. This is one technique that will not work with fish steaks or fillets.

---

1 whole fresh snapper or salmon (head and tail included), weighing at least 4 pounds, cleaned

4 pounds coarse sea salt

2 egg whites

Lemon wedges

Very fine extra virgin olive oil

PREHEAT the oven to 425°F.

RINSE the fish carefully, inside and out, in running water. Pat dry with paper towels. Measure the thickness of the fish at its thickest part.

POUR the sea salt into a large bowl, add the egg whites, and mix vigorously until all the grains of sea salt are coated with egg white. Spread about a third of the salt mixture over the bottom of a large rectangular or oval oven dish big enough to hold the whole fish. The bottom layer should be at least 1 inch thick. Place the fish on top, then cover it completely with the rest of the salt. It is important to encase the fish completely in salt, so that no part of it is visible. The topmost part of the fish should be covered at least 1 inch thick.

PLACE the oven dish in the preheated oven, turn the heat down to 400°F., and bake for 20 to 30 minutes, depending on the thickness of the fish—the so-called Canadian rule says fish should cook for 10 minutes per inch, measured at the thickest part.

REMOVE the fish from the oven. The salt will have formed a hard crust over the fish. It's nice to present the fish like this at the table, then dramatically crack the crust with the handle of a knife. Some people even add to the drama by using a small hammer to crack the crust. As you remove the crust, you will be pulling away the fish skin and, of course, any scales. The flesh will be pleasantly salty and very moist.

SERVE with wedges of lemon and a cruet of the finest extra virgin olive oil you can obtain for dressing the fish.

paper-wrapped fish for st. nicholas
ORATA OR TRIGLIE ALLA SAN NICOLA

1 serving

Presumably this is named for San Nicola because it's associated with Bari, where Nicholas has been patron since Barese merchants stole his saintly relics from Myra on the Aegean coast of Turkey in 1087.

In the original, small individual fish, weighing no more than ½ pound each, are dressed with olive oil, garlic, herbs, and lemon slices, then wrapped in parchment paper for roasting. Since whole fish of this size are difficult to find in this country, I often do this with fish steaks or fillets. Almost any fish responds well to the treatment—I have tried it with swordfish, halibut, and tuna steaks, as well as with boneless chunks of haddock and cod. Small, impeccably fresh tinker mackerel are splendid wrapped whole this way, as are small bluefish, sometimes called blue snapper, when they're in season.

---

2 teaspoons extra virgin olive oil

1 small whole fish, weighing approximately ½ pound, or comparable serving-sized fish steaks or thick fillets

Sea salt and freshly ground black pepper to taste

1 teaspoon minced flat-leaf parsley

1 sprig fresh oregano

3 or 4 pitted black olives, if desired

2 or 3 very thin lemon slices

2 or 3 garlic slivers

2 teaspoons fresh lemon juice

PREHEAT the oven to 400°F.

LAY out a length of parchment paper or aluminum foil—for each fish or piece of fish, you'll need enough to make a loose packet around it. Drizzle about ½ teaspoon of oil over the paper, then set the fish on it. Sprinkle with salt and pepper, then with the parsley. Add the oregano and olives, if desired, lay a few lemon slices and the garlic slivers on top, and drizzle the fish with the remaining oil and the lemon juice.

PULL up the edges of the aluminum foil or parchment paper and fold them together to make a loose but secure packet. Place each serving packet on a baking sheet and slide into the oven. Bake for 20 minutes. (If you use parchment paper, it will puff up and brown, a handsome thing to send to the table.) Open one of the packages to test if the fish is done. If not, return to the oven for another 5 to 10 minutes. Note that whole fish will take longer to cook than steaks or fillets.

SERVE immediately, in their individual packets.

NOTE: *If you are using whole fish, put some of the aromatics inside the opening as well as on top of the fish.*

sardines in a fennel-spiked tomato sauce
SARDE ALLA MARINARA

4 to 6 servings

In America, sardines are the young of *Clupea harengus,* the Atlantic herring; in Europe and the Mediterranean sardines are the young of the pilchard, *Sardina pilchardus.* Despite appearances, they aren't the same and some say the European is better, fatter, tastier. Whether baby herring or baby pilchard, however, sardines are hard to find, but well worth the effort. Fishmongers who cater to Italian, Greek, or Portuguese communities are your best bet. Oftentimes, what they're selling is in fact flown in from the Mediterranean.

If you can't find sardines, try this recipe with young tinker mackerel or small bluefish called snapper (not to be confused with red snapper). With oily fish like these, freshness is of even more critical importance, so let your nose be the judge before you buy.

---

1 onion, sliced very thin

3 tablespoons extra virgin olive oil, plus a little more for oiling the pan

1 pound ripe red tomatoes, peeled, seeded, and coarsely chopped

1 tablespoon fennel seeds, lightly crushed in a mortar

Salt and freshly ground black pepper to taste

1½ pounds impeccably fresh sardines, tinker mackerel, or blue snapper

1 tablespoon bread crumbs

⅓ cup dry white wine

PREHEAT the oven to 425°F.

IN a saucepan over medium-low heat, gently sauté the onion in the 3 tablespoons of oil until it is soft and golden but not beginning to brown. Add the chopped tomatoes and cook, stirring occasionally, for about 10 minutes, or until most of the juice has evaporated and the tomatoes have reduced to a thick jam. Stir in about half the fennel seeds and add salt and pepper as desired.

USE a little more oil to spread on the bottom of a rectangular or round oven dish large enough to hold all the opened sardines in one layer. Add all but about ⅓ cup of the tomato sauce and spread over the bottom of the dish.

OPEN each fish along the belly, making a complete cut from top to bottom, so that the two sides may be opened like a book. Bone the fish, rinse under running water, and arrange on top of the tomato sauce. Sprinkle a little salt, the bread crumbs and the remaining crushed fennel seeds on the fish. Drizzle on the wine, then dot with the remaining tomato sauce. Bake in the preheated oven for about 20 minutes. When the fish is done, serve immediately.

herb-marinated fillets of fish
PESCE ALLE ERBE MARINATE

2 to 3 servings

A quick and simple but effective technique, this can be expanded almost infinitely and adapted to almost any kind of fish. Moreover, you can vary the seasonings, using, for instance, more or less garlic, or other types of herbs—basil, thyme, even un-Pugliese herbs like lovage or tarragon. I call for haddock, but the recipe can serve for almost any kind of white-fleshed fish—monkfish, weakfish, Pacific cod, mahimahi, or others.

---

3 tablespoons finely minced flat-leaf parsley

1 bay leaf

1/2 garlic clove

1 small onion

3 tablespoons extra virgin olive oil

Pinch of salt

1 pound haddock fillets about 1/2 inch thick

3 tablespoons dry white wine, or a little more if necessary

1/4 cup golden raisins plumped in hot water for about 10 minutes

Freshly ground black pepper to taste

CHOP together the minced parsley, bay leaf, garlic, and onion until very fine—almost a paste. Mix with 2 tablespoons of the oil, add a little salt, and spread over the top of the fish fillets. Set the fillets in a deep dish and sprinkle with the wine. Cover and set aside in a cool place, or refrigerate, for at least 1 hour or up to 12 hours.

WHEN ready to cook, add the remaining tablespoon of oil to a frying pan and set over medium-high heat. When the oil is very hot, place the fish fillets in the pan, herbal side down. Add the marinade juices to the pan with the raisins and sprinkle the fillets with pepper. Turn the fillets once and cook on the other side—haddock fillets should take no more than 1½ to 2 minutes per side to be thoroughly done. Remove the fillets from the pan and transfer to a heated serving dish. Boil down the juices in the pan (adding a little more wine if necessary), scraping up any brown bits, and when the pan juices are reduced to a couple of tablespoons pour them over the fish fillets. Serve immediately, garnishing, if you wish, with some freshly minced herbs and lemon wedges.

oven-roasted fish with black olives
DENTICE ALLE OLIVE

6 servings

A whole fish makes a handsome presentation, but this dish may also be prepared with 1-inch-thick fish steaks (halibut or swordfish, for instance) or with thick fillets of haddock or cod.

¼ cup extra virgin olive oil

⅓ cup pitted, coarsely chopped black olives

⅓ cup finely chopped flat-leaf parsley, plus more parsley for garnish

1 garlic clove, minced

1 whole snapper, weighing at least 4 pounds; or six 1-inch-thick

halibut or swordfish steaks; or 3 pounds plump haddock or cod fillets

Salt and freshly ground black pepper to taste

Juice and grated rind of 1 lemon

PREHEAT the oven to 375°F. Use about 1 teaspoon of the oil to lightly oil a rectangular or oval oven dish large enough to hold the fish.

COMBINE the olives, parsley, and garlic. If using a whole fish, put half the mixture inside the fish, set the fish in the oiled dish, and strew the remainder of the olive mixture over the top. If using fish steaks or fillets, arrange in the dish and strew the olive mixture over the top.

SPRINKLE the fish with salt and pepper and pour on the remaining olive oil and the lemon juice. Place in the preheated oven and bake for 30 minutes, basting every 10 minutes with the pan juices.

WHEN the fish is done, remove from the oven and serve immediately, garnished with finely minced parsley mixed with the grated rind of the lemon.

oven-roasted fish with potatoes
ORATA ALLA PUGLIESE

4 to 6 servings

Orata is a type of bream with very fine flesh—again, snapper is an excellent substitute, and salmon, too, stands up well to this treatment, but, as in the preceding recipe, you could also adapt this to thick steaks of swordfish or halibut, or to thick fillets of haddock or similar fish.

I whole snapper or salmon, weighing at least 3 pounds; or 2½ pounds 1-inch-thick halibut or swordfish steaks; or 2 pounds plump haddock or cod fillets

½ cup extra virgin olive oil

3 garlic cloves

½ cup flat-leaf parsley leaves

4 medium russet potatoes, peeled and sliced about ¼ inch thick

3 tablespoons freshly grated pecorino or Parmigiano-Reggiano

Salt and freshly ground black pepper as desired

PREHEAT the oven to 400°F.

RINSE the whole fish inside and out, scale it if necessary, pat dry with paper towels, and set aside. Use about 2 tablespoons of the oil to brush liberally the bottom and sides of a rectangular oven dish large enough to hold the fish.

CHOP the garlic and parsley together until they are minced very fine. In a bowl, mix the garlic and parsley with about ¼ cup of the olive oil to make a loose paste. Toss the potato slices in this mixture to cover thoroughly.

ARRANGE about half the potatoes in the bottom of the dish, overlapping if necessary and spreading them out to distribute them evenly. Sprinkle with half the grated cheese. Add salt, if desired, and plenty of pepper. Now set the fish on the potato layer and cover with the remaining potatoes and grated cheese. Add more salt and pepper, and drizzle the remaining 2 tablespoons of olive oil over the top. Bake for about 40 minutes, or until the fish and potatoes are thoroughly cooked.

SERVE immediately.

VARIATION: *If you wish to make this with fish steaks or fillets, the roasting time will be much shorter—10 minutes should be plenty. In that case, to avoid underdone potatoes, parboil the potato slices for about 10 minutes in rapidly boiling water before you mix them with the garlic-parsley-oil paste and assemble the ingredients.*

A similar dish can be made with seppie ripiene, Stuffed Squid (page 30). Place slices of potato in the bottom of an oiled oven dish, as above, sprinkling with cheese and 1 tablespoon of dry bread crumbs, as well as salt and pepper. Place the stuffed calamari and their tentacles on top of the potatoes, cover with more potatoes, cheese, and bread crumbs, then pour on ¼ cup extra virgin olive oil and ½ cup dry white wine. Bake in a preheated 400°F. oven for about 1 hour.

steamed octopus
POLPO IN UMIDO

6 servings

I include this recipe just in case you come across a fisherman someday with an octopus for sale. If so, you can cook it Pugliese fashion in a tall earthenware *pignatta,* without water but with lots of garlic, chopped parsley, olive oil, sliced onion, little winter tomatoes (the kind that hang in clusters in shop doorways in Puglia), black pepper, hot red chile pepper, and a short piece of cinnamon stick—a very Greek sauce. When the octopus is tender, remove it, slice it, and serve it with its sauce, strained through a fine-mesh sieve.

Or make the following adaptation, as I do in America, with monkfish or another very firm-textured fish (marlin has proved an excellent choice).

---

4 garlic cloves, chopped

1/4 cup extra virgin olive oil

1 medium onion, sliced

6 small very ripe tomatoes, cut in half

1/4 cup finely minced flat-leaf parsley

1/2 small dried hot red chile pepper

Sea salt and freshly ground black pepper to taste

One 2-inch cinnamon stick

1 1/2 pounds boneless monkfish or other firm-textured fish

IN a saucepan over medium-low heat, gently sweat the garlic in the olive oil until it is very soft but not beginning to brown. Add the onion and continue cooking 5 to 7 minutes, until the onion is soft and turning golden. Raise the heat to medium-high and add the tomato halves, cut sides down. Cook the tomatoes, turning frequently, until they have released their juice and are very soft. Stir them into the other ingredients to make a sauce, adding a small amount of water (no more than 1/2 cup) if it seems necessary. Stir in the parsley, chile pepper, salt, black pepper, and cinnamon, cover the pan, and cook for about 15 minutes, or until the sauce is thick and flavorful.

REMOVE the cinnamon stick and chile pepper and push the sauce through a fine-mesh sieve or vegetable mill or process to a coarse purée.

Return the sauce to the rinsed-out pan over medium heat. Cut the monk-fish into 6 serving-size pieces and add to the simmering sauce. Cook, turning the fish pieces from time to time, until the fish is cooked thoroughly but still firm—about 7 to 10 minutes.

REMOVE from the heat and serve immediately, spooning the sauce over the fish pieces.

gratin of fresh anchovies, smelts, or other small fish
ALICI GRATINATE

6 servings

Paola Pettini, who has taught generations of Baresi how to cook, gave me this recipe for anchovies in the style of Bari. This should be made with fresh anchovies if you can find them—not an easy task in America. Otherwise, make it with small smelts no more than 6 inches long. The flavor of these freshwater fish is of course very different from the richness of anchovies, but it will still be a very fine dish indeed.

½ garlic clove, chopped

2 tablespoons chopped fresh flat-leaf parsley

2 tablespoons fresh bread crumbs

1 teaspoon dried oregano

1 tablespoon freshly grated Parmigiano-Reggiano

1 tablespoon pecorino Pugliese (or use Parmigiano)

Salt and freshly ground black pepper

Juice of 2 lemons

2 pounds medium (5 to 6 inches long) anchovies

2 or 3 tablespoons extra virgin olive oil

PREHEAT the oven to 375°F.

IN a small bowl, mix together the garlic, parsley, bread crumbs, oregano, and cheeses. Add salt and pepper to taste and set aside.

SQUEEZE the lemon juice into a small bowl. Slit the bellies of the anchovies and pull out and discard the backbone and innards. Rinse the anchovies briefly in the lemon juice.

SPREAD the olive oil over the bottom of an oven dish, preferably made of terra cotta, and add a teaspoon of water and a teaspoon of the lemon juice, mixing well with the oil. Arrange the anchovies in a circle in the oven dish and sprinkle the crumb mixture over the top. Bake in the oven for about 15 minutes or until they are just barely cooked.

Cozze (Mussels)

THE MUSSELS GROWN IN Puglia are Mediterranean black mussels, not the blue mussels common to our shores and in our markets. Blue mussels will do just fine in Pugliese mussel dishes if you can't get black ones. Black mussels, however, are cultivated in the Pacific Northwest (see page 255). Since they spawn in winter instead of summer, the opposite of blue mussels, true mussel lovers can be happy all year round.

Mussels, like clams, should be alive when purchased. To prepare for cooking, rinse them thoroughly under running water, scrubbing the shells together. Discard any with broken or gaping shells, or any that feel suspiciously heavy—they may be full of mud. If the mussels still seem very sandy after cleaning them, put them in a bowl of cool, salted water in which you've stirred a spoonful of cornmeal and leave them for an hour or so. Then rinse again and use a paring knife to pull off the beards. Prepare the mussels only when you're ready to use them.

To open raw mussels (assuming you are right-handed), cover your left hand with a heavy glove or towel and grip the mussel. Insert a small, strong, sharp knife between the two shells at the point on the straighter edge where they are joined by a small muscle. Slide the knife back and forth to cut and loosen the mussel muscle as much as possible, then twist the knife to separate the two shells. Do this over a bowl to catch the liquid in the shells—it's a tasty addition to any preparation.

This procedure requires a certain expertise that comes only with long experience. I'd be the first to confess that, when recipes require opening raw mussels, I usually cheat by steaming the mussels open first. I clean them as in the instructions above, then put them in a deep wide saucepan with a couple of tablespoons of water or dry white wine, cover the pan, and steam them over medium heat just until the mussels start to open, making it easier to get at them. Don't worry if the mussels aren't thoroughly cooked—that will come later in the process. But do discard any that do not open.

steamed mussels
PEPATA DI COZZE

4 to 6 servings

In Pugliese restaurants, these are often served as a first course, but they are equally satisfying as a main course, especially if served over slices of toasted country-style bread that has been rubbed with a little garlic and drizzled with olive oil. The abundance of black pepper is what makes them *pepata,* but for a more subtle flavoring, add a healthy pinch of ground cinnamon to the broth.

---

1 stalk celery, including green leaves

1 garlic clove

1/3 cup flat-leaf parsley leaves

1 green bell pepper

Zest of 1 lemon

1/4 cup extra virgin olive oil

1 small oil-packed anchovy fillet, coarsely chopped

1/2 cup dry white wine

1 teaspoon white wine vinegar or lemon juice

1 tablespoon (or more to taste) cracked black pepper

Pinch of ground cinnamon

4 pounds mussels, cleaned (see page 155)

COARSELY chop the celery, garlic, and parsley together. Cut the green pepper and lemon zest into slender strips. Using a saucepan that is large enough to hold all the mussels in a layer no more than two mussels deep, gently sauté the vegetables and lemon zest in the olive oil over medium heat until they are soft but not beginning to brown. Add the anchovy bits and continue cooking, mashing the anchovy into the oil with a fork.

ADD the wine and vinegar or lemon juice to the pan and as soon as it boils, stir in the cracked black pepper and a pinch of cinnamon. Now add the mussels, raise the heat to high, and cook, stirring and tossing, until the mussels are fully open. If after 10 minutes there are still mussels that have not opened, discard them.

USING tongs, remove the mussels from the pan to a deep serving bowl. Boil the pan juices down, if necessary, to about 1/2 cup, pour over the mussels in the bowl, and serve immediately.

deep-fried mussels
COZZE FRITTE

4 to 6 servings

Here's where steaming mussels open in a deep wide saucepan (see page 155), rather than using a knife, saves effort. Just as soon as the mussels start to open, remove them, and strain their liquid into the eggs, as indicated below.

---

4 pounds mussels, cleaned

2 eggs, lightly beaten with a fork

2 cups extra virgin olive oil for deep-frying

1 cup flour

$^1/_2$ teaspoon fine sea salt

OPEN the mussels, discarding the shells but reserving the liquid. Strain the liquid through a fine-mesh sieve or cheesecloth into the eggs, or strain the pan juices into the eggs.

HEAT the oil in a deep-frying pan to 370°F. Dip each mussel into the flour, then into the eggs, and then gently lower them into the hot oil and deep-fry until golden.

DRAIN on paper towels, sprinkle with salt, and serve immediately.

VARIATION: *Mix $^1/_2$ teaspoon fine sea salt with 2 eggs. Dip the mussels into the eggs and then roll each one in bread crumbs (you'll need approximately 1 cup). Fry as directed, drain on paper towels, and serve immediately.*

Tiella:
The Layered Casseroles of Puglia

A LAYERED CASSEROLE, CALLED tiella, taieddha, or tiedda in various dialects, is one of the most typical dishes found in the Pugliese kitchen. The tiella is both a way of cooking, that is, a specific type of preparation, and at the same time the dish in which that preparation is cooked. In traditional farmhouses, the tiella, a round, deep, straight-sided terra-cotta dish like an old-fashioned pie plate, was set to cook on the hearth amid the embers, with hot coals piled on the heavy metal lid, so that the fire was *sopra e sotto,* above and below, an ancient way of cooking that mimicked the oven. (However, I have seen tielle of metal, and rectangular tielle, too.)

Pugliese writers often insist that the tiella is related to Spanish paella, especially because the kind made in the Terra di Bari usually includes rice. But the more I look at these preparations, the more I am convinced that rice is, in fact, a fairly recent addition to a very old-fashioned dish, an attempt in bourgeois households to mimic the fancy cuisine of the aristocratic Neapolitan kitchen and give a gloss of chic to a traditional preparation. Throughout the Kingdom of the Two Sicilies, a complex timballo di riso, surprisingly rich and full of lush ingredients like veal meatballs and chicken livers and ragù, was the very symbol of the aristocratic table, as readers of Giuseppe di Lampedusa's *The Leopard* will remember. It isn't farfetched to imagine a parvenu household in nineteenth-century Bari putting on airs by adding rice to a humble local dish in an attempt to turn it into timballo di riso.

What makes a tiella today, however, is not so much rice as it is the presence of at least one layer of potatoes, especially creamy yellow-fleshed ones. These, too, are a late addition, for potatoes apparently didn't come into general use in this part of the Mediterranean until some time in the early nineteenth century. So what was the original tiella? There's a clue in a recipe in one of Luigi Sada's many publications on Pugliese traditions wherein he mentions a *teglia di grano,* made by layering pounded grain (see page 96) with vegetables and salt cod. If this cooking method, layering seafood and vegetables with wheat grains or rice or potatoes, is as ancient as I think it is, it may go back well before potatoes or rice to a Greek original. The evidence is there both in the name itself (Barbara Santich, an Australian food historian, suggests a relation between tiella and the Greek cooking utensil called *teganon,* or, more often *tagenon)* and in the process, for the Greeks were early masters of layered dishes like modern moussaka.

In any case, the three recipes that follow are just a small sample of the many forms a tiella can take.

In a traditional Pugliese tiella, mussels are served on their half shells. If you wish, you may discard the shells and use only the mussels themselves.

mussels, potatoes, and zucchini casserole
TAIEDDHA DI COZZE, PATATE, E ZUCCHINE

8 to 10 servings

Taieddha (Tie-EDGE-ah) is the name tiella takes in the Salento, where rice is rarely used and potatoes are always included.

4¹/₂ pounds mussels

2 pounds yellow-fleshed potatoes

1 pound small zucchini

1 pound white onions

Extra virgin olive oil

³/₄ cup bread crumbs

³/₄ cup freshly grated pecorino or Parmigiano-Reggiano

¹/₂ cup finely chopped flat-leaf parsley

Salt and freshly ground black pepper

PREHEAT the oven to 400°F.

CLEAN the mussels and open them (see page 155), leaving the mussels attached to their half shells and discarding the empty shells. Drain through a coffee filter and reserve the mussel liquid. Or use the steaming method. (For both methods, see page 155.)

PEEL and thinly slice the potatoes. Cut the zucchini into julienne strips. Peel the onions, cut in half, and slice thin.

LIGHTLY oil the bottom and sides of a terra-cotta oven dish 10 to 12 inches in diameter, or a rectangular roasting pan approximately 11 by 13 inches. Sprinkle the bottom of the dish with ¹/₄ cup of the bread crumbs.

LAYER half the potatoes, half the onions, and half the zucchini in the dish. Sprinkle with ¹/₄ cup of cheese, ¹/₄ cup of bread crumbs, and ¹/₄ cup of parsley. Add salt as desired and freshly ground black pepper. Arrange half the mussels on the half shell on top, then sprinkle with another ¹/₄ cup of cheese. Add the remaining potatoes, onions, and zucchini in layers, and top with the remaining mussels. Sprinkle the topmost layer with the remaining cheese, bread crumbs, and parsley, adding more salt and pepper to taste. Drizzle with the filtered mussel liquid and the oil. Cover with aluminum foil and bake for 30 minutes. Remove the foil and continue baking an additional 30 minutes, or until the potatoes are cooked through.

mussel and potato casserole
TIELLA DI COZZE E PATATE

4 to 6 servings

See information on an easy way to open raw mussels (page 155); you can get away with it in this one, too.

---

2 pounds mussels, cleaned as instructed (page 155)

¹/₄ cup freshly grated pecorino or Parmigiano-Reggiano

¹/₂ cup dry unseasoned bread crumbs

¹/₄ cup finely minced flat-leaf parsley

Salt and freshly ground black pepper to taste

¹/₄ cup extra virgin olive oil

4 medium (about 2 pounds) yellow-fleshed potatoes (yellow Finns or Yukon Gold), peeled and thinly sliced

1 large yellow onion (about 1 pound), halved and thinly sliced

2 large eggs

PREHEAT the oven to 400°F.

CLEAN the mussels and open them, draining and reserving their liquid, or steam them briefly. Once the mussels open, discard the empty shells, keeping the mussels in their half shells. Combine the cheese, bread crumbs, and parsley, adding salt and black pepper to taste.

HEAT the oil in a large 10-inch frying pan over medium heat, add the potatoes, and gently sauté, turning frequently with a spatula, for 5 minutes, or until the potatoes start to brown along the edges. (You may have to do this in two batches, combining all the potatoes with the onions at the end.) Add the sliced onion and continue to cook, turning, for an additional 5 minutes.

ADD the reserved mussel liquid to the pan with the potatoes and onions and continue cooking another 3 minutes. Layer the potato-onion mixture and the mussels on their half shells in a rectangular terra-cotta or glass oven dish in this order: potatoes, mussels, potatoes. Sprinkle each layer with about ¼ of the cheese and bread crumb mixture, not forgetting to save enough for the final layer (beaten egg).

BEAT the eggs with a fork until yolks and whites are thoroughly mixed, then spread over the topmost layer of potatoes. Sprinkle with the remaining cheese and crumb mixture. Set the dish in the oven and bake 45 to 50 minutes, or until the potatoes are thoroughly cooked and the top has formed a nice golden crust.

SERVE immediately or cool to just above room temperature.

potatoes, rice, and mussels casserole
TIELLA DI PATATE, RISO, E COZZE

6 servings

The presence of rice marks this as a classic tiella from Bari. The recipe comes from cooking school teacher Paola Pettini. Note that the ratio of mussels to other ingredients is much lower than in the recipe on page 159.

---

5 to 6 ounces (about ¾ cup) Carolina long-grain rice

1 pound mussels

¼ cup extra virgin olive oil

1 medium yellow onion, very thinly sliced

½ cup minced flat-leaf parsley

½ pound ripe red tomatoes, diced, or 1 cup canned tomatoes, drained and coarsely chopped

2 pounds yellow-fleshed potatoes (4 medium potatoes), such as

yellow Finns or Yukon Gold, peeled and thinly sliced

1 pound zucchini (2 medium zucchini), thinly sliced

¾ cup freshly grated Parmigiano-Reggiano or pecorino

Sea salt and freshly ground black pepper to taste

½ garlic clove, minced

½ pound ripe red tomatoes, thinly sliced

PREHEAT the oven to 425°F.

PUT the rice in a bowl and cover with water to a depth of 1 inch. Set aside while preparing the mussels. Clean and debeard the mussels as described on page 155. Open the mussels, leaving the mussel meat attached to the half shells and discarding the empty shells. Drain and reserve the mussel juice. Or steam the mussels just until open, then discard empty shells and strain the liquid left in the pan.

SMEAR a tablespoon of oil over the bottom and sides of a 10-inch round earthenware or glass oven dish. Layer the onion slices over the bottom. Scatter over them half the minced parsley and half the diced tomato. Layer half the potatoes and half the zucchini over this. Sprinkle the zucchini layer with about ¼ cup of the grated cheese, along with salt and pepper to taste.

PLACE the mussels in their half shells on the potato-zucchini layer. Drain the rice thoroughly, then distribute it in small handfuls over the mussels. Sprinkle with another ¼ cup of cheese and the remaining diced tomato and minced parsley. Add more salt and pepper and distribute the garlic over the top. Drizzle 2 tablespoons of oil over this layer.

LAYER the remaining potatoes and zucchini on top of the rice. Sprinkle with the remaining ¼ cup of cheese, adding salt and pepper. Use the sliced tomatoes as the topmost layer, completely covering the top. Drizzle over them the remaining oil, the reserved mussel liquid, and a little more salt.

ADD boiling water to the tiella to come halfway up the sides. Place the dish, uncovered, in the preheated oven for 45 to 60 minutes, or until the potatoes are tender and the rice is thoroughly cooked.

SERVE immediately, or cool to slightly warmer than room temperature.

farmyard bounty

*W*e met in Filippo Spinelli's butcher shop, just off the main piazza in Sammichele, a little town in the heart of the Murge, whose streets are paved with smooth blocks of white limestone. In a soft and misty winter night's rain, the paving stones glow like polished alabaster. Throughout the Murge, a rolling upland of broad, fertile wheatfields south of Bari, the town of Sammichele is famous for *zampina*, a type of veal sausage, very long and thin, that is cut into shorter sections for cooking. These segments are then curled round themselves, pinwheel fashion, before being set on the grill to crisp and brown over glowing embers. Sammichele zampine are lean, elegant, little more than seasoned and salted meat, and so slender they need nothing to hold them in their pinwheel shape when the butcher's boy sets them to roast on a gridiron over glowing charcoal.

Filippo the butcher is a mighty man, like most butchers in Italy, where it takes a well-developed set of muscles to heft the great sides of beef and pork, the whole lambs and baby goats and veal calves that come daily into the macelleria to be separated into joints and sliced, trimmed, rolled and tied, chopped into sausage meat, beaten into submissive scallops and cutlets. From a raised platform he looks down on his customers with a benevolent smile, like a priest about to bestow communion.

The macelleria, however, is one of those unassuming places you wouldn't think of venturing into unless you had been told. Small, chilly, bare, it is lit by a cold fluorescent light that bounces harshly off white-tiled walls. There was scarcely room enough for the six of us in front of the dais from which the butcher surveys his realm. And at the end of the day there was not a lot to choose from in the glass case before us. But once we declared our intentions the butcher went into action, opening the door to his walk-in cooler and like a jeweler from his safe extracting and displaying his treasures: the zampina, first of all, and then another fatter sausage, made of pork and tied in regular sausage links, called *al punto di coltello,* at the point of the knife, because the meat is chopped by hand with the knife blade. Then there were thick pork rib chops, the meat pink and lean but surrounded by a layer of cream-colored fat and rind that turns into crisp crackling at the swift touch of fire. There were little bundles of *turcinieddhi,* bits of lamb's liver-and-lights, wrapped around with papery strips of intestine to hold them together for grilling. There were *braciole,* thin scallops of pork rolled over chopped parsley and wild mint. And finally little garnet-colored lamb rib chops, no more than a bite or two at most in size, that looked like the ribs of a miniature toy lamb.

All this Filippo brought out, considered with us, weighed, advised against the pork chops because they might unbalance our palates (but we took them anyway), and then, piling it all on a sheet of butcher paper, transported it down a flight of stairs to the osteria below street level where his young assistant waited by a bed of glowing charcoal. We sat in the adjoining basement on benches at a long, paper-covered table, drinking a fragrant local rosato wine and eating wedges of soft, pungent pecorino cheese, chunks of the local semolina-flour bread, its crumb so yellow it looks like an egg dough, and olives, green and red ones, home-cured, of the most recent harvest. And meanwhile the butcher's boy cooked the meat.

One by one, he brought our selections to the table as he finished grilling them, each one hot off the fire and carefully balanced (it was, he admitted, his first day on the job) on a sheet of butcher paper, the grease shining through. We ate, with forks and knives, with our fingers, nibbling bones, wiping our hands on the bread, using the bread to mop up any juices left in the plate, passing greasy papers back and forth across the table, sampling, comparing, admiring, pouring more wine. We ate more meat in that one meal than most of us had eaten in the previous month, and we ate it happily and without apology.

crisp oven-roasted chicken and potatoes

POLLO ASSUTTE-ASSUTTE

6 servings

Assutto means *asciutto,* which means dry, in the sense of crisp and brown and cooked without a sauce. A similar preparation, called *agnello assutte-assutte,* is made with lamb—see page 177.

---

3 pounds baking potatoes, peeled and cut in chunks

½ cup extra virgin olive oil

½ cup minced flat-leaf parsley

Sea salt and freshly ground black pepper to taste

4 to 5 pounds chicken, cut in parts

PREHEAT the oven to 425°F.

MIX the potato chunks in a bowl with half the olive oil, half the parsley, and a generous amount of salt and pepper. Toss to coat well, then spread over the bottom of a roasting pan large enough to hold all the potatoes in one crowded layer.

IN the same bowl, mix the chicken parts with the remaining oil and parsley and more salt and pepper, again stirring to coat well. Arrange the chicken over the top of the potatoes. Place in the oven and bake for 30 minutes, then turn the chicken pieces over, at the same time stirring the potatoes, and return to the oven for an additional 30 minutes. The chicken is done when crisp and brown and the potatoes should be roasted to a fine golden color. If the potatoes have not browned, remove the chicken pieces to a heated platter, raise the oven heat to 500°F. and return the potatoes to the oven for 10 minutes or so, or until they are done to a turn.

roast stuffed chicken

POLLO ARROSTO

6 to 8 servings

The chicken roasted for a Pugliese Sunday lunch will be a plump, young farmyard bird, a *pollo ruspante*, her brief life spent in relative freedom, pecking away at the greens and grains, the bugs and worms, that give her juicy flesh so much savor. The stuffing speaks decisively of the Italian South and could be adapted for use with capons or even a small, fresh, free-range turkey. Slip a few slivers of garlic and some parsley leaves beneath the skin of the breast to make a handsome presentation. If the chicken you buy comes without giblets, buy a few chicken livers to add to the stuffing.

One 4½- to 5-pound free-range roasting chicken with giblets

1 medium onion, finely chopped

1 garlic clove, finely minced

3 tablespoons extra virgin olive oil

1 cup plain unflavored bread crumbs, preferably freshly grated

1 tablespoon coarsely chopped capers

¼ cup finely minced flat-leaf parsley

2 tablespoons freshly grated pecorino or Parmigiano-Reggiano

2 ounces Genoa salami, finely chopped

1 large egg

1 garlic clove, thinly sliced

8 whole leaves flat-leaf parsley

Sea salt and freshly ground black pepper to taste

1 cup dry white wine, at room temperature, plus 2 tablespoons for deglazing

PREHEAT the oven to 400°F.

REMOVE the giblets from the chicken and set the bird on a rack in a roasting pan. Tuck the gizzard in a corner of the pan; it will add to the flavor of the pan juices.

CHOP the liver and heart as finely as possible (or use about ¼ pound of chicken livers purchased separately) and place in a small frying pan along with the chopped onion, minced garlic, and 2 tablespoons of the olive oil. Over medium-low heat, sauté gently until the chicken parts are thor-

continues

oughly brown and the vegetables are starting to soften. Scrape into a bowl and mix with the bread crumbs, capers, minced parsley, cheese, and salami. Break the egg in a bowl, beat lightly with a fork, then stir into the stuffing mixture, using your hands to blend rapidly. The mixture should be moist but not runny. If necessary, add a little water or a few more bread crumbs to attain the right consistency. Stuff the chicken loosely with the stuffing mixture.

WITH your fingers, loosen the skin over both sides of the breast meat and gently slide a few slivers of sliced garlic and a few whole parsley leaves into place between the skin and the flesh. Tie the legs loosely over the opening with kitchen twine.

RUB the chicken all over with the remaining tablespoon of olive oil, then sprinkle with salt and pepper to taste. Place in the preheated oven and roast for 45 minutes, by which time the skin should be nicely brown. Turn down the heat to 350°F. and baste the chicken with 1 cup of the wine. Return to the oven to roast for an additional 30 to 45 minutes, basting with the pan juices every 10 minutes. The chicken is done when the juices around the thigh bone run clear yellow when the leg is pierced with a fork.

REMOVE from the oven and let rest for 15 minutes before serving. While the chicken is resting, pour the pan juices into a measuring cup. Deglaze the pan with the remaining 2 tablespoons wine and add to the juices in the cup. Skim off the fat that rises to the top of the cup (save this flavorful fat, if you wish, for sautéing potatoes). Put the juices in a small saucepan and boil a few minutes to reduce and concentrate the flavors. Serve as a sauce with the chicken.

rabbit with vegetables and dried mushrooms
CONIGLIO IN UMIDO ALLE VERDURE E FUNGHI SECCHI

6 servings

Modern methods of animal husbandry are not only questionable in terms of the environment and public health; they also mean that chickens or rabbits or veal calves taste nearly alike wherever they're raised in the world, because they're all raised in exactly the same way. In times past, every country family in Puglia (which must have included a good three-quarters of the population) kept its own chickens and rabbits, a ready stock for feast-day menus. Excess animals were sold off as necessary to butchers in nearby market towns. Thus, although meat was not consumed in great quantities, what was eaten by farmers and city dwellers alike was fresh and appropriately raised, without recourse to medicated feed and magic growth potions. Today wise cooks throughout Italy, and increasingly in other countries as well, insist on animals raised naturally for the appetizing flavors they provide.

One 2½-pound rabbit, cut into 6 pieces

1 cup white wine vinegar mixed with 1 cup water

One ½-ounce package dried funghi porcini (mushrooms)

2 medium carrots

3 stalks celery

1 medium onion

2 garlic cloves

3 very ripe plum tomatoes, peeled and seeded, or 1 cup drained canned tomatoes

2 ounces Italian pancetta, or blanched slab bacon

3 tablespoons extra virgin olive oil

4 bay leaves

1 or 2 sprigs fresh rosemary

1 cup dry white wine

Salt and freshly ground black pepper to taste

PLACE the rabbit pieces in a bowl with the vinegar and water and marinate for about 1 hour.

continues

MEANWHILE, put the dried mushrooms to soak in 1 cup of very warm water. Dice the carrots, celery, onion, and garlic together to make about 2 cups of chopped vegetables. Dice the tomatoes and set aside. Cut the pancetta or bacon into thin (matchstick) lardons.

WHEN ready to cook, sauté the pancetta lardons in the oil in a large skillet over medium heat for about 5 minutes, or until the fat starts to run and the lardons begin to brown along their edges. Add the diced vegetables (except the tomatoes) to the pan, lower the heat, and cook 10 minutes or so, stirring occasionally, until the vegetables start to soften. Do not let them brown.

WHILE the vegetables are cooking, drain the rabbit pieces and pat dry with paper towels.

PUSH the vegetables out to the sides of the pan, raise the heat to medium-high, and brown the rabbit pieces in the hot fat on both sides, about 5 minutes to a side. Strain the mushroom soaking water into the pan, using a fine sieve (lined with paper towel if it's not fine enough) to catch any grit. Lower the heat to simmer. Add the tomatoes, bay leaves, and rosemary and stir to mix well.

RINSE the mushroom pieces under running water to rid them of sand and chop coarsely. Add them to the pan along with the white wine. There should now be sufficient liquid to come just to the top of the pieces of rabbit; if there's not enough, add a little boiling water to top it off.

ADD salt and pepper, cover the pan, and cook until the liquid has reduced by two-thirds, about 1 hour. If necessary, during the last 10 minutes of cooking remove the lid, raise the heat, and boil to get rid of excess liquid and make a thick sauce.

REMOVE the bay leaves and rosemary sprigs and serve immediately. This is especially good with polenta, the diced vegetables topping the polenta as a sauce.

VARIATION: *To make rabbit with green olives* (coniglio alle olive verde), *omit the tomatoes and mushrooms. Add 12 to 15 pitted green olives and a spoonful of lightly toasted pine nuts (pignoli) in place of the mushroom pieces and increase the white wine to 1½ cups. Do not add more liquid, as this should be a drier preparation.*

rabbit braised with green and red peppers
CONIGLIO AI PEPERONI

6 servings

One 2½-pound rabbit, cut into 6 pieces

1 cup white wine vinegar mixed with 1 cup water

6 tablespoons extra virgin olive oil

2 large onions, halved and thinly sliced

¼ cup dry white wine

4 to 6 bell peppers, green and yellow or red combined, or about 2 pounds of peppers

Salt and freshly ground black pepper to taste

PLACE the rabbit pieces in a bowl with the vinegar-water mixture and marinate for 1 hour. Then drain and dry thoroughly with paper towels.

IN a pan large enough to hold all the ingredients, heat 3 tablespoons of the olive oil over medium-high heat. Add the rabbit pieces and brown on both sides, about 5 to 7 minutes to a side. As they brown, remove the pieces and set aside. (Sometimes rabbit gives off a great deal of moisture while sautéing; if this happens, remove the liquid and discard—otherwise the meat will not brown.) When the rabbit is done, lower the heat to medium-low and stir the onion slices into the pan. Cook until the onion is limp and golden, but don't let it brown. Add the wine to the pan, bring to a simmer, then add the rabbit pieces, nestling them among the onions, and cook, covered, for about 30 minutes.

WHILE the rabbit is cooking, cut the peppers in eighths, removing seeds, tops, and white membranes. Put the remaining 3 tablespoons of oil in a separate frying pan and over medium-low heat gently stew the pepper slices until they are thoroughly wilted and starting to brown—about 15 minutes uncovered and 15 minutes covered. Stir the peppers and their juices into the pan with the rabbit, add salt and pepper to taste, and cook together for an additional 30 minutes. Check the amount of liquid in the

continues

pan after 15 minutes—there should be a small amount of rather syrupy oil in the bottom of the pan, enough to keep the meat and vegetables from burning. Add a little more white wine, broth, or plain water if necessary to prevent sticking; if there's too much liquid, raise the heat to medium-high and continue cooking 15 minutes uncovered to evaporate some of the juices.

SERVE immediately.

VARIATION: *Chicken, cut into pieces, may be substituted for the rabbit, in which case the final cooking time should be 15 minutes.*

"beef" rolls
BRACIOLINE

4 servings

In the north of Italy, a braciole is a chop, whether of beef, veal, or pork; but in the South it is synonymous with a piece of lean meat, presumably originally cut from the chop bone, rolled around a filling. These are *braciolone* if they're big, *braciolone* or *braciolette* if they're small. In Puglia they might be made of lean veal, but more often they're made of horse meat. You probably won't be able to find horse meat for this dish, but young beef or veal will be an acceptable substitute.

This recipe is adapted from one given me by the Barese cooking teacher Paola Pettini, an energetic, enthusiastic exponent of her regional cuisine. Note that it is intended to be served as two courses, the first a sauce for pasta (often orecchiette), the second the meat, either on its own or with a little more of the sauce. While some might find it odd to serve two courses with the same flavors Pugliese think good things sometimes come in double doses.

---

8 thin boneless beef or veal scaloppine or cutlets (about 1 pound), pounded thin

8 very thin slices savory baked ham or pancetta, plus 2 tablespoons minced pancetta for the soffritto

1/3 cup finely chopped flat-leaf parsley

1 garlic clove, minced with the parsley

1 heaping tablespoon rinsed and drained capers

3 ounces pecorino or Parmigiano-Reggiano, cut in slender fingers

1/4 cup extra virgin olive oil

1 medium yellow onion, chopped

1 garlic clove, chopped with the onion

1 carrot, scraped and finely chopped

1/2 cup dry red wine

2 cups coarsely chopped canned whole tomatoes

1 small dried hot red chile pepper or 1/2 teaspoon crushed red pepper flakes

Sea salt and freshly ground black pepper to taste

Finely minced basil or parsley for garnish, optional

continues

POUND the beef cutlets with a meat pounder to stretch them and make them very thin (or ask the butcher to do this for you). Lay a slice of ham or pancetta on each cutlet, then sprinkle with a teaspoon of the garlic-parsley combination, a few capers, and a finger of cheese. Roll each cutlet up over the filling and secure with a toothpick or tie with thread.

IN a deep skillet over medium-high heat, brown the beef rolls on all sides in the olive oil. Remove as they brown and set aside.

ADD the minced pancetta to the pan together with the chopped onion, garlic, and carrot, lower the heat to medium-low, and cook, stirring occasionally, until the vegetables are soft but not brown. Add the wine, raise the heat slightly, and cook, scraping up any brown bits. When the wine has reduced by approximately half, add the tomatoes to the pan and continue cooking for about 5 minutes to reduce and thicken the tomatoes into a sauce.

THE recipe may be prepared ahead to this point.

WHEN ready to continue, heat the sauce over medium until it is simmering. Crumble the chile pepper and stir into the sauce. Return the beef rolls to the pan, spooning the sauce over them to cover well. Add salt and pepper. Cover the pan, lower the heat to medium-low, and continue cooking for 25 minutes, or until the beef rolls are thoroughly impregnated with the flavors of the sauce.

SERVE the beef rolls with the sauce; or, if you prefer, serve the sauce with pasta as a first course, reserving just a few spoonfuls to garnish the beef rolls, which are served as the main course. Garnish with minced herbs if you wish.

VARIATION: *In Foggia, bracioline are made as they are in Naples, with a few toasted pine nuts and some sultana raisins, plumped in hot water and drained, added to the stuffing.*

oven-roasted lamb with potatoes

AGNELLO ASSUTTE-ASSUTTE

6 servings

This is the lamb variation on pollo assutte-assutte (page 168). The meat and potatoes should be crisp and brown, with very little sauce.

---

2 pounds russet (baking) potatoes, peeled and cut in chunks about 2 inches long

6 tablespoons extra virgin olive oil

½ cup minced flat-leaf parsley

Sea salt and freshly ground black pepper to taste

½ cup freshly grated pecorino or Parmigiano-Reggiano

2 pounds boneless leg of lamb, cut in chunks similar in size to the potatoes

2 garlic cloves, finely chopped

PREHEAT the oven to 375°F.

MIX the potato chunks in a bowl with ¼ cup of the olive oil, ¼ cup of the parsley, and salt and pepper to taste. Toss to coat well, then spread over the bottom of a roasting pan or oven dish large enough to hold all the potatoes in one crowded layer. Sprinkle about ⅓ cup of grated cheese over the top of the potatoes.

IN the same bowl, mix the lamb chunks with the remaining 2 tablespoons of oil and ¼ cup of parsley and more salt and pepper. Add the remaining cheese and the chopped garlic, again stirring to coat well. Arrange the lamb on the top of the potatoes.

PLACE the uncovered pan in the preheated oven and bake for 30 minutes, checking after 15 minutes to be sure that no water is necessary. The lamb should have given off a certain amount of liquid, but if the potatoes are so dry they're sticking to the bottom of the dish, add a little boiling water. After another 15 minutes, remove the pan from the oven and turn the lamb pieces, at the same time stirring the potatoes. Return to the oven for an additional 30 minutes, then remove again and raise the oven heat to 425°F. Stir the meat and potatoes so that most of the potatoes are on top and return to the oven for 10 to 15 minutes to crisp and brown the potatoes to a fine golden color.

oven-braised lamb with greens

CUTTURÌEDDE

6 to 8 servings

There are probably as many variations on this dish as there are cooks in Puglia. Usually dandelion greens, escarole, or broccoli rabe are added to the lamb stew halfway through cooking, but sometimes the greens are omitted and the lamb is cooked with potatoes and onions. Or potatoes, onions, and greens may all be cooked together. Mushrooms may be sautéed in a little oil, then added, and a glass of wine tossed in and reduced. In short, this is an all-purpose stew or braise that can be varied depending on what's seasonally available, and if the dish has sufficient liquid, at the end it can be stretched to serve more appetites by pouring it over thick slices of country-style bread.

Wild dandelion greens, when available, will give the most authentically Pugliese flavor to this stew, but I have made it with cultivated dandelion greens and sometimes with Asian greens such as tatsoi or bok choy.

---

1 large onion, halved and thinly sliced

¼ cup extra virgin olive oil

2 pounds boneless lamb shoulder, cut in 1-inch cubes

1 tablespoon tomato concentrate or ¼ cup Tomato Sauce (page 14)

¾ cup dry red or white wine

About ½ cup coarsely chopped flat-leaf parsley

1 cup drained canned tomatoes, coarsely chopped (about 6 small canned tomatoes)

3 or 4 sprigs fresh marjoram or oregano

2 bay leaves

Salt and freshly ground black pepper to taste

1 stalk celery, including green top, broken in two

1 small dried hot red chile pepper

IF DESIRED:

15 to 18 small new potatoes, scrubbed and cut in half if large; or 4 or 5 baking potatoes, peeled and cut in chunks

1½ pounds carefully washed greens (see suggestions above)

1 pound small, pickling-size onions, peeled

1 cup thickly sliced mushrooms, preferably wild oyster mushrooms

1 tablespoon finely minced flat-leaf parsley

Handful of slivered pecorino cheese

PREHEAT the oven to 300°F.

IN a heavy kettle or casserole, over medium-low heat, gently sweat the sliced onion in 2 tablespoons of the oil until soft and starting to turn golden. Add the lamb pieces, raise the heat to medium, and cook, stirring frequently, until the meat has started to brown.

STIR the tomato sauce or concentrate into the wine and add to the pan. Raise the heat to medium-high and cook rapidly, stirring, until the wine has thrown off its alcohol. Add the chopped parsley and tomatoes, along with the marjoram, bay leaves, salt and pepper, celery, and the chile pepper, stirring to mix well. If you are using potatoes, add them at this time and stir into the stew. When the liquid in the pot comes to a simmer, cover and place in the preheated oven for 1 hour.

MEANWHILE, if you are using greens, clean them very well. Some greens may need to have tough stems removed; most will require coarse chopping. When the lamb has baked for 1 hour, add the greens, or the whole onions, or both, to the pot, setting them on top of the meat and its juices. (If the lamb appears very dry, add a little boiling water to the pan before adding the greens, remembering that most greens will also release quite a lot of liquid.) If using the mushrooms, sauté them quickly in the remaining 2 tablespoons of oil and add to the pan. Cover again and return to the oven for another 30 to 45 minutes, by which point both lamb and vegetables should be very soft. Remove from the oven, remove and discard the bay leaves, celery stalks, and chile pepper, and transfer the stew to a heated serving platter. Sprinkle with more black pepper, the minced parsley, and the cheese, which ideally should be shaved very thin, using a vegetable parer, rather than grated.

SERVE immediately.

easter lamb with fresh green peas and parmesan sauce

VERDETTO

6 servings

As it is in most of the Mediterranean, lamb is the great celebratory ritual food of Puglia, the very symbol of feasting and sacrifice. In the old, pre-Christian Mediterranean described in the verses of *The Iliad,* no feast began without a sacrifice, an offer of the best part of the meal to the gods. The Paschal lamb served at Easter and Passover, like the lamb for the great Id at the end of Ramadan, is a symbol meant, even if unconsciously, to recall this ancient pagan rite.

In the region around Bari, if the Easter lamb isn't roasted, then it will most likely be turned into *verdetto,* lamb cooked with peas—or sometimes with fresh green asparagus, or young, tender cardoons, the choice of vegetable depending in part on where in the spring season Easter happens to fall. At the end of cooking, this savory stew is made richer by the addition of eggs and grated cheese to coat the meat and vegetables with an unctuous cream.

This is a traditional dish for Easter (Pasqua) but more especially for the Monday following, called Pasquetta or Pasqualino, a national holiday.

---

2 ounces pancetta or blanched bacon, diced

2 tablespoons extra virgin olive oil

1 onion, halved and very finely sliced

2 pounds very young boneless lamb shoulder, or 2½ to 3 pounds lamb shoulder with bones, cut in pieces (see Note)

Salt to taste

1 cup dry white wine

1½ pounds (shelled weight) fresh green peas—about 2½ pounds peas in their pods (see Note)

½ cup finely minced flat-leaf parsley

Freshly ground black pepper to taste

3 large eggs

⅓ cup freshly grated pecorino or Parmigiano-Reggiano

PREHEAT the oven to 325°F.

IN a heavy ovenproof saucepan over medium-low heat, sauté the pancetta or blanched bacon in 1 tablespoon oil until the pieces are crisp and brown. Add the onion slices and continue cooking, stirring frequently until the onion is soft but not turning brown.

PUSH the onion and pancetta out to the sides of the pan, raise the heat to medium-high, and add the remaining tablespoon of oil and lamb pieces to the center. Sprinkle with salt to taste and brown the lamb on all sides— about 10 minutes. When the lamb pieces are thoroughly brown, stir in the wine. Let the wine boil rapidly to throw off the alcohol, then cover the pan and place in the preheated oven to bake for 1 hour, or until the lamb is very tender. Check from time to time and if the lamb juices are drying up add a very little boiling water.

AFTER 1 hour of cooking, remove the pot from the oven and stir in the peas and half the parsley. Add black pepper to taste, stir to combine well, then cover and continue cooking, on medium-low heat on top of the stove for about 20 minutes, or until the peas are tender, again adding boiling water from time to time if necessary.

FIVE minutes before you are ready to serve the dish, mix the eggs with the cheese and remaining parsley, beating with a fork. Quickly beat a few tablespoons of hot juices from the pan into the egg mixture to warm it up, then, off the heat, stir the egg mixture into the lamb and peas, using a wooden spoon to reach all the meat and vegetables and coat them well with the eggs. There should be sufficient heat to set the eggs into a creamy sauce, but not so much heat that they will scramble. If necessary, the dish may be returned to the heat, but be very careful. If the eggs scramble, there's not much you can do about it except pretend that's what you intended all along.

SERVE immediately. The dish should *not* be reheated.

NOTE: *In Puglia the lamb for verdetto is usually shoulder, cut into chunks with the bones, the wise observation being that bones add considerable flavor. In my experience, most Americans will be happier with boneless meat, in which case the quantity served should be no more than 2 pounds.*

If you wish to serve cardoons or asparagus instead of peas, clean the vegetable in the usual manner; the quantity used should be the trimmed weight. Cook the vegetable, like the peas above, until it is tender.

grilled calf's liver
FEGATELLI DI VITELLO

4 servings

In much of Italy, fegatelli means robust and delicious chunks of pork liver, wrapped in caul fat and threaded on skewers for grilling over live coals. At her tidy little restaurant in the heart of Lecce, Concetta Cantoro makes her fegatelli with more delicate calf's liver, an easier prospect for American cooks. Caul fat is the white lacy membrane that surrounds an animal's stomach. Specialty butchers or meat shops in Italian or Chinese neighborhoods often stock caul fat or are able to order it for you. It is essential in this preparation because the fat renders out while the meat cooks and keeps the liver from having the consistency of cardboard.

½ pound caul fat to wrap the liver
1 pound fresh young calf's liver

Sea salt and freshly ground black pepper
Bay leaves

CAUL fat should be soaked in tepid water for 10 minutes or so to make it more pliable. Simply set it in a bowl and cover with lukewarm tap water while you prepare the liver.

IF necessary, peel away the thin outer membrane from the liver. Cut the liver in chunky rectangles about 1 inch by 2 inches, discarding the veiny sections. Sprinkle each chunk of liver with a light dusting of salt and pepper.

DRAIN the caul fat and carefully unfold it. Cut pieces of caul fat large enough to wrap around each liver chunk in a single layer. Wrap the liver, tucking a little piece of bay leaf inside each packet. Sprinkle more salt and pepper on the outside and set on a rack for grilling; if you prefer, thread the chunks on skewers, separating each chunk with half a bay leaf.

FEGATELLI are best grilled over wood embers or charcoal, but an oven grill or broiler will do if you don't have access to live fire. If using wood or charcoal, start the fire at least 30 minutes in advance to build up a good bed of coals. If using an oven grill or broiler, preheat in sufficient time to make it really hot for cooking (you are the best judge of how long that will be) and set the rack so the meat will be at least 4 inches from the heat source.

GRILL until the packets are crisp and brown on one side, then turn and grill the other. Be careful not to overcook—ideally the liver will be nicely browned on the outside and still a little pink in the middle. This should probably take 3 to 5 minutes for each side, but the time can vary depending on the nature of the heat you're using. As the liver chunks cook, the caul fat will melt.

WHEN done, remove to a heated platter and serve immediately, with plenty of crusty country-style bread for sopping up the juices.

from the ovens of Puglia

BREADS, FOCACCIE, AND PIZZE

"They all come around asking about our bread. I've been interviewed by more Germans than I could count. Even the Milanese—they take our flour back to Milano with them but they can't get it right. It's the water, you see. Without the water of Altamura, there's just no doing it."
—BAKER'S ASSISTANT, ALTAMURA, DECEMBER 1995

*W*hether it's the water, or the flour, or the salt, or the wood that's burned in the smoky old ovens, or the baker's hands coaxing the living dough to swell and rise, or something in the very air itself, the bread of Altamura, Italians agree, is the best in Italy, a nation that takes its bread seriously. So seriously indeed that national leaders have been moved to poetry on its behalf, as in the following, printed on the paper sacks that wrap the bread at Francesco Picerno's Antico Forno in Altamura:

AMATE IL PANE
Cuore della Casa
Profumo della Mensa
Gioia dei Focolari

RISPETTATE IL PANE
Sudore della Fronte
Orgoglio del Lavoro
Poema di Sacrificio

ONORATE IL PANE
Gloria dei Campi
Fragranza della Terra
Festa della Vita

NON SCIUPATE IL PANE
Ricchezza della Patria
Il più Soave Dono di Dio
Il più Santo Premio della Fatica Umana*

Like most commercial Pugliese breads and many from home kitchens as well, the bread of Altamura is made from semola, a gritty, grainy flour milled from durum wheat *(Triticum durum)* and called semolina in English. The hardest wheat known, *Triticum durum* has a high ratio of protein to starch and a hard vitreous kernel. It produces a creamy yellow flour that, according to most authorities, is too hard for bread dough, which needs considerable give to it, but just right for pasta. (All commercial pasta made in Italy must by law use only durum wheat flour, one reason why it's superior to pasta made elsewhere.)

So how come the bakers of Puglia use durum wheat semolina for their bread? At least in part because that's what's available, what has always been available. The early history of wheat is not always clear (those who are interested, however, will find a fascinating discussion in Robert Sallares, *The Ecology of the Ancient Greek World,* Ithaca: 1991), but one fact stands out: Since antiquity, Puglia has been one of Italy's principal granaries, and the primary grain produced on the great, arid grasslands of the northern Tavoliere was and is hard durum wheat. The Tavoliere, the largest plain in Italy south of the Po, remains the major area of production, but durum wheat is grown today in many other parts of Puglia as well—some 1 million

* In a crude translation (my own): LOVE BREAD: Heart of the home, perfume of the table, joy of the hearth; RESPECT BREAD: Sweat of the brow, pride of labor, poem of sacrifice; HONOR BREAD: Glory of the fields, fragrance of the land, feast of life; DON'T WASTE BREAD: Wealth of the fatherland; the loveliest gift of God, the holiest prize of human labor. (This bit of verse was actually composed by Il Duce himself. Mussolini, it seems, could get as sentimental as any modern food writer over the epic romance of traditional foods.)

acres are planted to wheat each autumn. By February, on the undulating uplands of the Murge, south of Bari, and the sweeping plains of the Tavoliere, the winter wheat, most of it durum, is already ankle-deep, the rippling waves of green a spectacular sight, a vast ocean of growing grain.

It may be true that flour ground from durum wheat is more difficult to work than ordinary flour, although I remain unpersuaded of this, as I explain below. In any case, improved modern strains and modern milling practices have taken much of the labor out of it. Pugliese bakers learned long ago that the superior flavor and nutritional value of durum wheat were worth the effort. The carotenoids in durum semolina make a bread with a pleasantly rich buttery yellow color, so golden that you might think eggs had been added to the dough. Finally, durum wheat, because of its low water content, is more long-lasting than other, softer wheats, whether as whole grains, wheat flour, baked bread, or pasta. I have kept loaves from the Altamura bakeries for two weeks or more with no deleterious effects.

If bread this good were made in America, it would quickly be picked up and mail-ordered all over the country, but in Italy, if you want it, you have to go to Puglia. Pane pugliese is a type of bread displayed on the shelves of smart bakeries all over Italy, but the real stuff is not easy to find except in places like Altamura, Laterza (where they specialize in giant loaves weighing about twenty-two pounds), Mandúria, and the Gargano peninsula. That's partly because, in addition to the durum wheat flour from which it's made, the bread is baked in wood-fired ovens, preferably a great old masonry oven like the one in the Picerno bakery in Altamura, a dark, vaulted cavern redolent of woodsmoke, of bread, of the sweetness of grain, where, at 1:00 P.M. of any weekday, there's a sense of bustle as last-minute shoppers rush to get their daily bread before the lunchtime closing.

A friend who lives in the Salento south of Lecce calls the making of bread "a fundament of rural life." In the Salentino countryside, bread is often still made from wheat or barley grown on the family farm and baked in a stone beehive oven built next to the farmhouse. Heated the night before with two or three bundles of vine or olive prunings, the oven is relit next morning with fresh bundles of twigs. Often the dough is also worked and set to rise in its wooden trough the night before.

Once the oven is hot, the coals are brushed aside and in go the quick breads, like *puccie,* small breads made from a wet dough with black olives added, pits and all, and *cuccuzate,* with onions, tomato, and *cucuzzi* (zucchini) incorporated. Then the loaves themselves are put in, and finally, so as not to waste any of the oven's heat, a large quantity of Friselle (page 209) are thrust into the oven. These little spirals of barley dough are baked twice. After the first baking, they're pulled from the oven, then split in two by drawing them, while hot, through a loop of suspended wire; then they're replaced in the now slower oven, where they remain till late afternoon, slowly drying and becoming harder.

"Long ago, wood-fired ovens of this kind were declared unhygienic, in order to advantage 'modern' electric ovens, which naturally produce a poorer bread," my friend writes. "This drama has been going on for decades, and only yesterday in the town of Maglie a number of 'private' breadmakers working in the traditional way were denounced and fined on hygienic grounds. Their delicious breads had been passing surreptitiously to eager clients and at early morning were on sale in Maglie's beautiful covered market."

Having recounted all this, I may be more than a little presumptuous to offer the following recipes. They are by no means intended as ways to reproduce Pugliese breads in American kitchens, whether domestic or professional. Rather, they are good breads, all of them, that teach something about the qualities of flour, leaven, salt, water, heat, and air that bakers are always learning and relearning. And for those who have sampled Puglia's breads on their home turf, I hope they will recall, at least, some of the splendid flavors to be found there.

Ingredients

FLOUR. The best flour for any purpose, whether durum wheat semolina, regular bread flour, or finer, softer pastry flour, is freshly milled from organically raised wheat without added bleach or bromates. Live yeasts have a better chance to grow in this kind of medium. Organically raised wheat is not always easy to find, however, and in the absence of other characteristics, I settle happily on a high-quality, unbleached, unbromated, strong all-purpose flour like King Arthur, which is widely available in good grocery stores in the Northeast and by mail order to the rest of the country (see page 256).

King Arthur also has semolina available by mail order, and here a word of explanation is in order. In Italian, the term for the gritty textured flour used for pasta, and for many Pugliese breads, is *semola;* semolina, a diminutive, refers to a more finely ground flour, also from durum wheat. In American English, confusingly, the coarser grind is semolina and the finer grind is called durum wheat flour. When buying flour for making a Pugliese-style hard wheat bread (or pasta), be sure to ask for semolina and not durum wheat flour. Even though both types of flour are made from durum, it's the grainier semolina (semola) that you'll need.

LEAVENING. In general, for my own home baking, I use a leavening method that's often called old-dough or reserved-dough. A related method, using a slow-rising sponge, is called *biga* in Italian. (Neither of these makes sourdough, which properly comes about as the result of wild natural yeasts captured in a mixture of flour and water that's left out to trap the wildings.)

Using the old-dough method, you first make a regular bread dough with flour, water, and a commercially available yeast. (Best of all is fresh yeast, the little cubes wrapped in foil, but it is difficult to feel confident about this. Too much of what I've bought in recent years has been moldy, and store managers seem not to know or care. Health food stores with a high turnover are probably the best sources for fresh yeast. In the absence of good fresh yeast, dry granulated yeast is fine to use.) Before the final rise, you remove about a cup of the dough, put it in a jar with a little more flour and water, and set it aside to act as the starter the next time you make bread. If it's not used within a few days it should be refreshed, like sourdough starter, with more flour and water.

Using the biga method, you simply make a fresh starter or biga each time you bake, mixing together a loose batter of flour, water, and yeast; in this case, you must figure in an additional eight hours or overnight for the starter to get to work.

It may seem like splitting hairs, but the yeast bacteria in such cultures are different from those in sourdough, which is why it doesn't get to be called sourdough. The point of it all is a long, slow development of the culture, which gives the resulting bread better flavor, texture, and keeping qualities. Think of quick breads like muffins, leavened with phosphates and bicarbonates and flavored with sugar and other ingredients, as one end of the baking spectrum, and long, slow-rising bread with a crisp crust, a dense but holey texture (what the French call, suggestively, *bien alvéolé),* and a good wheaten flavor as the other. It's the far end of the spectrum that the best bread-bakers aim for.

WATER.   Ordinary tap water is often full of chemicals that may, curiously, help to make the water cleaner but often create an environment that is as hostile to yeast as it is to good coffee beans. That's why I usually use bottled water (Poland Spring in New England, but many other brands are equally good) for both bread-baking and coffee-making.

SPECIAL EQUIPMENT.   A baking stone (or baking tiles) is pretty much de rigueur for mimicking the action of old-fashioned masonry ovens. *The stone should always be put into a cold oven before turning the heat on*—if you heat the oven first, then put the stone in, you risk cracking it. The bread, of course, is cast right onto the stone, without any intervening pans or baking sheets. However, you can also make pretty good bread without a baking stone, using an ordinary baking sheet to hold the loaves.

Baking stones, and lots of other good baking equipment, as well as flours and other ingredients, are available from The Baker's Catalogue, published by the King Arthur Flour Company (see page 256).

Bread recipes are of necessity imprecise. Much depends on the temperature and humidity of the location where you're baking, not to mention the temper and patience of the baker. Thus you will find a range of quantities, especially where flour and water are concerned. Start with the smaller of these, and work your way gradually to the greater as it seems necessary.

semolina bread
PANE DI SEMOLA TIPO ALTAMURA

Two 2- to 2¹/₂-pound loaves

In commercial bakeries like those in Altamura, bread is made with 100 percent du-rum wheat flour, called semola in Italian, semolina in English, which makes a beautiful creamy golden crumb that looks as if eggs had been mixed in the dough. At home it's easier to work by starting with a biga made with normal all-purpose flour. This bread reminds me of those from Altamura and other parts of Puglia. Note that the quantity of flour needed can vary depending on a number of factors, including the ambient humidity in the kitchen in which you are working.

FOR THE STARTER OR BIGA:

1 cup warm water, preferably unchlorinated (i.e., pure spring water)

¹/₂ teaspoon dry yeast

1¹/₂ cups unbleached all-purpose flour

2 cups warm water, preferably spring water

6 to 8 cups semolina (Italian semola), plus additional

1¹/₂ cups room-temperature water, preferably spring water

1 tablespoon sea salt

Extra virgin olive oil

FIRST, make the biga. Put the water in a small bowl, sprinkle the yeast over the top, and let set for 2 to 3 minutes, then gently stir the yeast and water together. Add the all-purpose flour and, using a wooden spoon, stir the flour into the liquid—the resulting mixture should be thicker than heavy cream. Set aside, loosely covered with plastic wrap or with a damp-ened kitchen towel, for a couple of hours, then refrigerate overnight.

NEXT morning, turn the biga into a larger bowl. Add 2 cups of warm wa-ter and, using your hands, break up the biga in the water. (It will make a rather sloppy mixture.) Add 2 cups of semolina and work it gradually into the liquid to make a thick slurry. Cover with a damp cloth or towel and set aside in a cool place (do not refrigerate) to work and rise for 2 to 3 hours, or until the mass in the bowl has puffed and looks thicker, with bubble holes over the surface. This is the first rise.

AFTER the first rise, add the remaining 1½ cups of water and about 4 to 5 cups of semolina to the mixture, a little at a time—a little flour, then a little water, and so on. Add the salt and mix well, using your hands to knead in the bowl. Sprinkle a wooden bread board with a cup of semolina and turn the dough out on it. Work the dough well, kneading to incorporate everything thoroughly. Knead the dough for about 5 to 10 minutes, or until it feels silky and smooth, with no hint of stickiness.

BRUSH a little olive oil around the inside of the cleaned bowl and add the dough to it, turning to coat it thoroughly. Cover once more with a damp cloth or towel and set aside to rise till doubled, about 1 to 2 hours. This is the second rise.

SET the baking stone in the oven and preheat at 450°F.

PUNCH down the dough and form it into 2 loaves, round or elliptical or long, whatever you prefer. (Pugliese bakers sometimes spread the dough in a rather flat ellipse, then, when it has risen and is ready to bake, flip one half of the ellipse over the other, like a wallet. If you do this, do not slash the loaf as in the directions below.) Scatter a little cornmeal or semolina over the bread board and set the loaves on the board, covered lightly with a dry cloth, while the oven heats for at least 45 minutes. (The oven light will go off before 45 minutes are up, but continue heating anyway to make sure the stone is heated through.) Just before putting the loaves in the oven, slash the tops in 3 or 4 places with a very sharp knife to let the dough expand. Transfer to the baking stone and close the oven door. Bake for 15 minutes at 450°F., then turn the heat down to 350°F. and continue baking 45 minutes longer, by the end of which time the loaves should be crisp and golden, with a pleasant hollow knock when they're rapped against the bread board. Remove from the oven and cool on a rack.

homemade bread from bari
PANE CASARECCIA BARESE

2 loaves weighing 1¹/₂ to 2 pounds each

The directions could not have been clearer: Mix together flour, leavening, and clean sea water (specifically, so you wouldn't need to purchase salt, which government taxes made prohibitively expensive). Knead the dough first thing in the morning, before anyone else is up, then put it to rise in a bed still warm from the bodies of those who've slept therein. But don't worry—the sheets will have been rinsed in water perfumed with bay leaves, which will give the bread a special flavor. When the dough has risen a couple of hours, shape it into loaves, stamp them with an identifying mark, and give them to the baker's boy along with a pan of focaccia and a tiella with potatoes, rice, and mussels. The whole to cook together all morning in the baker's oven, and as soon as the youngest son comes home from school he's sent on the run to the baker's to bring back the family lunch. That's the way bread used to be made in Bari's old town years ago when sea water was still clean, rinse water was scented with laurel, housewives stayed home to bake bread, and schoolboys (and girls) came home for lunch. If you have a source of clean sea water, by all means use it for the salted water in this recipe.

---

2 cups water, preferably
   unchlorinated (i.e., pure spring
   water)

6 bay leaves

1 tablespoon sea salt

1 teaspoon dry yeast

5 or 6 cups unbleached all-purpose
   flour

Cornmeal

IN a small saucepan, bring 1 cup of water to a boil, add the bay leaves, and set aside in a warm place to steep for about 30 minutes. Heat the remaining cup of water in another saucepan, add salt, and stir over heat until the salt has dissolved completely. Set aside to cool to lukewarm.

REMOVE the bay leaves from the water and discard them. Sprinkle yeast over the water and set aside for about 5 minutes to let the yeast dissolve.

POUR 4 cups of flour into a large bowl. Make a well in the middle and add the water with the dissolved yeast. Start mixing it into the flour, using a wooden spoon or your hands to pull the flour gradually into the well of liquid in the middle. Once the dissolved yeast is incorporated with flour, add the salty water, and continue pulling flour into it. When the flour and liquid are thoroughly combined, spread a cup of flour on a bread board and turn the dough out onto the board. Knead thoroughly for 5 to 7 minutes, or until the dough has lost its stickiness and become soft and pliable. Add more flour as you knead, if it seems necessary. When the dough is ready, form it into a large oblong and set it on a board or baking sheet sprinkled with cornmeal. Using a knife, or a baker's razor if you have one, make a cut the length of the loaf and about $\frac{1}{2}$ inch deep. Cover lightly with a damp towel and set aside to rise in a warm place until doubled, about $1\frac{1}{2}$ hours. The two sides of the cut will be fully opened.

NOW cut the dough, across the first cut, into 2 pieces. On a lightly floured board work each piece rapidly into a long rectangle, then fold one end of the rectangle lightly over the other. Cover with a dry cloth and let rise about 2 hours.

AFTER the first hour and 15 minutes of rising, start to preheat the oven to 450°F. and continue heating it for at least 45 minutes. Place the loaves in the preheated oven, either on a baking sheet or casting them directly onto a stone. Bake for 15 minutes, then lower the heat to 350°F. and continue baking another 45 minutes.

REMOVE the loaves from the oven and let cool on a rack.

potato bread from foggia
PANE DI PATATE

2 loaves weighing approximately 2 pounds each

Throughout northern Puglia, mashed potato is often added to bread dough to make a softer, denser loaf. Pane di patate has a tender crumb (it makes wonderful toast) with a crisp, crackly crust that is at its finest when fresh from the oven. This is sometimes used to make a double-crusted pizza or focaccia, but it's also used for ordinary household bread, shaped either in loaves or in small rolls, or panini.

FOR THE BIGA:

1 cup very warm water

1 teaspoon dry yeast

1½ cups unbleached all-purpose flour

FOR THE BREAD DOUGH:

1 medium potato, about 6 ounces, peeled

6 to 7 cups unbleached all-purpose flour

2 cups warm water

1½ teaspoons sea salt

Extra virgin olive oil for the bowl

Cornmeal

FIRST make the biga: Place the water in a small bowl and scatter the dried yeast over it. Leave until the yeast is thoroughly dissolved, then, using a wooden spoon, beat in the flour, a little at a time. Cover with a dampened kitchen towel and set aside for an hour or so, then place in the refrigerator for 6 to 8 hours or overnight.

WHEN ready to continue, remove the biga from the refrigerator and transfer to a large mixing bowl.

BOIL the potato in water to cover over medium-high heat until it is soft, about 20 minutes. When the potato is done, drain it well, then mash thoroughly with a potato masher while still hot. Stir the warm potato into the biga.

STIR 1 cup of warm water into the potato mixture, then start to incorporate the remaining flour, 1 cup at a time. When you reach 4 cups, the dough will be quite stiff. At this point add another cup of warm water, the salt, and 1 or 2 more cups of flour, mixing well. By now the dough should be stiff enough to knead on a board. Scatter 1 cup of flour on the bread board, turn the dough from the mixing bowl onto the board, and knead for 5 to 10 minutes, or until the dough is soft and very smooth, incorporating the flour from the board gradually into the dough.

RINSE out and dry the mixing bowl and rub the inside with a few drops of olive oil. Turn the kneaded dough into the bowl, cover with a damp cloth, and set aside to rise in a warm place—the ambient temperature of most American kitchens should be sufficiently warm—for $1\frac{1}{2}$ to 2 hours, or until the dough has doubled in bulk.

HEAT the oven to 450°F. for 45 minutes. Punch the dough down and shape it into 2 rectangular or elliptoid loaves. Scatter a little cornmeal on the bread board and set the loaves on the board to rise while the oven is heating. When ready to bake, slide the risen loaves onto a peel and shake them onto the baking stone.

(IF you are using a baking sheet instead of a stone, simply set the loaves to rise on the sheet, on which you will have scattered cornmeal. Then set the sheet in the oven when ready to bake.)

BAKE at 450°F. for 15 minutes, then turn the oven down to 350°F. and continue baking an additional 40 to 45 minutes, or until the loaves are golden brown and have the hollow ring of thoroughly baked bread. (The potato gives this bread quite a dense crumb that may take longer to bake than a normal loaf. When in doubt, bake an additional 10 to 15 minutes: It's always better to overbake than to underbake.)

TURN the loaves out onto a rack and cool somewhat before cutting them.

olive-studded panini from the salento

PUCCIA

4 to 6 puccie

These little round breads, with black olives or bits of flavorful ham embedded in the dough, are a specialty of the Salento. I first saw them being made at the Caroppo bakery in the tiny hamlet of Specchia Gallone near Minervino, where the baker was deftly working with a dough so wet and viscous that it slipped and slid between my fingers when I tried to maneuver it. Mr. Caroppo had a big bucket of this dough right by the wood-fired oven and as fast as he shaped and dropped the breads onto a wooden peel, his assistant flipped them onto the floor of the oven to bake very quickly.

It seemed like a technique for commercial bakers, and in fact anyone who has the opportunity to bake in a wood-fired masonry oven (as more and more American restaurant chefs and bakers have) quickly understands that these loose, wet doughs produce better bread. But Adriana Bozzi-Colonna, a fine cook from Lecce, achieves much the same results with a small electric oven at home. Using her hand as a paddle, Adriana beats extra water into a normal bread dough to make the batterlike dough for puccia. She adds whole olives, stones and all (but the Leccese know what to expect when they bite into puccie; for Americans, it seems wiser to pit the olives before adding them to the dough). Once she finishes making puccie, Adriana uses the remaining dough, mixed with a little hot pepper relish, to make pittule (page 44), small deep-fried dough balls that are served with a glass of wine before lunch.

FOR THE BIGA:

1 teaspoon dry yeast

1 cup very warm water

1 cup unbleached all-purpose flour

2¹/₂ to 3 cups warm water, preferably spring water

1 cup whole wheat flour

3 to 4 cups unbleached all-purpose or bread flour

A few drops of extra virgin olive oil

Sea salt

1 cup coarsely chopped black olives, or very savory baked ham, or finely slivered onion, or minced flat-leaf parsley—or a mixture of these, but use no more than a cup in all

Cornmeal

TO make the biga, sprinkle the teaspoon of dry yeast over the cup of very warm water and leave for a couple of minutes to dissolve, then stir lightly to make a creamy, cloudy mixture. Stir in the cup of flour and set aside at room temperature, covered with a damp cloth, for about 1 hour so the yeast will start working. Once the surface of the mixture is bubbly and slightly depressed, the biga is ready to use, but you may also leave it, covered with the damp cloth, in the refrigerator for 6 to 8 hours or overnight—the flavors will only get better. This will make about 1½ cups of biga or starter.

TRANSFER the biga to a large mixing bowl and add 1½ cups of warm water. Using a wooden spoon, or your hands, break up the biga and mix it with the water to make a sloppy slurry. Add the whole wheat flour and about 2½ to 3 cups of the regular flour. Mix the flours into the watery biga, using a wooden spoon or your hands. Then turn out onto a lightly floured board and knead for 5 to 7 minutes, or until the dough is springy and soft and has lost its stickiness. Put a few drops of oil in the bottom of the clean, dry mixing bowl and turn the dough in the oil. Cover with a damp cloth and set aside for 2 to 3 hours to rise until more than doubled in bulk.

WHEN ready to continue with the dough, set the oven at 450°F. You may use a baking stone, but I find that this slippery dough is less problematic with a flat cookie sheet.

PUNCH the dough down in the bowl and add another cup of warm water to it. Add sea salt—1 teaspoon should be plenty, but if you are not planning to add salty olives or ham, 1½ teaspoons will be better. Using your hands, mix the water with the dough to a sloppy, slurrylike consistency. If you have a mixer with a dough hook, use it to knead the water into the dough for 3 to 5 minutes, to make a viscous dough that is nonetheless smooth and satiny on its surface. If you do not have a dough hook, beat the water into the dough with a stiff, flat hand used like a paddle.

WHEN the dough has reached the right texture, it will be more like a viscous batter than a normal bread dough, and you will be able to feel the strands of gluten as you mix it with your hands. Add the black olives, ham cubes, and/or onion and parsley, and mix them in with your hands, turning the dough over and over to combine the addition as thoroughly as possible.

HAVE ready a large baking sheet with a little cornmeal sprinkled over it and a bowl of water in which to dip your hands to keep the dough from sticking. Wet your hands and take up as much dough as you can handle in two hands cupped together. Using an under and over motion with your hands, quickly form it into the shape of a bulky roll and drop it onto the

continues

baking sheet. Working quickly, continue with the rest of the dough—you should get 4 to 6 breads out of this, each one large enough for two people. As soon as all the breads are formed, put the baking sheet into the oven and bake 45 minutes.

WHEN done, remove from the oven and cool on a rack.

VARIATION: *Back in Toronto and using her home oven, Naomi Duguid, a superb baker who was with me in Specchia Gallone, devised the following method for duplicating a little more closely the action of the masonry oven: She took a large black iron skillet, one with low sides, and heated it in a 450°F. oven till it was very hot, then dropped one or two of the little bread doughs right into the hot skillet and put them back in the oven to bake. It's more time-consuming, since you can only do a couple of breads at once, but the texture of the finished crust is delicious.*

double-crusted onion calzone
SCALCIONE DI CIPOLLA

1 calzone about 12 inches in diameter

Why this is called scalcione when similar savory pies are called focaccie is a question for a diagnostic dialectician and not for me. Scalcione is typical of the region around Bari, especially during Lent, when the long, slender, white sponsale are in season. Also called cipolle porraie (leek-onions), sponsale are a type of allium that look like thin leeks (see page 112). Don't be tempted to increase the amount of stuffing—it's a perfect balance to offset the delicious richness of the pastry itself.

Rosa Granozio, who lives in Triggiano on the outskirts of Bari, showed me how to make scalcione. Rosa worked in Chicago for several years when she was a young woman, so we discussed what an American substitute for sponsale might be. Scallions are, on the whole, too thin and too sweet, so seeking out the thinnest of leeks seemed to us to be the best solution. While the dough differs quite a bit from those previously given, you may use one of them if you prefer.

FOR THE DOUGH:

¹/₄ teaspoon dried yeast

1¹/₄ cups very warm water

4 cups flour plus a little more for rolling out the dough

¹/₄ cup dry white wine

¹/₄ cup extra virgin olive oil

Salt and freshly ground black pepper to taste

FOR THE FILLING:

¹/₄ cup extra virgin olive oil

2 pounds leeks, very thinly sliced to make about 5 cups

3 tablespoons whole milk

I teaspoon sugar

6 salted anchovy fillets, cleaned and chopped

¹/₂ cup pitted black olives, chopped

¹/₄ cup finely minced flat-leaf parsley

2 or 3 small tomatoes, peeled, seeded, and chopped

¹/₂ cup golden raisins soaked in hot water to plump

About ¹/₄ cup extra virgin olive oil for the pan and the top crust

I teaspoon sugar

continues

SPRINKLE the dried yeast over ¼ cup of very warm water in a small bowl; when it has "bloomed," add the remaining water to it.

IN a larger bowl, mix the flour with the wine, olive oil, salt, and pepper. Stir in the yeast water and work it into the dough with your hands. Transfer to a lightly floured board and knead the dough just until it loses its stickiness. Set aside, covered with a damp cloth, while you prepare the filling.

TO make the filling, warm the olive oil in a sauté pan over medium-low heat. Add the leeks and sauté very gently for about 15 minutes, or until the leeks are soft but not brown. Add the milk and continue cooking another 5 minutes. Then stir in the sugar and cook 5 minutes more. At the end of this time, the leeks should be very soft, almost melting into a sauce. Add the anchovies, black olives, parsley, and tomatoes. Stir to mix well and continue cooking until the sauce is thick and all the liquid has evaporated. Remove from the heat and stir in the drained raisins.

SHAPE the calzone on a lightly oiled baking sheet or in a round shallow 12-inch pizza pan, lightly oiled. Punch down the dough and divide it in two, one part slightly larger than the other. Roll out the larger part on a lightly floured board until it is about ⅛ inch thick. Set it on the baking pan—if using a pizza pan, the dough circle should come up over the sides. Spread the filling mixture on the circle, leaving a border of about 1 inch or less around the edge. Roll out the second portion of dough and top the filling. Fold together the top and bottom edges of dough, pulling the bottom edge up over the top edge and pressing evenly to seal. Brush the remaining oil over the top crust, sprinkle with the sugar (it will help brown the crust), and prick with a fork. Set aside, covered with a damp cloth, while you heat the oven.

TURN the oven on to 450°F. and heat for at least 30 minutes, then slide in the scalcione. After 15 minutes, turn the heat down to 350°F. and continue baking another 30 minutes. May be served immediately or left to cool to room temperature.

VARIATION: *Some Pugliese cooks add ½ pound of mozzarella or scamorza cheese, or baked ham, cut into small cubes or slivers. Some also add about ½ pound of ricotta, dabbed here and there over the surface of the filling.*

focaccias

FOCACCIE

1 double-crust focaccia 10 inches in diameter

In most parts of Italy, focaccia is a flat bread, often dotted with oil and sprigs of rosemary or bits of tomato, that is quickly baked, like a pizza, on the floor of a wood-fired oven. Traditionally, this was the bread that went in first, to test the oven's heat. In Puglia, however, things are a little different. Here, the same word, focaccia, also stands for a double-crusted free-form pie, something like a Spanish empanada, that is stuffed with a great variety of fillings. I give some of these below, though the one most often encountered is the Pugliese favorite, onions, tomatoes, black olives, and capers stewed in olive oil, like the filling for panzerotti on page 46. You'll also find a focaccia on page 207 that's more like other focaccie—a flat dough with a tasty topping.

The dough for focaccia is always a leavened bread dough; in fact, both the Homemade Bread from Bari (page 192) and the Potato Bread from Foggia (page 194) make excellent focaccia doughs. When you're making one of those breads, simply set aside about a quarter of the dough for a good-sized focaccia, roughly 10 inches in diameter, enough for 4 to 6 servings as a main course, 8 to 12 servings as an appetizer with a glass of wine before dinner. Or use the following recipe, which gives enough dough for a focaccia roughly 10 inches in diameter.

Focaccie are ideally made as free-form savory tarts on a flat baking sheet; if you use a round, low-sided tart pan about 10 inches in diameter, be careful to make the crust as thin as possible. In either case, the metal surface should be lightly brushed with olive oil before the focaccia is formed.

No matter what recipe you use, simply roll the dough out into two disks no more than ⅛ inch thick, one a little smaller than the other. Top the larger disk with one of the fillings, put the smaller disk on top, fold the bottom edge over the top edge and seal together, then prick the top crust to let steam escape. Set the focaccia aside, loosely covered with a cloth, to rise for 1½ hours. When ready to bake, preheat the oven to 450°F., brush the top layer with a little olive oil, and bake the focaccia until the top is golden and crisp, about 45 minutes.

continues

dough for a single focaccia:

FOR THE BIGA:

½ teaspoon dry yeast

½ cup very warm water

½ cup unbleached all-purpose
flour

FOR THE BREAD DOUGH:

1 cup very warm water

1 teaspoon sea salt

3 to 3½ cups unbleached all-
purpose flour

Drops of extra virgin olive oil

FIRST make the biga in the usual manner: Sprinkle the dry yeast over the surface of the warm water in a mixing bowl and leave to dissolve. Once the yeast has "bloomed," stir in the flour. Cover with a damp cloth and set aside to work for a couple of hours or overnight. The biga is ready when the surface is bubbly and has collapsed just a little, but it will develop more flavor if you keep it longer, refrigerated and covered with plastic wrap or a damp cloth.

WHEN ready to make the dough, mix the water, salt, and flour into the biga until it is well combined, then turn out on a lightly floured board and knead until the dough is satiny and has lost its stickiness. Put a few drops of oil in the clean, dry bowl and turn the dough in it. Then cover with a damp cloth and set aside to rise for an hour or so, or until doubled in bulk.

PROCEED with the recipe, following the instructions above for shaping the focaccia and using one of the fillings below. Each of the fillings should be sufficient for this much dough.

fillings for focaccia:

sweet red, yellow, and green pepper filling
PEPERONI MULTICOLORI

3 bell peppers, preferably 1 yellow,
1 red, 1 green

½ medium yellow onion

2 tablespoons extra virgin olive oil

Sea salt to taste

½ small dried hot red chile pepper

4 medium very ripe tomatoes,
peeled and seeded, or 2 cups
drained canned tomatoes

Freshly ground black pepper to
taste

¼ cup freshly grated pecorino or
Parmigiano-Reggiano

CORE and trim the peppers, discarding seeds and white membranes. Chop the peppers with the onion to a coarse blend.

IN a sauté pan over medium heat, gently sauté the peppers and onion in the olive oil for 10 to 15 minutes, or until the vegetables are very soft but not turning brown. Add salt and chile pepper as desired.

WHILE the peppers are cooking, chop the tomatoes. Add to the peppers when they are soft and continue cooking until the tomato liquid has evaporated and the sauce is thick and naps the peppers well. Set aside and cool to lukewarm before spreading on the bottom crust of the focaccia. (If there's still a lot of liquid in the peppers, drain in a sieve before spreading.) Sprinkle with black pepper and the freshly grated cheese before adding the top crust.

fish and sweet leek filling
PESCE E PORRI

To make thin shavings of pecorino, use a vegetable parer, drawing it toward you over the cheese in short spurts.

---

1 or 2 medium leeks, trimmed and sliced (about ¾ cup)	3 tablespoons coarsely chopped basil leaves
⅓ cup plus 2 tablespoons extra virgin olive oil	3 tablespoons coarsely chopped flat-leaf parsley
¼ cup golden raisins	½ cup thin shavings of pecorino
½ pound white-flesh fish fillets (hake, cod, haddock, or the like)	Sea salt and freshly ground black pepper to taste
About ¾ cup all-purpose flour	

IN a sauté pan over medium-low heat, very gently sweat the sliced leeks in 2 tablespoons of the olive oil, stirring frequently, until they are melted into a sauce, about 45 minutes. Do not let brown.

WHILE the leeks are slowly cooking, set the raisins in a small bowl of hot water to plump.

CUT the fish fillets into small pieces, about ¾ inch to the side. Place the flour on a plate and roll the fish "nuggets" in the flour. Heat the ⅓ cup of olive oil in a skillet or sauté pan over medium-high heat and when it is hot enough, quickly fry the fish pieces until crisp and golden, draining them on paper towels when done.

continues

SPREAD the leeks over the bottom crust of the focaccia and top with the fish pieces. Drain the raisins and dot the fish with them. Then scatter the chopped herbs and shavings of pecorino over the top. Add salt and pepper to taste, then top with the second crust.

ricotta filling

I pound fresh ricotta, preferably sheep's or goat's milk (see page 256)

2 large eggs, well beaten

Pinch of salt

½ pound very flavorful baked ham or mortadella, cut in thin slivers

¼ cup freshly grated pecorino or Parmigiano-Reggiano

Freshly ground black pepper to taste

IF you are using ordinary commercial ricotta, drain it overnight in a colander lined with a double layer of cheesecloth. (Otherwise, the whey will leak out and make the bottom crust very soggy.)

MIX the ricotta with the eggs and salt. Spread on the bottom crust of the focaccia and top with the ham or mortadella. Sprinkle the cheese on top, add pepper to taste, and top with the second crust.

pizza rustica

One 12-X-16-inch pizza

Like the scalcione and focaccie that precede, this is a two-crusted savory pie, with a stuffing of sweet and hot peppers. Throughout the winter, Silvana Camisa, an accomplished cook in Lecce, uses a sauce made from her own preserved peppers, long, slender ones that she grows and puts up each year in the early autumn. Silvana says they're piccante, meaning hot—but her idea of hot peppers is not Thai, or even Mexican. She preserves them in the following manner: She half opens each pepper, fills it with salt, then puts the peppers in a colander with a weight on top, exactly as you would for eggplant, to rid them of excess water. After a couple of days, she puts the salted peppers in a terra-cotta crock, layering them with more salt, and keeps them like this throughout the winter.

Keeping in mind that most American cooks won't have access to salted peppers like these, I've adapted Silvana's recipe somewhat.

DOUGH FOR THE BIGA:

½ teaspoon dried yeast

1 cup warm water

1½ cups unbleached all-purpose flour

1 cup warm water

3½ cups unbleached all-purpose flour

1 teaspoon sea salt

Oil for the pan and the top crust

STUFFING:

3 red or yellow bell peppers, seeded and coarsely chopped

2 small green jalapeño peppers, seeded and coarsely chopped

1 medium onion, coarsely chopped

⅓ cup extra virgin olive oil

One 28-ounce can whole tomatoes, drained and coarsely chopped

⅓ cup minced flat-leaf parsley

⅓ cup chopped black olives

1 tablespoon brine-preserved capers, drained and rinsed

½ teaspoon oregano

Salt, optional

MAKE the biga in the usual manner: First dissolve the yeast in the cup of warm water. When the yeast has "bloomed," stir in the flour for the biga and mix well. Set aside, covered, to develop for a couple of hours until the dough is bubbly, then refrigerate overnight.

continues

NEXT morning add the remaining water, 2½ cups of the remaining flour, and the salt; mix well with a wooden spoon but do not knead. Set aside, covered, in a warm place to rise, about 2 hours. While the dough is rising, prepare the stuffing.

TO make the pepper stuffing: In a sauté pan over medium-low heat, gently sauté the peppers and onion in the olive oil until they are very soft but not brown—about 20 to 30 minutes. Add the tomatoes, raise the heat to medium, and cook until the liquid has evaporated and the tomatoes have thickened into a sauce. Stir in the parsley, then the olives, capers, and oregano. Let cook for 5 minutes, to meld the flavors, then taste and add salt if necessary. Lower the heat to medium-low, cover the pan, and cook for about 20 minutes. If the stuffing is still too liquid, drain it in a sieve before filling the pizza.

PREHEAT the oven to 450°F.

WHEN the dough has risen and the stuffing is ready, spread the remaining cup of flour on a board. Remove the dough from the bowl and knead it on the board just a little, no more than 25 or 30 strokes, incorporating into the dough about half the flour on the board. When the dough is still soft but no longer sticky, divide it in two, one part a little greater than the other. Roll out the larger portion in an oval roughly 12 inches by 16 inches for the bottom crust, which should be about ⅛ inch thick. Set the crust on a well-oiled aluminum baking sheet and prick it all over with a fork.

SPREAD the stuffing over the crust. Roll out the remaining dough, placing it on top of the filling. Bring the upper and lower dough edges together and press with your fingers or a fork to seal, then prick the top all over with a fork. Rub some oil into your hands and smooth it over the top crust, just as if you were rubbing in hand cream. Then bake in the preheated oven until brown on top, about 30 minutes.

potato focaccia from triggiano
FOCACCIA DI PATATE

Two 11 - X - 13 - inch focaccias

This "focaccia," of course, does not fit my earlier description of a Pugliese focaccia as a double-crusted savory pie. But focaccia is what Rosa Granozio and her daughter Nicla call this, and focaccia it will be. In any case, it's more like what's called focaccia in the rest of Italy, and in America.

Rosa and Nicla think nothing of whipping up a potato focaccia at the last minute for supper or an afternoon snack. They made this for me one late afternoon at Pino's house when they dropped in for tea.

This is a very wet dough; the potato helps keep it soft. The point here is to be able to taste the flavor of the dough rather than drown it in the topping. You may be tempted to add more tomatoes and mozzarella, but try to resist, at least the first time you make it.

I large potato, about ½ pound

I teaspoon dried yeast

I tablespoon sea salt, plus more to top the focaccia

2½ cups very warm water

5 to 6 cups unbleached all-purpose flour

½ cup extra virgin olive oil, plus a little more to oil the pans

½ pound freshly made mozzarella, sliced

½ pound fresh ripe tomatoes, sliced; or 6 to 8 canned whole tomatoes, drained and coarsely chopped

Dried oregano to taste

BOIL the potato until it is very soft, peel it, and mash it while still hot in a large bowl.

PUT the yeast and salt in a 2-cup measuring cup and add very warm water to make 2 cups. Mix together until the yeast and salt are thoroughly dissolved in the water.

SET aside about ¾ cup of flour for the bread board and pour the rest of the flour on top of the potato. Start mixing the potato and flour together,

continues

using your hands, adding about ¾ cup liquid at a time, first the water with the yeast dissolved in it, and then plain warm water until you have added about 2½ cups of liquid in all. When all the water has been mixed in, you will have a very wet and sticky dough, but never mind.

SPREAD the reserved flour on a bread board and start to work the dough vigorously on the board, incorporating all the flour on the board. Do not add more flour, however, even though you may be tempted to do so—the dough is meant to be very loose and wet. Keep kneading the dough vigorously until it holds together nicely and has developed a soft, elastic, but compact consistency—like a baby's bottom, Nicla says. When the dough is ready, place it in a clean, dry bowl, cover with a clean kitchen towel, and set aside in a warm place to rise for at least 1 hour, or until it has doubled in bulk.

PREHEAT the oven to 500°F. Use a little olive oil to oil two rectangular pizza pans, each about 11 by 13 inches. Punch the dough down and divide it in half. Roll each dough half into a rough rectangle, then spread the halves in the prepared pans so that they reach all corners. Over the top of each rectangle distribute slivers of mozzarella and the tomatoes, bearing in mind that a Pugliese focaccia is very restrained compared to an American version. Sprinkle the focaccie with crumbled dried oregano and sea salt, then drizzle with an abundance of olive oil—at least ¼ cup on each focaccia.

PLACE the focaccie in the preheated oven and bake until the dough is crisp and the top is melting with cheese and tomato, about 15 minutes.

friselle
F R I S E D D E

32 friselle

This is a very old way of making a bread to last forever, and bread that would last forever was once necessary for survival all around the Mediterranean. Partly this was a matter of simple domestic economy: The more bread you could produce in a single baking, the less fuel you would use in the long run. Partly, too, it was a matter of the vast distances, in time and miles, people customarily traveled in order to accomplish what had to be done. In the days when countryfolk lived in villages and walked, often many long miles, out to their fields and back each day, this was the bread that accompanied them, to be dipped in spring water to soften it and eaten with a *companatico* (that which goes with bread) of sliced onions or tomatoes or whatever vegetable was at hand in the fields, and perhaps a drop or two of precious olive oil from a little stoneware container the field worker carried with him. But it was also the bread sailors and fishermen tucked in their sacks when they put out to sea, and it accompanied shepherds on their long springtime treks as they followed the flocks up the ancient *tratturi* that led to the high cool mountain pastures of the Abruzzi.

A few years ago I saw similar breads being made in a mountain village on the island of Crete, yet another in the great number of customs that link the folk culture of Puglia with that of Greece. There, too, barley flour was part of the mixture, and there, too, the breads were twice-baked to make a kind of long-keeping rusk.

Friselle are often served with a topping of very ripe tomatoes, chopped and mixed with oil, salt, and fresh oregano.

FOR THE BIGA:

1 teaspoon dry yeast

1½ cups very warm water

1½ cups unbleached all-purpose flour

2 cups warm water, preferably spring water

3 cups unbleached all-purpose flour, plus more for the board

2 cups barley flour, preferably organic

1 cup whole wheat flour, preferably organic

Sea salt

2 teaspoons extra virgin olive oil

FIRST make the biga: Sprinkle the dry yeast over the surface of the warm water and leave until the yeast is thoroughly dissolved, then stir in the flour. Combine thoroughly, stirring with a wooden spoon. Cover with a damp cloth or plastic wrap and set aside to "work" for 1 hour or more. When the surface is covered with bubbles and starting to depress, the biga is ready to be used, but it will develop more flavor if you refrigerate it, covered, for several hours or overnight.

WHEN ready to make the friselle, place the biga in a bowl and add to it 1 cup of warm water, 1 cup of the all-purpose flour, 1 cup of the barley flour, and the whole wheat flour. Mix together well and leave to rise, covered with plastic wrap or a dampened cloth, for several hours or overnight.

WHEN the dough is well risen, add the remaining cup of warm water, 1 more cup of all-purpose flour, the remaining barley flour, and the salt. Mix together well. Spread the final cup of all-purpose flour on a board or wooden counter top and knead the dough, gradually incorporating the flour on the board into the dough. When it's sufficiently kneaded and the dough has lost its stickiness and become soft and resilient, place the dough in a bowl that has been rubbed with 1 teaspoon of extra virgin olive oil. Cover the bowl and set aside to rise for 2 hours.

PREHEAT the oven to 450°F. Punch down the dough in the bowl and divide it into 4 pieces. Roll a piece out in a long thick roll like a snake. Cut it into 4 pieces and roll each piece into a thinner snake. Bring the two ends of each snake together, overlapping slightly, to make a ring. As you finish each ring, set it aside on a board lightly dusted with flour. When all the dough is finished, cover the dough rings lightly with a dry towel and let rise while the oven heats up. (The oven should heat for at least half an hour; longer is better.) The rings will close up, leaving not much of a hole in the center—don't worry.

WHEN ready to bake, fill a bowl with cold water, adding a few ice cubes. Lightly oil a baking sheet with the remaining oil. Dip the risen dough rings in ice water and set them on the sheet. Place the sheet in the oven. After 15 minutes, turn the oven temperature down to 350°F. and continue baking an additional 45 minutes, or until the friselle are crisp and golden. Remove from the oven and turn the oven temperature down to 225°F. As soon as you can handle the friselle, slice them in half and lay the halves, cut side up, on the baking sheet. Return to the oven for 1 hour to dry out thoroughly. Properly stored, in a biscuit tin or similar container, they will keep for weeks.

taralli

4 to 5 dozen taralli

"Tutto finisce a taralli e vino." It's an old Pugliese saying that means no matter what the argument, it can all be resolved over a glass of wine and a handful of taralli, little rings of semolina dough, sometimes flavored with fennel seeds, crushed red chiles, black peppercorns, or only with the olive oil that goes into them. You can serve them at any time—with a glass of wine or an aperitif before dinner, with coffee at breakfast, with a substantial salad at lunch, to hungry children looking for a snack between meals, whenever it seems suitable. This recipe was given to me by Paola Pettini.

---

2 teaspoons dried yeast

1 cup dry white wine, warmed to about 100°F.

3 cups unbleached all-purpose flour

2 cups semolina flour

1/2 cup extra virgin olive oil, warmed to about 80°F.

1 teaspoon salt

2 tablespoons fennel seeds, lightly crushed in a mortar; or 1 tablespoon crushed black peppercorns; or 1 teaspoon crushed red pepper flakes, if desired

SCATTER the yeast over the warm wine and leave for several minutes, then stir to mix well. Put in a large bowl with all the other ingredients, adding seasoning if you wish. Use your hands to mix the ingredients well, then turn out onto an unfloured board and knead until the dough is smooth and elastic. Return to a clean, dry bowl, cover the dough with plastic wrap or a dampened towel, and let rise for 30 minutes or longer in a warm place.

DIVIDE the dough into small pieces. Take a piece and roll it with your hands on a work board into a long, slim pencil about the thickness of your little finger. Cut the pencil into lengths of about 4 inches and bring the two ends of each length together and join them to make a round doughnutlike shape. Continue until you have used up all the dough.

PREHEAT the oven to 375°F. Bring a pot of water to a rolling boil and drop the taralli in, a few at a time. Have ready a folded kitchen towel. When the taralli rise to the surface, skim them out and drop on the towel to dry.

ARRANGE the boiled taralli on a cookie sheet and bake in the oven for 15 to 20 minutes, or until they are golden brown and crisp.

from the pantry

*C*ountry wives in Puglia take pride in a larder sparkling with jars of colorful and deliciously tasty vegetables, each one preserved, in olive oil, at the flavorful height of its season. These *sott'olii* (literally, "under oil") are brought out throughout the winter months as part of an antipasto or to add savor to pasta sauces and winter stews. Some of these will be difficult, if not quite impossible, to achieve in this country, but I offer the recipes for those who are up to the challenge.

Preserving Tips

JARS AND LIDS MUST be clean and sterilized for preserving. Wash the jars in hot suds and rinse in scalding water. Place the hot jars on a baking sheet and set in a preheated 225°F. oven at least 20 minutes before filling. Or, place the jars in a saucepan of water, bring to a simmer, and simmer for 10 minutes. Dry the jars with a clean towel before using. Separate the metal rings from the lids, place the lids in a shallow bowl, and cover with boiling water to soften the rubber seal. Soak the lids for 3 minutes before using.

Tightly pack ingredients into the hot jars. If adding a liquid, pour to within $1/2$ inch of the top of the jar to allow for expansion of the food when processed.

To seal the jars, wipe the rim of each jar with a clean, damp towel and fit with a hot lid. Tightly screw on a metal ring.

A hot-water bath destroys microorganisms that cause spoilage. Place the jars on a rack or folded dish towels without touching, in a deep pot with water to cover by 1 inch. Cover the kettle and boil as indicated in the recipe. Remove the jars to a cooling rack, taking care not to burn yourself, and allow to cool completely. A pop or a ping sound after the contents have cooled indicates that the seal is complete. When completely cool, tighten the rings if necessary, label the jars, and store in a cool, dry place.

canned peeled tomatoes
POMODORI PELATI

3 or 4 quart jars of tomatoes

This simple canning method is the one used all over Italy at the luscious height of summer when plum tomatoes are big and ripe. It really isn't worth doing with less than 10 pounds of tomatoes. If you have a garden or a good farmers' market, get a bushel of tomatoes and plan to spend a summer afternoon putting them up. Come January, you'll be glad you did.

---

1 bunch fresh basil

At least 10 pounds very ripe tomatoes, preferably San Marzano plum tomatoes

Salt to taste, if desired

PICK the leaves off the basil, rinse them, and dry them on paper towels.

BRING a large pot of water to a rolling boil. Dump in the tomatoes (do this in two batches if it's easier to manage), count to 12, then immediately drain the tomatoes in a colander, running water over them to cool down. The skins should easily slip off.

IF they're very large, cut the peeled tomatoes in halves or quarters. Place in 1-quart glass jars, packing the tomatoes down firmly without squashing them. Add salt, if you wish, and put a few basil leaves in each jar. Close tightly and place the jars upright in a large stockpot. (If the jars don't fit snugly enough to keep them from falling over, stuff crumpled newspaper between them.) Fill the pot with water to cover to a depth of 1 inch and set over medium-high heat. Bring to a boil and boil for 30 minutes, topping up the boiling water as needed. Cool completely before removing the jars from the water. (For more information, see page 214.)

dried tomatoes preserved in oil
POMODORI SECCHI SOTT'OLIO

Quantity depends on how many tomatoes you use

For those who live in a warm, dry, Mediterraneanlike climate such as parts of California and the Southwest, with access to first-class tomatoes at their peak of flavorful ripeness, this is the Pugliese method for sun-drying tomatoes. Not living in that kind of climate, I have to confess that I have never tried it in North America, but this is the way I was taught to do it in Puglia.

The best tomatoes to use have a healthy proportion of pulp to juice. They should be as ripe as possible but still firm, not too soft or overripe, and without any bruises or other anomalies that might turn quickly to rot. San Marzano (Sammarzano) plum tomatoes, shaped like an overweight hourglass, are the type most often recommended, an Italian variety developed for the tomato industry that is easy to find in this country from seed suppliers and in farmers' markets.

Tomatoes	Whole garlic cloves
Fine sea salt	Crushed red pepper flakes,
White wine vinegar	optional
Fresh mint leaves	Extra virgin olive oil

CUT ripe tomatoes in half lengthwise, sprinkle the cut halves with fine sea salt, and set them, cut side up, in the sun, preferably on reed mats (you can also use trays or clean boards), to dry for at least 4 days. Turn the tomatoes from time to time, more frequently the first day, then less so as time goes by. If you're bothered by flies, bees, and other critters, lay a cheesecloth over the tomatoes—but don't overdo it to the extent that you shade them from the sun. Be sure the mats are always in full sunlight and bring them inside as soon as the sun sets or if any clouds come up.

IF you're frustrated by unforeseen bad weather midway in this process, remove the partially dried tomatoes and place them either in an electric drying cabinet, if you have one, or in a very slow oven. They won't be as tasty, but at least you won't lose your entire crop.

WHEN the tomatoes are thoroughly dried, place them in a bowl and cover with white wine vinegar that you have brought to the boil, then let cool to a little warmer than room temperature. Leave the tomatoes for 20 minutes, then drain thoroughly and press down in scrupulously clean (rinsed with boiling water) 1 quart glass canning jars. Layer the tomatoes with fresh mint leaves, whole garlic cloves, and, if you wish, a few crushed red pepper flakes. Press the layers down firmly. Now pour in olive oil to cover and tightly close the jars. Put a layer of folded dish towels (to keep the jars from cracking) in a deep pan, put the jars on the towels, and pour in water to cover. Bring slowly to a boil. Process in a hot-water bath (page 214) by boiling for 10 minutes. Remove, cool, check seals, label, and store.

NOTE: *If, like me, you don't have the right weather or the right tomatoes, you can still preserve commercially produced sun-dried tomatoes, available in specialty foods stores, by following the directions above. The flavor is much better than those preserved commercially.*

tomato conserve
CONSERVA DI POMODORO

Four or five ¹/₂-cup (4-ounce) jars of conserve

Tomato conserve is used in small quantities—no more than a tablespoon or so—to boost the flavor of tomato-based soups and sauces throughout the winter months. It's also sometimes spread on bread for a quick and healthy snack. This conserve is what tomato paste should be but seldom is, deeply rich and savory, without the metallic flavor of tinned commercial tomato paste.

---

10 pounds very ripe tomatoes, preferably San Marzano plum tomatoes

1 bunch fresh basil

3 medium yellow onions, quartered

2 tablespoons sea salt

About ¹/₂ cup extra virgin olive oil

WASH the tomatoes, cut them in half, and squeeze out the seeds and most of the juice. Put the seeded tomato halves in a big pot with the fresh basil, the onion quarters, and the salt. Bring to a boil over medium heat and cook, uncovered, until the tomatoes are thoroughly melted and most of their liquid appears to have boiled away.

LINE a colander with a double layer of cheesecloth and turn the tomato mixture into it. Set aside, over a bowl or in the sink, to drain thoroughly. (Do not squeeze the tomatoes; simply let them rest in the colander for 1 hour or so.) Discard the watery liquid that comes out. Put the drained tomatoes through the fine disk of a food mill and return to the cheese-cloth-lined colander to drain a second time—again, without squeezing the cheesecloth bag. You will have about 3 or 4 cups of thick purée. Taste the purée and add more salt if it seems necessary, although the drying process will increase the saltiness.

SPREAD the purée about ¹/₂ inch thick on large, flat platters—originally, these were of terra-cotta, although ordinary serving platters or even clean boards will do. Set the platters outdoors in full sunlight to dry, protecting from flies with a layer of cheesecloth. Each night, or in inclement weather, bring the plates inside, first stirring the conserve to mix together the part that's thoroughly dried with the part that's less so. When the conserve is dark brick red in color and very thick, it's done. Spoon into 4-ounce glass jars and cover with a thin layer (¼ to ½ inch) of olive oil.

IF you lack the right climate, you can make something similar by putting dishes of tomato purée in a clean pan and boiling it for another 30 minutes, stirring constantly to keep it from sticking, to get a very thick paste. While the paste is still hot, spoon it into clean half-pint canning jars, leaving enough space to add ¼ to ½ inch of olive oil. Make sure the tops of the jars are completely clean of any tomato residue, so there'll be nothing to attract mold. The paste should be smooth on top and completely covered with the layer of oil. Screw down the lids.

PUGLIESE cooks don't feel the need to process their conserve further, but for American cooks who are anxious about keeping unprocessed food in the cupboard, here's how to do it: Place the jars upright in a stockpot large enough to hold them all and cover with water to a depth of 1 inch. Bring to a boil and process for 20 to 30 minutes, then cool down before removing. (Page 214 gives detailed instructions.)

THE conserve may be kept, unopened, for several months in a cool, dark place—a pantry or cellarway is fine. Once a jar has been opened, however, it should be refrigerated and there should always be sufficient olive oil to cover the paste.

green pepper preserve
PEPERONI VERDI SOTT'OLIO

3 to 4 pints

If you wish, use an assortment of different kinds of green peppers for this, mixing sweet bell peppers with Italian long green peppers and even a few hot green chile peppers, such as jalapeños or serranos.

2½ pounds assorted green peppers

1 large white onion

½ small bunch celery

5 to 6 cups white wine vinegar

3 tablespoons sea salt

3 or 4 stalks fresh mint (1 stalk for each jar)

2 or 3 garlic cloves, sliced (a few slices for each jar)

Extra virgin olive oil

CORE and seed the peppers and remove the white internal membranes. Chop the peppers rather coarsely on a cutting board—the pieces should be fairly uniform and no more than about ¾ inch square. Peel the onion and chop it with the celery in finer dice than the peppers—or process in the food processor till the mixture is coarse. Put all the vegetables in a deep bowl and add vinegar to cover to a depth of 1 inch. Set a plate on top of the vegetables and weight it to keep them under the vinegar. Cover the bowl with plastic wrap or foil and set aside to marinate for 2 days.

DRAIN the vegetables well but do not rinse. Return to the bowl and stir in the salt, mixing well. Have ready 3 or 4 clean 1-pint canning jars. Spoon the salted vegetables into the canning jars and top each with a stalk of mint and several slices of garlic. Pour olive oil into the jars to cover the vegetables. Screw down the jar lids and set aside in a cool place for 2 weeks. For longer keeping, place the jars in a stockpot with water to cover to a depth of 1 inch. Bring to a boil and boil for 20 to 30 minutes to process (see page 214).

pepper relish

P E P O N E

4 pints or 8 half-pints

This may look like a labor-intensive recipe, but the labor is spread out over several days and the result is so delicious that you may find yourself making it several times over the course of a season. And it *is* seasonal: Despite the fact that peppers are in our produce markets nearly all year, success with this recipe will come when the peppers in your market are fresh from local gardens, not shipped from Mexico or even farther afield.

The balance of sweet and hot peppers is a matter of personal taste and also depends on the relative piquancy of the peppers used. If you have a mildly spicy chile pepper like New Mexico or Anaheim, for instance, make the relish with that alone; if, on the other hand, the only chiles available are fiercely hot Scotch bonnets, you might decrease the quantity of chiles and increase the amount of bell peppers.

---

6 pounds fresh bell peppers, green and red combined

15 fresh hot red chile peppers

3 stalks celery

2 medium carrots, scraped

1 large white onion

4 garlic cloves

2 tablespoons sea salt

4 cups white wine vinegar

2 cups extra virgin olive oil

WASH the sweet and hot peppers and dry thoroughly with paper towels, then cut in half, discarding the tops, seeds, and white internal membranes. Chop the peppers, celery, carrots, peeled onion, and garlic rather coarsely by hand, put them in a bowl, and add about 2 tablespoons of salt. Set aside for a day, but do not refrigerate. They will give off quite a lot of liquid. Turn the vegetables into a colander, rinse the salt off thoroughly under running water, and set aside to drain.

PUT the drained vegetables into a bowl, cover them with the white vinegar, and set aside for another 24 hours.

HAVE ready 8 half-pint (or 4 pint) glass canning jars with their lids, prepared as described page 214. Drain the vegetables in a colander, but do not rinse them. Fill each jar about ⅘ full with the chopped vegetables. Add the olive oil, which should completely cover the ingredients and top off the jar. (Push a table knife down into the jar in several places to get rid of any air bubbles.) Screw down the lid and proceed with the rest of the jars.

PLACE the jars upright on a layer of newspaper in a large stockpot and fill with water to cover to a depth of 1 inch. Bring to a boil and process for 20 minutes. Remove from the heat and let the water cool until you can remove the jars—or remove them with a set of canning tongs. When the jar lids ping, it's a sign that they have sealed.

preserved artichokes

CARCIOFI O CARCIOFINI SOTT'OLIO

2 pints

In Puglia, the smallest artichokes, called *carciofini,* are used to make a lovely preserve or sott'olio that's often included as part of the antipasto. Baby artichokes are very hard to come by in this country. If necessary, use larger artichokes cut in quarters.

2½ lemons

8 or 9 globe artichokes

1½ cups white wine vinegar

3 bay leaves

1 teaspoon whole black or white peppercorns

½ teaspoon (8 or 10) whole cloves

Extra virgin olive oil

1 garlic clove

SQUEEZE the juice of 1 lemon into a bowl of water. Clean the artichokes, trimming away the hard outer leaves and cutting off the tops so that only the tender artichoke heart remains. Cut the artichoke hearts in quarters, rubbing the cut surfaces with a lemon half. Scrape away every bit of choke, using a serrated spoon. As the quarters are prepared, toss them into the bowl of acidulated water to keep them from turning brown.

IN a saucepan large enough to hold all the ingredients, mix the vinegar with 2½ cups water. Add the bay leaves, peppercorns, and cloves. Slice a lemon and add to the pan. Bring the liquid to a boil. Drain the artichoke quarters and add them to the boiling liquid. Return to a boil and cook the artichokes for 5 to 10 minutes, or until they are tender but not mushy. Remove from the heat and drain, discarding the lemon slices.

TRANSFER the artichokes to clean 1-pint canning jars, distributing the bay leaves, peppercorns, and cloves among the jars. Cover with olive oil and top each jar with a few slices of garlic. Screw down the jar lids and store in a cool place for 2 weeks. For longer keeping, follow the instructions on page 214: Place the jars in a stockpot with water to cover to a depth of 1 inch. Bring to a boil and boil for 20 to 30 minutes. Let cool in the stockpot before removing the jars.

quince curd or butter
C O T O G N A T A

45 to 60 lozenges

Cotognata is an old-fashioned sweet, a thick quince paste. Made in the autumn when the quinces were ripe and full of flavor, the little squares of quince curd, covered with sifted powdered sugar, could be kept for months in special small wooden boxes to be produced when children were to be amused or one's ladyfriends gathered for tea. Serve it at the end of the meal in place of a rich dessert or as part of the elegant little farewell plate that the best restaurants send to the table with the bill.

6½ pounds fresh quinces

6½ pounds granulated sugar

1 cinnamon stick about 3 inches long

Almond oil for oiling the trays

About 2 cups powdered sugar for sifting

PEEL and core the quinces and cut in pieces. Place the quince pieces in a very large saucepan with a little water (no more than ¼ cup—just enough to keep the quinces from burning before they start to release their own juices) and half the sugar. Set the pan over medium heat and cook, stirring continually, until the quinces are very soft and have released a lot of rosy liquid. Remove from the heat and pass through a fine-meshed sieve to purée. (You may also purée in a blender, but the purée should be sieved before returning to the pan.)

RETURN the purée to the clean pan, add the remaining sugar and the cinnamon stick, and continue to cook slowly over medium-low heat, stirring frequently. When the purée has become a nice rosy color and starts to pull away from the sides of the pan, remove from heat and discard the cinnamon stick. Have ready flat trays or baking sheets that have been lightly oiled with almond oil. Turn the paste onto the trays and smooth the surface with a spatula or palette knife. The paste may be sun-dried, loosely covered with cheesecloth, as for the sun-dried tomatoes (page 216). Or, the trays may be set in a very low oven, about 200°F., with the door left ajar so that humidity doesn't build up. When the quince paste is dry and no longer feels sticky on the surface, cut into lozenges or other shapes, set on a cake rack, and sift over completely, top, bottom, and sides, with powdered sugar. Store in dry containers.

pear marmalade

MARMELLATA DI PERE

4 or 5 half-pint jars of marmalade

The nuns of the convent of Saint John the Evangelist in Lecce are said to have originated a sweet made of almond paste, originally made for Easter but now available throughout the year. It takes the form of a fish or lamb, beautifully shaped and filled with pear marmalade. The marmalade is similar to quince paste (preceding recipe), but looser and more spreadable. In fact it makes a nice jam to have on toast in the morning, not a particularly Pugliese thing to do, but comforting nonetheless.

2 pounds pears, peeled and cut in small pieces

$1^1/_3$ cups granulated sugar

MIX the fruit and sugar together thoroughly, cover with a kitchen towel, and set aside for at least 3 hours to let the juices start to run. Transfer to a large nonreactive saucepan and cook over moderate to medium-low heat for about 45 minutes, stirring with a wooden spoon to prevent sticking. Remove from the heat when the mixture is dense.

FOLLOW the guidelines on page 214: Turn the hot marmalade into sterilized canning jars, screw down the caps, and seal. (If you are planning to keep the marmalade for more than a few weeks, it's safest to seal the jars in a boiling water bath, simmering in the water bath for 15 minutes.)

lemon liqueur
LIMONCELLO

About 1¹/₂ quarts

Liqueurs like this one were once made by country housewives in order to have something strong, sweet, and reinforcing to offer guests after a meal. They were also served at weddings, baptisms, and especially funeral receptions when this kind of pick-me-up seems particularly called for. Fragrant with mint, bay leaves, basil, coffee, citrus, or green walnuts, they were the pride of the country housewife's larder, and were displayed in crystal decanters in elaborately carved glass-fronted cabinets that had been handed down from mother to daughter over the generations, along with the decanters and the recipes for the liqueurs to fill them. The most popular of these confections in recent years has been limoncello, a rosolio of lemons that is served after a copious meal, whether at home or in restaurants. This recipe comes from Concetta Cantoro's father. When he found me drinking her homemade limoncello in her delightful Lecce restaurant, he said proudly, "Mine is better."

---

8 large lemons, preferably organic	3 cups spring water
1 bottle (⁴/₅ quart) 100-proof vodka	1¹/₄ cups granulated sugar

IF you cannot find organically raised lemons, scrub the lemons with soap and water to rid them of any pesticide or wax residue, then rinse and dry them thoroughly.

CAREFULLY peel the yellow rind from the lemons in very thin strips, leaving behind the white part (pith). (You won't need the lemon juice here. If you have no other immediate use for it, squeeze the peeled lemons and put the juice in the freezer, or freeze it as ice cubes and store in a plastic container, using each cube as you need it.)

PUT the lemon rinds and the vodka in large glass jars, screw down the lids, and set aside in a cool place (but not refrigerated) for 1 week.

STRAIN the vodka through a sieve, discarding the lemon rinds. Bring the spring water to a boil and dissolve the sugar completely in the water. Cool to room temperature, then mix with the strained vodka. Bottle in 2-pint containers and seal for 24 hours. Then refrigerate and serve the limoncello well chilled in tiny glasses after dinner.

sweet celebrations

*S*weet things, historically, were a privilege, consumed only by the higher clergy and the aristocracy, whose position at the apex of society required a suitably elevated style of display. This was true in Puglia, as it was throughout the Mediterranean, right up until modern times when the new bourgeoisie began to ape aristocratic customs. Sugar was expensive to produce in its own right, and transforming sugar into elaborate confections was something for which most households had neither time nor money. Still, there were celebratory feasts like Christmas and Easter, weddings and funerals, that demanded validation in the form of special foods, and most of those foods were sweet, often of very ancient lineage.

One such is a renowned confection from Lecce, elaborately and elegantly modeled of sweet almond paste in the shape of a fish or a lamb (both with obvious and ancient Christian symbolism), and stuffed with a filling of pear marmalade (see page 225) or sweet pastry cream. Made by the convent nuns, these are still sold in Lecce at Christmas and Easter. They were invented, historian Luigi Sada tells us, at the Benedictine convent of St. John the Evangelist in the late seventeenth century, specifically by one Anna Fumarola, abbess of the convent at the time. Yet the use of sweet almond paste, or marzipan, almost surely has antecedents in Arab confectionery, although whether it came to Puglia directly from the East, or indirectly via Spain, is unclear. There is no mystery, however, about its aristocratic origins, whether in the form of elaborate convent sweets, or as marzipan pure and simple, or as a kind of almond brittle still served today after meals.

But there were popular sweets, too, often with an even more ancient lineage. *Coliba,* a pudding of wheat berries, nuts, and pomegranate seeds, made for the Day of the Dead or All Souls' Day (November 1), connects with similar dishes all over the Mediterranean, even among Turkish Moslems who eat it at Ramadan. Like Greek *kolyva,* coliba is descended from offerings of sweetened grain made to Demeter, the great mother goddess of the harvest and, indeed, of all growing things; the presence of pomegranate seeds in the dish is a direct reminder of Demeter's beloved daughter Persephone, Queen of the Dead, who was consigned to remain in the underworld half the year because she ate a pomegranate while she was Hades' captive. Coliba is made of grano pestato (see page 96) in some parts of Puglia, of soft wheat berries in others, but wherever it's made, it's sweetened with mosto cotto or *vincotto,* a syrup made by simply boiling down crushed grapes and their juice—another indication that it's a rustic, rural kind of treat, but one with ancient and noble ancestry.

For the most part, however, and certainly for less ritualistic occasions, the sweets served in Pugliese homes were made up of common, everyday ingredients, ricotta for instance, or strips of fried dough, sweetened with that same mosto cotto or *cotto di fichi,* a similar syrup made from crushed figs. These two syrups, with flavors somewhere between molasses and sorghum, are still widely used in Puglia today, and available in almost every market, especially around Christmas.

I haven't given recipes for many of these traditional sweets, because to my mind they're often of much greater interest as anthropology than they are actually to eat. The following ones, I hope, will be delicious as well as, quite possibly, interesting.

sponge cake with pear marmalade
CIAMBELLA PUGLIESE

One 2-layer 8-inch cake (6 to 8 servings)

A simple, not very sweet country cake, such as is made in many parts of Italy, this derives its Pugliese character from the olive oil used as shortening and the pear marmalade in the middle; you may also use another marmalade or jam to fill the cake—it's equally delicious with strawberry jam. Compared to some rich American-style cakes, this is rather dry. It's intended to be served with a cup of strong black coffee or a potent after-dinner liqueur.

Butter and flour for two 8-inch round cake tins

$^1/_2$ teaspoon sea salt

2 teaspoons baking powder

$2^1/_2$ cups cake flour

5 tablespoons extra virgin olive oil

$^3/_4$ cup less $1^1/_2$ tablespoons sugar

3 eggs

1 tablespoon grated lemon zest

$^1/_2$ cup whole milk

$^3/_4$ cup Pear Marmalade (page 225), or other jam

Powdered sugar to sprinkle on top

LIGHTLY butter and flour the cake tins. Preheat the oven to 350°F. Add the salt and baking powder to the flour and toss with a fork to mix well.

IN a mixing bowl, beat the oil and sugar together, then add the eggs, one at a time, beating thoroughly after each addition. Put the dry ingredients in a sifter and sift about a third into the egg mixture. Add the lemon zest and fold in the flour and zest, then add about a third of the milk. Continue with the remaining thirds of flour and milk until all the ingredients have been incorporated and blended together.

TURN into the prepared cake tins, set in the preheated oven, and bake for about 25 minutes, or until the cakes are set, pull away from the sides of the pans, and spring back when pressed lightly in the center with a finger. Remove from the oven, turn the cakes out, and cool on racks. When cool, spread marmalade or jam between the layers and press the layers together. Sprinkle the top of the cake with powdered sugar.

fried christmas pastries
CARTELLATE/CARTEDDATE

40 pastries

One rainy, windswept day between the Feast of the Immaculate Conception (December 8) and Christmas, I took refuge with some friends from America in a humble bar on the seafront in Trani where we had gone to visit the magnificent Apulian Romanesque cathedral for which the town is famed. Unable to find a restaurant open for lunch, we persuaded the barkeeper to fry up a few pieces of fish and serve them with a little salad, which he did with great enthusiasm. In a room behind the bar, a woman named Maria was making cartellate, the traditional sweets of the Christmas season, and complaining bitterly about her husband who, it turned out, was the barkeeper himself, a silent witness to her dirge. As she worked, weaving the strips of dough around themselves, and bemoaned her lot, Maria wept, and the salt of her tears fell and mingled with the oily dough, adding a special savor to the cartellate that year.

Cartellate are deep-fried rosettes of dough served dripping with a thick syrup called mosto cotto, or with a similar syrup of honey flavored with lemon peel and powdered cinnamon. This sweet is only eaten at Christmastime, especially in the Terra di Bari, and then it's eaten in great quantities.

½ cup dry white wine, at room temperature

¼ teaspoon dry yeast

About 5 cups (1 pound) unbleached pastry flour, or half pastry flour and half all-purpose flour

½ teaspoon salt

½ cup extra virgin olive oil plus more for deep-frying

4 cups honey

Rind of 1 lemon, thinly peeled

Pinch of powdered cinnamon

WARM the wine over gentle heat to body temperature. Remove from the heat and sprinkle the dry yeast on the wine. Allow to set for a few minutes, then stir the yeast into the wine until creamy.

PUT the flour in a large mixing bowl and make a well in the center. Pour in the wine-yeast mixture and, using a wooden spoon, gradually pull the flour from the sides of the well to mix in the middle. Once the wine is thoroughly mixed, add the salt and olive oil. Continue mixing and kneading the dough, adding a little warm water if necessary. Turn the dough out on an unfloured wooden board (the oil will keep it from sticking) and knead for about 10 minutes, until the dough is smooth and elastic.

WHEN the dough is thoroughly kneaded, put it through a pasta machine, decreasing the size each time until you have a thin sheet of pasta. (Or roll the pastry dough out on a lightly floured board.) Using a fluted pastry cutter, cut strips of pasta about 2 inches wide and 10 to 12 inches long. Take a single strip and fold it lengthwise so that the two fluted edges come together. Do not press the pasta strip—it should be a loose fold—but very lightly pinch the fluted edges together every couple of inches just to hold in place. Now roll the folded strip on itself to make a spiral or pinwheel, pinching the fluted edges together every inch or so, so that the spiral stays in shape. Continue with the remaining pasta strips. As you finish each spiral, set it on a rack to dry. When all the spirals have been formed, leave them to dry, uncovered, for about 10 hours, longer if the weather is very humid.

ANOTHER way to shape it, a good deal easier and less time-consuming, is to cut the pasta sheet in 3-inch squares, then pinch two sides together to make a bow tie or butterfly. These too should dry on a rack.

WHEN ready to cook, fill a deep-frying pan with olive oil to a depth of about 3 inches. Heat over a medium-hot burner to frying temperature—about 360°F. Handling the fragile spirals with care, drop a few in the boiling oil and fry until they are crisp and golden. Remove with a strainer or a spatula and set on a rack to drain.

WHEN all the cartellate have been fried, mix the honey in a saucepan with a cup of water, adding the lemon peel and pinch of cinnamon. Bring to a boil, then turn the heat down to a gentle simmer. Dip each cartellata in the hot honey, working carefully because they are very fragile, then remove and set, dripping, on a platter. They may be served immediately or set aside in a dry place to be served at room temperature.

sweet ravioli for christmas
CALZONCELLE

These were also made by the weeping Maria. She used the same dough, rolling it out and cutting it in circles about 2 ½ inches in diameter. Each circle was then filled with a teaspoonful of jam. The circles are then folded over to make little half-moon-shaped ravioli and sealed by pressing the edges with a fork. They are then set aside on a rack to dry overnight.

Next day, the ravioli or calzoncelle are deep-fried until golden in extra virgin olive oil heated to about 380°F., then removed, drained on a rack, and sprinkled with powdered sugar.

ricotta torte or cheesecake
TORTA DI RICOTTA

One 10-inch torte

Two ways to make a ricotta torte, one with a pastry casing, one without. Which is better? You decide.

If you're using commercial ricotta, it should be drained overnight in a cheesecloth-lined colander in order to keep the whey from oozing out and spoiling the pie.

FOR THE PASTRY:

1$^{1}/_{2}$ cups unbleached all-purpose flour, plus a little more for the board

$^{1}/_{4}$ cup dry white wine

$^{1}/_{4}$ cup ($^{1}/_{2}$ stick) unsalted butter

2 tablespoons sugar

FOR THE FILLING:

2 pounds fresh ricotta, preferably sheep's milk

12 eggs, separated

$^{3}/_{4}$ cup sugar

Grated zest of 2 lemons

$^{1}/_{2}$ cup candied citron or peel

$^{1}/_{2}$ cup golden raisins plumped in hot water

MAKE a crust with the flour, wine, butter, and sugar, working the ingredients together well until they resemble coarse meal. Gather the pastry into a firm ball, wrap in plastic wrap or foil, and refrigerate for 1 hour.

PREHEAT the oven to 375°F. Roll the chilled pastry out between 2 sheets of wax paper and line the bottom and sides of the pan. Cover the crust with wax paper or aluminum foil and weight it down with dried beans or rice. Place the pan in the oven and bake for 12 to 15 minutes. Remove from the oven, remove and discard the wax paper and beans, and set the crust aside.

PUT the well-drained ricotta through a food mill or sieve to get rid of any lumps. In a large mixing bowl, beat the egg yolks with the sugar until the mixture is very thick and lemon-colored, then beat in the sieved ricotta. Fold in the lemon zest and candied fruit. Drain the raisins and fold in.

BEAT the egg whites until they are stiff but not dry. Fold gently into the ricotta mixture, turn into the pie shell, and bake for about 1 hour, or until the top of the torte is golden brown.

REMOVE and let cool to room temperature before serving.

ricotta torte without pastry

Unsalted butter and fine dry bread crumbs for the torte pan

2 pounds fresh ricotta, preferably sheep's milk

$\frac{1}{2}$ cup sugar

$\frac{1}{3}$ cup honey

4 eggs, separated

6 tablespoons fine, dry bread crumbs

Grated zest of 1 lemon

$\frac{1}{2}$ cup toasted slivered almonds

Powdered sugar and cinnamon to sprinkle on top

BUTTER the bottom and sides of a 9-inch springform pan and sprinkle liberally with bread crumbs. Preheat the oven to 375°F.

PUT the drained ricotta through a sieve or food mill to get rid of any lumps. Beat the sugar and honey together and gradually beat in the ricotta, a little at a time. Add the egg yolks, one at a time, beating after each addition. Stir in the bread crumbs, lemon zest, and almonds, distributing them thoroughly throughout the mixture.

IN a separate bowl, beat the egg whites until they are stiff. Fold the whites into the ricotta mixture and turn into the prepared springform pan. Place in the oven and bake 30 minutes, or until the top is golden brown and the sides have pulled away from the pan a little. Remove from the oven and let cool in the pan. When cool enough to handle, remove from the pan and transfer to a plate or serving platter. Sprinkle with a combination of powdered sugar and cinnamon.

sponge cakes with pastry cream
BOCCONOTTI ALLA CREMA

1 dozen bocconotti

Bocconotti (the name means "big mouthful"), sometimes simply called *pasticcione* or big pastries, are served for dessert, but even more often as a kind of late-morning pick-me-up with a tiny cup of exquisitely strong black coffee. The mouthfuls are usually filled with a classic pastry cream *(crema pasticciera)* but they may also be filled with a dollop of delicious jam.

The following recipe comes from cooking teacher Paola Pettini. Little round straight-sided molds called darioles are best for these, but they may also be baked in small muffin tins. Bocconotti are best eaten fresh from the oven, or within an hour or so of baking.

Butter and flour for the molds
or muffin tins

FOR THE FILLING:

Two 2-inch strips lemon zest

2 cups whole milk

4 eggs

1/2 cup sugar

1/2 cup unbleached all-purpose
flour

1/2 teaspoon pure vanilla extract

FOR THE CAKE BATTER:

1 cup less 2 tablespoons sugar

1 cup less 2 tablespoons butter, at
room temperature

1 whole egg

3 egg yolks

1/2 teaspoon pure vanilla extract

Grated zest of 1/2 lemon

3 cups pastry flour

4 teaspoons baking powder

Pinch of salt

LIBERALLY butter and flour 12 dariole molds or muffin tins.

MAKE the filling: Add the lemon zest to the milk in a saucepan and bring heat almost to a boil over medium heat. As soon as the milk starts to shimmer, remove from the heat and set aside to cool slightly while the lemon zest steeps and flavors the milk.

BEAT the eggs in a large mixing bowl, adding sugar a little at a time, until the mixture is thick and forms a ribbon. Fold in the flour and vanilla.

Remove the lemon zest from the milk and discard. Fold the milk into the egg mixture. Return to the saucepan and set on low heat, or set the pan in a larger pan of simmering water, and cook, stirring frequently, until it's a thick custard. As the custard thickens, stir it continuously. Be very careful not to let the custard come to a boil or it will curdle. When it is the consistency of heavy cream, remove from the heat, strain through a sieve, and let cool to room temperature or refrigerate while you make the cake batter. The custard will continue to thicken as it cools.

MAKE the batter: Beat together the sugar and butter until they are very creamy, then beat in the whole egg and egg yolks, 1 at a time, beating well after each addition. Fold in the vanilla and lemon zest. Put the flour, baking powder, and salt in a flour sifter, stirring with a fork to mix together. Sift about a third of this over the egg batter and fold it in. Continue with the remaining thirds, until all the flour mixture has been blended in.

PREHEAT the oven to 400°F. Put a dollop of cake batter in the bottom of each mold or tin. Top with about 2 tablespoons of the custard cream, then with another dollop of cake batter. When all the molds (or as many as you can bake at one time) are filled, place in the oven for 30 minutes, or until the little cakes are golden and perfume the air with their fragrance.

REMOVE from the oven and set the molds or muffin tins on a cake rack to cool. The cakes may be served immediately, sprinkled with a little powdered vanilla sugar if you wish, or left to cool to room temperature.

NOTE: *Instead of pastry cream, the cakes may be filled with a little jam, or a combination of jam and pastry cream.*

lemon tart

CROSTATA DI LIMONE

One 9-inch tart (6 to 8 servings)

A devastatingly elegant and delicious country dessert or teatime treat made with *pasta frolla,* a sweetened pastry. The almonds give it added crunch. To toast them, simply place in a dry pan in a preheated 350°F. oven for 15 to 20 minutes, stirring occasionally and watching closely lest they overbrown, until the almonds have toasted a golden color.

A little butter for greasing
a 9-inch pan

FOR THE PASTRY:

1³/₄ cups unbleached all-purpose
flour

¹/₂ cup ground toasted almonds

¹/₂ cup sugar

1 stick unsalted butter

1 egg

Pinch of salt

FOR THE PIE FILLING:

4 eggs, separated

³/₄ cup less 1¹/₂ tablespoons sugar

Grated zest of 2 lemons

Freshly squeezed juice of 3 lemons

A straight-sided pie or torte pan, preferably a springform pan, is best for this. Grease the bottom and sides with a small amount of butter and set aside.

TOSS together the flour, almonds, and sugar. Cut the butter into the dry mixture until it is the consistency of fine bread crumbs. Add the egg and salt and mix well, kneading slightly. Form the pastry into a ball, wrap in plastic wrap, and refrigerate while you make the filling.

TO make the filling, beat the egg yolks with the sugar until very thick, then beat in the lemon zest and juice. Transfer the mixture to the top of a double boiler and set over barely simmering water. Cook, stirring constantly, until the mixture becomes thick—15 to 20 minutes. Remove from the heat and set aside to cool slightly. Preheat the oven to 450°F.

ROLL the dough, if you can, between 2 sheets of wax paper; if the dough is difficult to work, press it with your knuckles in a thin layer over the bottom and up the sides of the buttered pan. Prick the dough with a fork all over the bottom, line with wax paper, and fill with dried beans or rice to keep the bottom from puffing. Place in the oven and bake 10 minutes, then remove the paper and beans and continue baking an additional 5 minutes.

MEANWHILE, beat the egg whites until very stiff and fold them into the cooled lemon mixture. Remove the pie casing from the oven and lower the oven temperature to 325°F. Spread the lemon filling over the pie shell and bake for 10 to 15 minutes, or until the filling is thoroughly set.

when you go to Puglia

*P*uglia is at its finest in spring, when wild flowers—scarlet poppies and pale asphodel, yellow mustard and early blue cornflowers—carpet the countryside, or in the fall when the surrounding sea, still warm from the summer sun, keeps days balmy and nights crisp until late in the season. Summer's heat can be oppressive to all but the most confirmed desert rat, while in winter visitors risk an endless succession of chill, gray, rainy days only occasionally sparked by sunshine.

Puglia is well off the beaten tourist path, but visitors are increasingly attracted to the region's unspoiled beaches interspersed with stretches of dramatically rugged coastline, especially along the Gargano peninsula, the spur of Italy's boot. Art lovers and history buffs also find much of interest here, from the great chain of Apulian Romanesque churches linking more northerly cities like Tróia, Bitonto, and Ruvo, to the treasures of Taranto's Museo Nazionale, repository of a dazzling collection of red-figure and black-figure ceramics from the hegemony of Magna Graecia. There are prehistoric dolmen sites scattered throughout the region, as well as rupestrean chapels where, it is said, Anatolian monks fleeing the iconophobia of Greek Byzantium found refuge in limestone caves that they carved and painted with their fervid visions. There are massive stone fortresses built at the command of Frederick II, the thirteenth-century Swabian emperor who reigned over a territory that extended from the North Sea to the Mediterranean and may have been the greatest ruler of medieval Europe. There are the honey-colored baroque fantasies, pouting angels, and garlanded arches of Lecce and Martina Franca. And, it must be confessed, there are also stretches of the most thoughtless and depressing modern development, what Italians call "abusive" construction, especially around Bari and Taranto and on the outskirts of the northern towns. Still, the worst of this is not extensive, and easy to overlook except when you're in the midst of it.

You will be warned repeatedly by the Pugliese themselves about the dangers of the cities, especially Bari, Foggia, and Taranto. It's true, purses get snatched and cars get broken into, but my twentysomething son and I both felt that, in terms of personal safety alone, we'd take Bari any day over New York, Washington, or Los Angeles. And if you miss Bari, you'll miss two jewels of Apulian Romanesque architecture, the cathedral church of San Sabino and the even more glorious San Nicola di Bari, as well as the intricate maze of Old Bari, a cobblestoned warren of alleys and overarching lanes that recalls, more than anything else, a North African medina. Just strap your purse tight, don't leave cameras or, heaven forbid, passports in your car, and enjoy!

Cities like these have hotels of every size and shape and to fit all sorts of budgets, but for the most authentic flavor of the region, stay in a masseria, a type of fortified farmhouse complex or rural hamlet, often walled and gated; many of these have been restored with great charm and attention to detail. Comfort levels are often very high and there's the bonus in these places of feeling very much in tune with the region. There are a number of these, and that number is constantly growing, but I mention four that I know to be outstanding. (Telephone numbers are for dialing from outside Italy. Within Italy, drop the country code [39] and dial 0 before the city code [e.g., 080, 0837].)

Accommodations

IL MELOGRANO, Contrada Torricella, 70043 Monópoli (Bari); tel. 39-80-690-9030; fax 39-80-747-908; E-mail: melogra@mbox.vol.it. A member of the Relais & Chateaux organization, Il Melograno, just outside Monópoli on the Adriatic coast, midway between Bari and Brindisi and an easy drive to Taranto, is one of Italy's great hotels, with swimming pool, spa facilities, access to a nearby beach, and a first-rate dining room.

TORRE CASCIANI, strada provinciale Felline-Torre S. Giovanni, 73059 Ugento (LE); tel. 39-833-931-661. A newly refurbished establishment near the coast south of Gallípoli (with its fascinating fish market in the old town), Torre Casciano is within easy walking and biking distance of the sea. If you don't stay here, at least drop by for lunch or dinner in the rustically comfortable dining room where Giovanna Greco serves a high level of local cuisine.

IL FRANTOIO, Strada Statale 15, Km. 874, Fasano, 72017 Ostuni; tel. 39-831-330-278. North of Brindisi and close to the upland plain of the Murge, Il Frantoio, like Masseria Lo Spagnuolo (see below) is in a first-rate location for exploring this fascinating trulli-bespeckled region, including the hill towns of Locorotondo, Martina Franca, Ceglie Messápico, and the charming white city of Ostuni.

MASSERIA LO SPAGNUOLO, Strada Statale 15, Ostuni; tel. 39-831-333-756. Lo Spagnuolo is still a working farm; thus guests are apt to dine on oil, wine, and other products from the surrounding terrain.

Restaurants

YOU'D be hard put to find many restaurants serving fancy international cuisine in Puglia, but the region abounds in good, simple places that serve the food of the place, and a number of these have achieved fame outside the region as well. The following is at best a partial list of restaurants where I've enjoyed the local cuisine.

In the heart of the trulli country of the Murge:

AL FORNELLO, contrada (hamlet) Montevicoli, just outside Ceglie Messápico; tel. 39-831-377-104. This is one of Italy's great restaurants but firmly tied to local foods and cuisine. Dora Ricci is the chef, her husband Angelo is in charge of the dining room and the extensive and interesting wine list. Trust him for a first-rate introduction to Pugliese wines.

IL POETA CONTADINO, via Indipendenza 21, just outside the walls of Alberobello, the capital of trulli land; tel. 39-80-721-917. Leonardo Marco runs the dining room, his wife the kitchen, and the surprise is that Mrs. Marco is Carol Emerson, a Canadian, though you'd never know it from the gifted way she handles Pugliese traditions; a fine selection of Pugliese wines.

TRATTORIA CENTRO STORICO, via Eroi di Dogali 6, but you can't miss it; tel. 39-80-931-5473. In the heart of Locorotondo's centro storico or historic center, this is one of those little nothing places travelers like me are always hoping to discover, simplicity personified, but with a wonderful kitchen turning out delicious local food.

TRATTORIA SANTUDD, via S. Marco 176, just outside Locorotondo; tel. 39-80-723-110. The restaurant is in an actual trullo, one of the domed stone cottages that are such a feature of the local landscape; it is open evenings only except on weekends. Pizza from a wood-fired oven is the great attraction here, though the rest of the menu is equally interesting.

MACELLERIA SPINELLI, via Venezia 17, Sammichele; tel. 39-80-891-7314. This has the appearance of a humble butcher shop, which in fact it is, but Filippo Spinelli, the butcher, will dress out sausages, chops, steaks, and other cuts, then carry them down an adjacent flight of stairs to a basement dining hall where his assistant grills the meats over wood embers and serves them up with wine, cheese, bread, olives, and other simple accompaniments (see pages 165–166).

In Lecce:

CUCINA CASARECCIA, via Costadura 19; tel. 39-832-245-178. You will find this just off one of Lecce's main squares and around the corner from a baroque masterpiece, the church of Santa Chiara. The name means home cooking and Concetta Cantoro runs the kitchen of this tiny, enormously popular restaurant exactly as if it were her own at home; her husband Marcello is the affable host, but you're apt to find either one in charge. Its popularity means reservations are necessary.

RISTORANTE ACAYA, via Rugge n. 11, Acaia; tel. 39-832-861-104. (Open for dinner only.) Acaia is a tiny fortified village just a few kilometers east of Lecce on the road to the coast. Oranza Quarto, the cook here, is proud of a cuisine that is not just regional, but strictly of the place.

On the Adriatic coast:

RISTORANTE N. VAN WESTERHOUT, via de Amicis 3–5, Mola di Bari; tel. 39-80-644-253. The site is a fishing port just south of the city of Bari and a whole lot easier of access; the odd name honors a famous local composer and musician of Dutch parentage. The parentage of the kitchen however is strictly Barese, with an emphasis on seafood, handled with great skill and attention to detail.

TRATTORIA PANTAGRUELE, Salita di Ripalta 1/3, Brindisi; tel. 39-831-560-605. Brindisi, known in classical times as the end of the Via Appia and to generations of modern backpackers as the embarkation point for ferries to Greece, is graced with few restaurants of any interest, but Pantagruele is an exception, with first-rate seafood selections.

On the Ionian coast:

TRATTORIA GAMBRINUS, via Cariati 24, Taranto; tel. 39-99-471-6552. If you find the place where the fishing boats tie up along the docks of the Città Vecchia (the old city of Taranto), the restaurant is just opposite; Aldo Missiani, who speaks five or more languages, runs the kitchen of this delightful hole-in-the-wall (almost literally) with, naturally, an almost exclusive concentration on seafood.

Not to Be Missed

PAOLA Pettini has been teaching the traditional dishes of Puglia to eager students for the best part of the last twenty-five years. Her Scuola di Cucina, at via Amorusa, Bari, 7 (tel. 39-80-513-498) operates all year. Classes are in Italian only but translators are also available.

The town of Grottaglie, east of Taranto, is famous for its decorated ceramics and terra-cottas. Nicola Fasano Ceramiche (not to be confused with a number of other Fasanos in the town), via Caravaggio 45 (tel. 39-99-866-1037; fax 39-99-862-3069), is said to be Giorgio Armani's favorite; here you'll find a selection of traditional and modern designs that can be confidently ordered for shipment to the United States.

On the Menu or in the Market

WITH some exceptions, Puglia has so far escaped the worst of mass modern tourism with its degrading effects on local food traditions. A more dangerous threat comes from television and other forms of mass media, bringing news of a vapid but nonetheless seductive world where margarine and vegetable oils are more prestigious than the good richly flavored olive oil of Puglia, where industrial cheeses oozing with butterfat are preferred over the dry, crumbling cheeses meant to be grated sparsely over a bowl of hard wheat pasta, where tomatoes are raised in Dutch greenhouses to be shipped south and sold at prices that undercut local tomatoes even at the height of the season. But the people of Puglia continue to resist. Many of their most beloved dishes are almost impossible to replicate elsewhere and should be sought out by travelers who are interested in local food and local culture and where the twain meet. The following, then, is a list of dishes and food products to enjoy on their home ground.

PANE DI ALTAMURA. The bread of Altamura, made from hard durum wheat flour (semolina), is famous, and available in many of the nearby towns. In Altamura itself, I especially like the Antico Forno di Francesco Picerno at Corso Umberto 15, but there are several other good bakeries, still shaping the big loaves each morning and putting them to bake in dark old wood-fired ovens. And there are good bakeries in other towns too: Panetteria Caroppo, for instance, in the tiny hamlet of Specchia Gallone, part of the town of Minervino di Lecce, makes puccia, a traditional small bread made with a very loose, wet dough; and Giuseppe Preite bakes in a wood-fired oven at the Panetteria Tiziana, via Marconi, in Ruffano, in the heart of the southern Salento.

RICCI (SEA URCHINS).   In season throughout the spring months, these spiny critters are sold ready to eat at beachside restaurants and in markets up and down the Adriatic coast. You use bits of bread to tease out the bright crimson roe with its extraordinary briny fresh flavor. But are they safe to eat? As with other raw seafood (clams, mussels, oysters, all favorites in Puglia) throughout the Mediterranean—and, indeed, throughout the world—only you can be the judge. Some people are extraordinarily sensitive to water-borne parasites, while others can consume just about anything with the greatest of ease. I would be less than honest if I didn't admit that there have been cases of cholera and hepatitis traceable to raw seafood from Mediterranean waters, so caution is recommended.

RICOTTA FORTE.   A fiercely strong, double-fermented ricotta cheese, this is most decidedly an acquired taste, yet many Pugliese, especially from the Bari area, can't conceive of a plate of pasta without a dollop of ricotta forte on top, or a spoonful of this confection stirred into a tomato sauce at the last instant before serving.

BURRATA.   This is one of the few recently invented food traditions of Puglia. Pino Marchese, my number one authority and consultant, says that when he was a boy in the 1950s, burrata didn't exist. Who first made this delectable confection? No one seems to know for sure but the droopy sack of freshest mozzarella enclosing a creamy interior has quickly become a regional specialty. The best comes from Andria, an otherwise undistinguished town west of Bari, but burrata from Andria is sold in cheese shops and served on restaurant tables (more often as a first course than at the end of the meal) throughout the region.

GNEMERIÈDDE OR TURCINIEDDE.   A series of grilled, skewered ur-sausages made with different types of innards (e.g., pieces of lung, spleen, heart, and liver), almost always from lamb or kid, often rolled in lamb tripe to make a little sausage which is itself wrapped in the rinsed-out lamb's intestines or chitterlings. These are then skewered alternately with fragrant bay leaves and grilled over a charcoal fire until the outside is deliciously crisp and the inside is thoroughly cooked and juicy. A similar preparation, steamed in the oven, is called *cazzamarra*. This time, the rolls of innards are set in a terra-cotta baking dish with a little water, then placed in a wood-fired oven with embers piled around and atop the dish.

CAVALLO OR PULEDRA (HORSE MEAT).   Puglia is known for its consumption of horse meat, which is most often served as meatballs or rolls with a savory stuffing, both of which are often cooked in a tomato sauce to accompany pasta or polenta. Restaurants advertise on outside hoardings: "Oggi: Pezzi di

Cavallo con Polenta!" You'll find recipes for similar preparations, using beef or veal, in this book, but for the real thing, you'll probably have to go to Puglia.

CECATELLI DI GRAN'ARSO. A hand-rolled pasta made with flour from burned grain. In the old days, once the harvest was done the fields of wheat were burned to clear them, after which the gleaners went through, collecting every precious grain of wheat that the harvesters had missed. This, because it was burned, produced a dark, smoky-flavored flour that was esteemed for pasta-making in the Tavoliere, the great granary of northern Puglia. Gran'arso remains a mystery to me, for though I heard about it from many people, I never found any being sold or served.

Another grain used in traditional baking and pasta-making is barley (orzo), especially in the Salento, the southern part of Puglia, where Greek influences predominate. Macaroncini d'orzo is a pasta made with barley flour, and in many parts of Lecce province you will find friselle, crisp rounds of biscuit bread, made entirely or partly from barley flour.

DRIED FIGS. Well, yes, of course you can find dried figs in America, but the delicacies piled up in Pugliese markets and sold by vendors of dried fruits and nuts around Christmastime are something quite special. Made by cutting green figs in half (leaving them attached at the stem end), they are dried on cane mats in the sun. Once dried, the figs are stuffed with toasted almonds and fennel seeds, sometimes with walnuts and little bits of chocolate flavored with clove, or with thin strips of lemon rind and a few wild fennel seeds. Then the two halves are closed up and the finished figs are pressed into layers between fragrant bay leaves in a willow basket or a big terra-cotta jar.

BELLA DI CERIGNOLA OLIVES. These very large, green, brine-cured olives are a deliciously meaty specialty of Cerignola, in the heart of the northern zone of olive culture. You can find them at the Bella di Cerignola Cooperativa, in the town of Cerignola, tel. 0885-422-007, but they are also available in America at specialty stores like Balducci's.

LAMPASCIONI. The bulbs of the wild tassel hyacinth (*Racemosum muscari*), these can be purchased fresh throughout the winter in Pugliese markets. Boiled, braised, or pickled, they are often served as an accompaniment to the purée of fava beans that is a regional staple.

MOSTO COTTO. A thick, molasseslike syrup made by boiling down fresh grape must, mosto cotto is served as a kind of poor man's honey, to garnish crisply fried sweets like cartellate and to top fresh ricotta puddings.

OLIO SANTO. Olive oil in which tiny, fiery, red chile peppers have been put to steep, olio santo is often served in a little glass jug and intended to be used as a searing condiment for plates of pasta or bowls of soup. The Pugliese are more enamored of hot chile peppers than are other Italians. The story, according to

Patience Gray, whose book *Honey from a Weed* details many Pugliese food traditions, is that peperoncini amari, as they are called, were introduced by the Turks, who hoped that their consumption would kill off the inhabitants. The people of the Salentino peninsula took to them with a passion instead, "but there is a very high incidence of stomach problems in consequence."

Olive Oil

THERE are, it is said, 50 million olive trees in Puglia, or one for every man, woman, and child in all of Italy. Not all of these trees are productive, or as productive as they could be, although in 1992 Puglia produced 12,815,000 *quintale* (a little short of a million and a half tons) of oil, far more than any other region of Italy—and Italy itself is the world's largest, or second largest, producer, constantly jockeying with Spain for first place. Although statistics weren't yet available for the 1995–96 season, it was predicted to be a record for Puglia, with an even higher yield of high-quality oil.

Wherever you go in Puglia, the landscape is graced with olive trees, many of them great gnarled giants as much as three stories tall and so big around it takes several men, arms outstretched, to encircle them. Olive trees, like sequoias, are famously long-lived. People are always claiming that this or that one goes back to the time of Christ or the time of Caesar or some other more or less venerated historical figure, but on the grounds of Il Melograno, a lovely country inn outside Monópoli, there's a tree that's been analyzed by experts from the University of Bari who say it really is some two thousand years old. It's kept in a protected courtyard outside the dining room and, it doesn't produce many olives these days, but a living creature of such hoary endurance is awesome, and few who see the tree are unmoved in its presence.

Olive oil is produced throughout Puglia, and used lavishly in the cuisine, but the north, the Terra di Bari, is the great zone of commercial production. The autostrada that runs from Naples south of Foggia to Bari passes through vast groves, a splendid sight at any time of the year but especially in November when the harvest begins. Pugliese oil is made, for the most part, from two varieties of olives, coratina (named for the northern town of Corato, a center of production) and ogliarola, also called cima di Bitonto, whose tall, slender trees, their high branches pruned to bend like weeping willows, distinguish the landscape around Bitonto, another northern town. The oil from coratina olives is distinguished by a grassy bitterness with a flavor of artichokes, an indication of lots of good polyphenols in the oil, while ogliarola produces a soft, sweet, fat oil, sometimes with hints of rosemary. Good producers blend the two to make a well-balanced oil with a long shelf life, lush in flavor, golden in color, with a fine fruity flavor and a fresh olive aroma. Much of it is bottled and sold under Pugliese brand names, like Masseria di Sant'-

Eramo, but even more is shipped north to be used in blending with more expensive northern oils, like those from Lazio, Tuscany, and Umbria.

Unfortunately, much of the oil produced in Puglia is not of such high quality. Good olive oil is made from olives that are picked and rushed to the mill, within forty-eight hours of harvest. Olives left to lie around will go rancid quickly and develop off flavors, producing an oil with an unacceptably high level of free oleic acid—far too high to be classified as extra virgin, which is oil with less than 1 percent acidity. One of the strangest sights in Puglia is of massive old olive trees, their trunks gnarled and twisted by wind and time, row on row in winter fields of red earth, while beneath them lie great orange nets full of black olives, many of them close to rotting and already oozing oil. Even with the price of olive oil at an all-time record, it seems, some farmers just don't see any point investing in labor-intensive, hand-harvesting of olives.

Like many agricultural problems, this is one farmers have created for themselves, ignoring the market and insisting that the way things have always been is the right way. The market demand is for extra virgin oil, but far too many of Puglia's olives are harvested by waiting for them to drop from the trees. Sometimes the acidity level of olives brought into the local mill is so high that producers prefer to be paid in cash rather than in an oil they consider unusable, an oil that must be refined into "pure" oil before it can be used. And the odor emanating throughout the winter months from olive oil refineries outside Bari is enough to convince me, at least, of the virtues of unrefined extra virgin oil.

There is no reason why fine extra virgin oil can't be made from Pugliese olives. One such excellent example is Masseria Sant'Eramo, one of the few brands of Pugliese oil being marketed as such in the United States. Antonio Ferro, the manager of the facility, gave me a tour of Masseria Sant'Eramo, which is located in an industrial suburb of the little city of Sant'Eramo in the Terra di Bari.

Masseria Sant'Eramo's oil is a blend of about 80 percent coratina and 20 percent ogliarola olives. Coratina on its own is too strong, Ferro said, and ogliarola is too soft, but together, they're nearly perfect. This is what the company calls "gusto classico," but they also produce a "gusto delicato" that's made with the reverse, 80 percent ogliarola, to give a softer, more delicate finish to the oil.

Interestingly, the factory does not own its own olive groves, but instead buys olives mostly from producers north of Bari. "If you own land," Ferro told me, "then you become a victim of your harvest. It's much better to select from others, to seek out and buy the best." What he looks for, naturally enough, is a sound product, and he looks not just at the olives themselves, he explained, but even more critically at the land on which they are produced. Good ferrous soil, with a high level of iron—which is what turns Pugliese soil a striking red color—is an indication of good olives.

"At Masseria Sant'Eramo," Ferro said, "we didn't discover oil. We just discovered the right way to produce—and market—it. The secret is cleanliness—that's really all it takes. Of course, you have to keep the oil away from light and heat. Our oil doesn't see light until the moment it goes into the bottle. It's produced and stored in absolute darkness. The more light the oil gets, the more quickly it spoils."

Masseria Sant'Eramo's oil is produced by a mixture of modern and traditional methods. The olives are crushed at room temperature the old-fashioned way with giant millstones, but instead of being pressed, the thick black paste is put into slowly turning stainless steel drums to express the oil, a system oil people call the continuous cycle method. A centrifuge separates out the water, and then the oil is stored. It is decanted periodically, as the sediment settles to the bottom of the tanks, but never filtered. Beneath the great barnlike warehouse in which the oil is produced are enormous stainless steel storage tanks. Here the oil sits and is brought up only for bottling and shipping.

There are other fine extra virgin oil producers in Puglia, but the oil is not easy to find in this country. Some names to keep in mind, however, and to look for if you go to Puglia are the following:

Azienda Calogiuri extra virgin olive oil from Antico Podere il Boschetto, via L. da Vinci 4, 73023 Lizzanello (LE); fax 0832-65-17-29; decanted but not filtered, golden yellow with green highlights; intense and fruity, good body, acidity no greater than 0.3 percent. Production is limited and bottles are numbered.

Antiche Masserie Amati extra virgin olive oil, Contrada S. Angelo, Fasano (BR); tel. 80-713-471. The oil is from five estates owned by the company in Fasano, south of Monópoli; olives are guaranteed hand-picked and pressed within forty-eight hours of harvest. Quality certified by Coassol, a consortium of regional producers. At company headquarters in a seventeenth-century villa in S. Angelo de' Graecis (Fasano), there's a fascinating olive oil museum (Museo dell' Olio di Oliva), open to the public on Sundays and holidays, well worth a visit if you're in the area between Bari and Brindisi.

APROL is an association of producers of extra virgin oil in the province of Lecce; each producer's name is on the bottle, which is marketed by the association. I tried extra virgin olive oil from an estate called Labbate in Ugento, southeastern Puglia, and found it excellent, golden with green highlights, like most southern oil, but with a fine soft fruit flavor.

Olive oil is the preferred fat, indeed almost the only fat, used in Pugliese cooking, as a quick glance through the recipes in this book will confirm. But two uses of freshly pressed extra virgin oil stand out as peculiar to the region. One is bruschetta, a slice of country bread toasted, preferably over a wood fire, and lavishly drizzled with oil. In that it's not so very different from other parts of Italy, but the Pugliese like their bruschetta with an abundance of freshly ground black pepper, or crushed tomatoes, or both, on top. Another version of bruschetta is made by soaking slices of stale bread in beaten egg, as for French toast, then frying them in olive oil. And then there's a kind of pick-me-up salad that reminds me precisely of a similar salad from Andalucia, the great oil-producing region of southern Spain:

Sliced oranges, immersed in boiling water to soften them slightly, then drained and dressed with olive oil, salt, and lots of black pepper—a tonic, Luigi Sada says, to refresh the comatose.

Wine

PUGLIA has always been a major Italian producer of wine, but until recently the wines of the region were better known for quantity than for quality. Much of the annual production of high-alcohol red wine, typical of a hot southern climate, was shipped out by the tankload, either to strengthen and give character to thinner northern wines or to be converted to aperitifs and other fortified drinks. The city of Lecce, I was told, is called "the Florence of the South," not because it is so beautiful (which it is) nor because it has so many monuments to a great age of Italian art (which it does), but because of the historic connection between Tuscan and Pugliese wine-makers. Each year in late autumn or early winter, when the new wine was ready for tasting, Tuscan negociants would descend on the Pugliese wineries to sample the crop and make their selections for blending with the Tuscan wine of the year. Historic relationships grew between particular Tuscan buyers and particular Pugliese wineries, and these relationships persisted over generations, often to this very day.

As in many other southern regions, however, the exclusive production of high-alcohol bulk wine is starting to change, and some fine, well-balanced Pugliese wines, robust reds often of great character, are the result. Many of these have been made in recent years under the direction of Severino Garofano, an enologist of exceptional talent who has had an important and welcome influence on Pugliese wine-making.

Unfortunately, few of the new-style Pugliese wines have so far made it into American wine shops and restaurants, although there are some noteworthy exceptions, including Cosimo Taurino's Patriglione and Francesco Candido's Duca d'Aragona, both powerful (and expensive) red wines, full of warm, rich, spicy flavors, both made with a base of negroamaro, the typical Pugliese varietal, and both attracting the attention of astute connoisseurs, especially the recently released 1988 vintages. Candido's Cappello di Prete and Taurino's Notarpanaro are also among Pugliese reds to be found in this country; again, big, spicy wines that are reminiscent of well-made California zinfandels.

The most prominent DOC (denominazione di origine controllata, the official Italian guarantee of a wine's origin, similar to the French apellation controllée) red from Puglia to be found in U.S. markets is probably Sàlice Salentino, produced in the province of Lecce from a blend of negroamaro and malvasia nera vines. But another Pugliese red, of special interest to travelers in the region, is made from a local vine called primitivo, thought by some ampelographers to be the mysterious ancestor of California's zinfandel. At its best (and not always easy to find), primitivo, like zinfandel, produces a rich, chewy wine with a notably fruity character and a high alcohol content.

Pugliese white wines are less interesting, but travelers will want to try the DOC white wines from Locorotondo and Martina Franca, fresh and crisp at their best and very pleasant at the height of summer in the trulli country.

Aleatico is a very special red dessert wine produced in Puglia from vines of this old varietal with grapes that taste of moscato; made from late-harvested grapes, the wine is not drunk before the third year of age, when it develops a mahogany color, a velvety texture, and a rich and complex aromatic flavor. Again, it is not an easy wine to find, even in Puglia, but well worth the effort when properly handled.

acknowledgments

In speaking of the qualities that make Puglia and its cuisine so special, I cannot conclude without mentioning a rare regional asset, the hospitality, generosity, and good-natured curiosity of the Pugliese themselves. Like ancient Greeks, the country people of this distant region welcome strangers as if it were a moral or religious obligation. When you walk out along the stone-walled lanes of the countryside, people invariably stop to ask where you've come from and where you're going, not out of suspicion but out of kindly interest: *"Ma, chi è Lei, signora?"* the old ladies ask, with an innocent curiosity, the way a child would ask: Who are you? And then they welcome you with old-fashioned grace into their homes and lives. To them all, I offer my deepest gratitude.

My special thanks also to the following very special people: Roberta Guerra and Matthew Watkins, Anna Longano and Pino Marchese, Claudia Bacile and Benedetto Cavalieri, Gigliola Bacile, Patience Gray and Norman Mommens, Adriana Bozzi-Colonna, Concetta Cantoro and Marcello Grua, Dora and Angelo Ricci, Franco Fasano, Paola Pettini, and Nicla and Rosa Granozio.

I'm also grateful to the International Olive Oil Council and Oldways Preservation & Exchange Trust for providing an early introduction to the flavors of Puglia, and to my editor, Harriet Bell, for her immediate enthusiasm and continuing energy in support of this book. Thanks, also, to Nelda McClellan and Frances Holdgate for expert recipe testing. Finally, as always, thanks to Faith, Carol, Corby, Fred, and Ed, who together comprise that unique support group, La Banda Italiana.

bibliography

Allen, Edward, *Stone Shelters,* Cambridge, Mass.: MIT Press, 1962.

Davidson, Alan, *Mediterranean Seafood,* 2nd Edition, Baton Rouge: Louisiana State University Press, 1981.

Douglas, Norman, *Old Calabria,* Marlboro, Vt.: Marlboro Press, 1993.

Fascarini, Antonio Eduardo, *Il Salento in Cucina,* Pesce, Galatina: Congedo Editore, 1995.

Gray, Patience, *Honey from a Weed,* New York: Harper & Row, 1987.

King, Shirley, *Fish: The Basics,* New York: Simon & Schuster, 1990.

Panza, Giovanni, *La Checine de nononne: U mangià de baise d'aiire e de iosce,* 3a edizione, Fasano (BR): Schena Editore, 1989.

Pignatelli Ferrante, Maria, *La Cucina delle Murge: Curiosità e tradizioni,* Padova: Franco Muzzio Editore, 1995.

Pinto, Domenico, and Severino Garofano, Vittore Fiore, Luigi Sada, and Nicola Borri, *Puglia: Dalla terra alla tavola,* Bari: Mario Adda Editore, 1990.

Ramage, Craufurd Tait, *Ramage in South Italy,* ed. by Edith Clay, Chicago: Academy, 1987.

Sada, Luigi, *La Cucina della terra di Bari,* Padova: Franco Muzzio Editore, 1991.

Sada, Luigi, *La Cucina pugliese,* Roma: Newton Compton Editore, 1994.

Sada, Luigi, *Cucina pugliese alla poverella,* Foggia: Edizione del Rosone, 1991.

Schneider, Elizabeth, *Uncommon Fruits and Vegetables,* New York: Harper & Row, 1986.

Stanziano, Angelina, and Laura Santoro, *Puglia: La tradizione in cucina,* Fasano (BR): Schena Editore, 1991.

Stoja Muratore, Maria Rosaria, *La Cucina salentina: Feste e ricette per 365 giorni,* Galatina (LE): Congedo Editore, 1993.

source guide

Balducci's
424 Avenue of the Americas
New York, NY 10011

Balducci's Shop from Home Service
P.O. Box 10373
Newark, NJ 07193-0373
(800) BALDUCCI or 225-3822
Fax (718) 786-4125
Web site: www.balducci.com

Dean & Deluca
560 Broadway
New York, NY 10012
(800) 221-7714
Personal Shopper Line:
(212) 226-6800 ext. 268

Todaro Brothers
555 Second Avenue
New York, NY 10016
(212) 679-7766
Fax (212) 689-1679

Vivande Porta Via
2125 Fillmore Street

San Francisco, CA 94115
(415) 346-4430
Fax (415) 346-2877

Williams-Sonoma
Catalog available from:
P.O. Box 7456
San Francisco, CA 94120
(800) 541-2233
Carries Benedetto Cavalieri pasta

Zingerman's Delicatessen
and Mail Order
442 Detroit Street
Ann Arbor, MI 48104-3400
(313) 769-1625
Fax (313) 769-1235

SPECIAL ITEMS:

Mussels
Taylor Shellfish Farms
SE 130 Lynch Road
Shelton, WA 98584
(360) 426-6178

Baker's supplies and flours

King Arthur Flour Baker's Catalogue
P.O. Box 876
Norwich, VT 05055
(800) 827-6836

Mozzarella and other cheeses

Mozzarella Company
2944 Elm Street
Dallas, TX 75226
(800) 798-2954

Sheep's milk ricotta and other sheep's milk cheeses

Hollow Road Farms
Route 1, Box 93
Stuyvesant, NY 12173
(518) 758-7214

index